CROSSING

CROSSING

A MEMOIR

DEIRDRE
McCLOSKEY

THE UNIVERSITY OF CHICAGO PRESS

CHICAGO & LONDON

The University of Chicago Press, Chicago 60637
The University of Chicago Press, Ltd., London
© 1999 by The University of Chicago
All rights reserved. Published 1999
Paperback edition 2000
08 07 06 05 04 03 02 01 00   3 4 5
ISBN: 0-226-55668-9 (cloth)
ISBN: 0-226-55669-7 (paperback)

Library of Congress Cataloging-in-Publication Data

McCloskey, Deirdre N.
  Crossing : a memoir / Deirdre McCloskey.
     p.   cm.
   ISBN 0-226-55668-9 (alk. paper)
    1. McCloskey, Deirdre N. 2. Transsexuals—United States—
Biography. 3. Transsexuals—United States—Psychology.
4. Gender identity—United States—Psychological aspects. I. Title.
HQ77.8.M39A3   1999
305.9'066—dc21   99-19450
                                                CIP

THAT WOMANLY SOLIDARITY
AND GRACE

Joanne Mc., Helen Mc., Lucy, Robin P., Susan
R., Laura Mc., JoAnn R., Janet B., Barbara Jean
W., Stephanie V., Anna, Rebekka, Angela, Bren
P., Ruthann P., Cari B., Roxanne D.,Alice E.,
Michelle P., Lola L., Jenifer G., Carol F., Nancy
H., Sharon M., Ann R., Kim P., Linda C., Leola
B., Kitch A., Nadine C., Helen R., Santhi H.,
Mary Beth C., Marty O., Esther H., Elyce R.,
Diana S., Naomi L., Claudia G., Margalit M.,
Cynthia T.-M., Mary G., Ruby O., Susan C.,
Evelyn Mc., Virginia P., Laura L.-G., Jeri,
Mira,Judith M., Janet L., Mary S., Ginny, Ginny
O., Mary L., Connie N., Sarah M., Riva R., Denis
L., Louise P., Susan W., Connie B., Sarah H.,
Susan L., Hélène L., Gayle S., Alice S., Marijke
P., Renée J., Anna K., Jani K., Gonda K.,
Theresia K., Marianne K., Luz-Eugenia C.-F.,
Mary M., Anna de B., Nienke G., Corinne V.,
Linda W., Marian V., Livia P., Kathleen D.,
Marian van der B., Irene van S., Lieke M.,
Nancy F., Fieke van der L., Coco B., Tineke O.,

Rolien v. D., Nelleke v. D., Marlite, Simone, Margeth H., Judith S., Vicky A., Christine B., Sheila B., Susan M., Marlena C., Barbara C., Jackie B., Katherine M., Mary, Katherine H., Françoise S., Katherine C., Carmel M., Leena M., Marie M. R., Marilyn B., Lynn J., Tineke B., Nicole B., Nancy W., Corine van D., Elizabeth T., Suzanne J., Barbara G., Gail V., Noe V., Hedie S., Consuela W., Susannah M., Monique, Marianne D., Bernadette, Jeanne G., Teri S., Pat T., Saskia de V., Rita S., Françoise, Marthe, Tjietschede, Edith K., Jolien H., Eva K.-v. d. D., Marja L., Timmie T., Paivi O., Jagi G., Linda R., Mariette B., Pien v. d. B., Antoinette B., Marianne B., Anneke v. B., Anne Irene v. d. B., Janka F., Astrid H., Else K., Paula M., Maria H., Anja d. J., Ria O.-v.D., Wendela v. B., Annemarie U., Corinna d. W., Marti T., Annemarie V., Jennifer R., Guje S., Karen K., Rae Ann, Diane R., Deb R., Katherine T., Linda W., Judy van H., Lin L., Julie S., Suzanne Z., Fiona R., Annie, Patty H., Samantha H., Amanda H., Kathy E., Karen T., Caroline J., Paola B., Irina, Kathryn M., Irma, Bregje v. E., Betsy H., Mary T., Lori R., Joanie Z., Fran A., Alice H.-F., Lori E., Judith C., Joanne P., Sharon Mc., Doris W., Linnea P., Anne T., Iulie A., Charlotte K., Anna M.-S., Christine M., Maxine B., Starrlett C., Barbara W.-B., Hanna G., Emily C., Evonne, Dorothy H., Julianna C., Shari T., Renea J., Sharon S., Cheryl G., Kathleen F., Paddy Q., Anya R., Mary Ellen H., Amy A., Joyce B., Amy D., Sara R.-W., Cathy C., Sharon B., Paula M., Marisa R., Nuala Z., Cynthia F., Dorothy H., Elena G., Mary G. H., Valerie H., Valerie L., Ayhan L., Alison O., Beth I., Grace J., Linda K., Pat C., Jean L., Lois C., Anne T., Jean L.-J., Minnette D., Mary N., Barb O., Helena D., Mary D., Carin G., Robin S., Adriana M., Maggie R., Sister Dorothy Ann, Sister Marilyn B., Sister Irene M., Gabriella M.

CONTENTS

ACKNOWLEDGMENTS

Theresia Ketting, Marianne Ketting, Arjo Klamer, Marijke Prins, and Elaine Pfefferblit told me in August 1996 that the first draft needed work. An audience at the Project on Rhetoric of Inquiry at the University of Iowa heard the beginnings of a new version in the late winter of 1997 and was encouraging. Patricia Hersh read several versions, offering encouragement and suggestions. David Joel and my agent Gordon Massman offered excellent professional advice, most of which I've taken. Helen McCloskey, Lori Erickson, Carrie La Seur, Alan Venable, Barbara Olson, Kate Cummings, Arjo Klamer, Gabriela Maya, Joanne Meyerowitz, and Jan Radway gave me advice as the book came out of the oven. Alice Bennett at the University of Chicago Press did the frosting. My brother John writes so much better than I do that I wish he could have written it all; he did rewrite many paragraphs. Readers should thank all these people for their love and their judgment. I do.

PREFACE *CROSSINGS*

I want to tell you the story of a crossing from fifty-two-year-old man to fifty-five-year-old woman, Donald to Deirdre.

"A strange story," you say.

Yes, it's strange, statistically. All the instruments agree that what's usually called "transsexuality," permanently crossing the gender boundary, is rare. (The Latin in "transsexuality" makes it sound sexual, which is mistaken; or medical, which is misleading; or scientific, which is silly. I'll use plain English "crossing.") Only three in ten thousand want to cross the boundary of gender, a few of them in your own city neighborhood or small town. Gender crossing is no threat to male/female sex ratios or the role of women or the stability of the dollar. Most people are content with their birth gender.

But people do after all cross various boundaries. I've been a foreigner a little, in England and Holland and on shorter visits elsewhere. If you've been a foreigner you can understand somewhat, because gender crossing is a good deal like foreign travel. Most people would like to go to Venice on vacation. Most people, if they could magically do it, would like to try out the other gender for a day or a week or a month. The Venice visitors as a group can be thought of as all the "crossgendered," from stone butch dykes to postoperative male-to-female gender crossers, all the traversers, permanent or temporary, somber or ironic. A few people go to Venice regularly, and you can think of them as the crossdressers among these, wearing the clothing of the opposite gender once in a while. But only a tiny fraction of the crossgendered are permanent gender crossers, wanting to *become* Venetians. Most people are content to stay mainly at home. A tiny minority are not. They want to cross and stay.

On a trip to New York to see a friend after my own crossing I stood in the hall of photographs at Ellis Island and wept at the courage. Crossing cultures from male to female is big; it highlights some of the differences between men and women, and some of the similarities too. That's interesting. My crossing was costly and opposed, which is too bad. But my crossing has been dull, easy, comfortable compared with Suyuan's or Giuseppi's outer migrations.

Or compared with some people's inner migrations. Some people cross this or that inner boundary so radically that it would look bizarre, a slippage in the normal order of the universe, Stephen King material, if it were not so common. The most radical one is the crossing from child to adult, a crossing similar to mine that we all experience. I once saw a spoof scientific paper titled "Short Stature Syndrome: A Nationwide Problem." The strange little people, whose thoughts and actions were so different from normal, requiring the compulsory intervention of psychiatrists, and lots more money for the National Institute of Mental Health, were . . . children.

The word "education" means just "leading out." People are always leading themselves out of one life and into another, such as out of childhood and into each new version of adulthood. Not everyone likes to keep doing it, but the women I most admire have. My mother educated herself to earning her income and writing poetry after my father died. My roomer for a year in Iowa educated herself as a hospital chaplain after a third of a century teaching elementary school. My sister got a second degree in psychology, my former wife made herself into a distinguished professor. May Sarton, so glad to become by forced crossing an American rather than a Belgian woman, an English rather than a French poet and novelist and memoirist, kept crossing, crossing and looked forward at age seventy to "what is ahead — to clear my desk, sow the annuals, plant perennials, get back to the novel . . . like a game of solitaire that is coming out."

It's strange to have been a man and now to be a woman. But it's no stranger perhaps than having once been a West African and now being an American, or once a priest and now a businessman. Free people keep deciding to make strange crossings, from storekeeper to monk or from civilian to soldier or from man to woman. Crossing boundaries is a minority interest, but human.

■

My crossing—change, migration, growing up, self-discovery—took place from 1994 to 1997, beginning in my home in Iowa, then a year in Holland, then back in Iowa, with travels in between. As Donald and then as Deirdre I was and am a professor of economics and of history at the University of Iowa. From age eleven I had been a secret cross-dresser, a few times a week. Otherwise I was normal, just a guy. My wife had known about the crossdressing since the first year of our marriage, when we were twenty-two. No big deal, we decided. Lots of men have this or that sexual peculiarity. Relax, we said. By 1994, age fifty-two, I had been married those three decades, had two grown children, and thought I might crossdress a little more. Visit Venice more too.

I visited womanhood and stayed. It was not for the pleasures, though I discovered many I had not imagined, and many pains too. But calculating pleasures and pains was not the point. The point was who I am. Here the analogy with migration breaks down. One moves permanently from Sicily to New York because one imagines the streets of New York are paved with gold, or at least better paved than the streets at home, not mainly because back in Catania since age eleven one had dreamed of being an American. Migration can be mod-eled as a matter of cost and benefit, and it has been by economic his-torians. But I did not change gender because I liked colorful clothing (Donald did not) or womanly grace (Donald viewed it as sentimental-ity). The "decision" was not utilitarian. In our culture the rhetoric of the very word "decision" suggests cost and benefit. My gender cross-ing was motivated by identity, not by a balance sheet of utility.

Of course you can ask what psychological reasons explain my de-sire to cross and reply with, say, a version of Freud. Some researchers think there is a biological explanation for gender crossing, because parts of the brains of formerly male gender crossers in postmortems are notably female. But a demand for an answer to why carries with it in our medicalized culture an agenda of treatment. If a gender crosser is "just" a guy who gets pleasure from it, that's one thing (laugh at him, jail him, murder him). If it's brain chemistry, that's another (commit him to a madhouse and try to "cure" him).

I say in response to your question Why? "Can't I just be?" You, dear reader, are. No one gets indignant if you have no answer to why you are an optimist or why you like peach ice cream. These days most people will grant you an exemption from the why question if you are gay: in 1960 they would not and were therefore eager to do things to you, many of them nasty. I want the courtesy and the safety of a why-less treatment extended to gender crossers. I want the medical models of gender crossing (and of twenty other things) to fall. That's the politics. I am ashamed that from the 1960s to the 1990s, in the political movements for black civil rights, women's liberation, gay rights, and opposition to the war in Vietnam, I had sound opinions but never really took a chance on them. Telling you my story is my last chance to be counted.

And incidentally, Why *do* you think you are the gender you were officially assigned to at birth? Prove it. How odd.

Ah. I think you need some treatment.

■

After a year of hesitation, and two years from well beginning, I found to my delight that I had crossed. Look by look, smile by smile, I was accepted. That doesn't make me a 100 percent, essential woman—I'll never have XX chromosomes, never have had the life of a girl and woman up to age fifty-two. But the world does not demand 100 percents and essences, thank God. An agnostic since adolescence, in my second year of crossing I came tentatively to religion and then could thank God in person, who made me inside in my comfort a woman.

I get weepy sometimes as I walk to the office, pick up my dry cleaning, shop at Prairie Lights bookstore, so pleased to Be. It's like someone who thought herself more French than American and one day was able to be French; or someone who always hoped to be a professional athlete and finally became one; or someone who felt herself a businesswoman and at last was seen as one. My game of solitaire came out.

I apologize for romanticizing sometimes the goodness of women and criticizing sometimes the badness of men. It's how I felt at the time. Forgive me, new to this place and starry-eyed. Perhaps my stories of Donald and then Dee and then Deirdre show enough bad women and good men to offset my romantic theories. In contrasting how men and women "are" I do not mean to recruit stereotypes or essentialisms that have been used to the disadvantage of other women. Women are not always more loving, or less interested in career. And certainly they are what in detail they "are" not on account of some eternal Platonic ideal or the imperatives of genetics. I am reporting how the difference in social practice seemed to me, admitting always that the difference might be, as the professors say, "socially constructed." Gender is not in every way "natural." "Feminine" gestures, for example, are not God's own creation. This of course I know. The social construction of gender is, after all, something a gender crosser comes to know with unusual vividness. She does it for a living.

I apologize, too, for any inaccuracies that remain despite my earnest attempts to get them out. I have tried to tell a true story. Yet none of the conversations and descriptions in the book are court transcripts. Each is something I believe I remember, ordered in the sequence I believe I remember, and intended to show how I heard and saw and thought at the time—my recollections, my ardent opinions, how I felt as I remember how I felt. I have been as careful as I can and have offered to show the manuscript to the main parties, some of whom could help.

The world does not tell stories. Men and women do, and I am merely a woman telling. It would be impossible to recount every single thing about your hour just passed, tiny things that illustrate character or position, much less to tell every single thing about three crowded years, or one side of a tangled life. Whether the result is God's own truth I don't know. Telling any story, from physics to fiction, is like placing stepping-stones through a garden, choosing what spots to miss in showing the path.

■

After the crossing I was eating lunch in Iowa City with a woman friend, another academic, and we spoke about how talk normalizes. She said, "This is the age of the candid memoir." So it seems. It's a good thing, we agreed, because talking to each other about who we are can make us mutually all human. Demonizing Others is the first stop on the railway to the gas chambers. Nowadays there are many books about the crossgendered. Movies and television have stopped portraying them as dangerous lunatics in the mold of Anthony Perkins in *Psycho*. Since the 1960s, detested by those who value order above freedom, many kinds of people have spoken up: the raped women who kept their secrets, the unmarried mothers who kept theirs. In the 1950s a lot of people were keeping secrets, personal and state: the obedient wives, the hidden handicapped, the closeted homosexuals, the silenced socialists, the blacks under Jim Crow. After the liberation and the talk that followed they are no longer disgraceful Others or pathetic victims, or merely invisibles—"We don't have any homosexuals in Oklahoma" — but people whose stories are heard and talked about and might even be imagined as one's own. It's the difference between shame and life.

For this age of openness I praise the Lord, blessed be her holy name. I began to see that Christianity resembles the secular stoicism circa the 1930s in which I was raised, A. E. Housman to Hemingway, in that it promises no bed of roses. The world is mysterious from a human point of view, as both the stoic Housman and the Christian Gerard Manley Hopkins would say, and it contains bad news as well as good. I found Christianity in this way grown up, admitting sin. That *is* God's own truth.

And slowly as the story ended I began to hear the good news of forgiveness, the duty to offer it and the grace to receive.

PART ONE

DONALD

MOTHER

FATHER

SISTER, *ELEVEN YEARS YOUNGER*

BROTHER, *THIRTEEN YEARS YOUNGER*

WIFE

SON, *BORN 1969*

DAUGHTER, *BORN 1975*

LUCY, *CROSSDRESSER*

ROBIN, *GENDER CROSSER*

FRANK, *PSYCHOLOGIST*

ARJO KLAMER, *FRIEND*

I

BOY TO MAN

*D*eirdre remembers Donald's mother taking him at age five into a tea and ice cream place called Schraft's, in Harvard Square. After a hot fudge sundae and a watery Coke he had to go to the bathroom, so she took him into the ladies' room. It was nothing out of the ordinary. She wasn't going to leave her five-year-old son in a strange men's room when he needed to wee-wee, not even in the safe world of 1947. What's not ordinary was Donald's sharp memory of it, the ladies in the tiny room speaking kindly to the boy as they straightened their seams and reapplied their lipstick.

His mother took him everywhere, all over Boston to her voice lessons at the Longey School in Cambridge and to rehearsals downtown with the opera director Sarah Caldwell. Sarah took him to his first circus, and at Longey he used to slide down the banister, or imagined it. His father was a graduate student at Harvard and then an assistant professor, not doing much baby-sitting. Donald's mother took him at age six to a rehearsal of *Henry V* in Memorial Hall, down the street from their married students' housing in Holden Green. He was fascinated by the swords in the play. He loved swashbuckling, and in college he joined the fencing team. The team photo hangs on Deirdre's office wall at home, under the mask and sword, an arrangement of artificial flowers beside it. Unfazed by her male past, she puts her coffee cup on a little brass plaque, "1889–1989. Harvard. One hundred years of fencing." As a boy Donald organized armies for mock battles, with wooden swords and trash-can lids for shields. The armies were cozy—families—though families with a lot of dramatic keeling over dead like in the movies. No girls. She's all right.

His mother also took him along to Filene's Basement in downtown Boston for sale days, when the women in the aisles tried on dresses in their slips and less. It was annoying, her mother said in recollection, that men would stand at the edge of the crowd and watch silently while the women worked to clothe themselves at prices they could afford. There was nothing out of the ordinary about a mother with a full-time job, also studying singing, and therefore with child-care problems, taking her little boy along to Filene's. It was Donald's sharp memory of it that was out of the ordinary. He kept the memory, not yet wanting to dress as the women did, to be as the women were. He was half conscious of it: *Swordplay, yes, what boys and men do. Not that other. No.*

He loved the MGM musicals that he and his mother would see at matinées at the University Theater. He would come out tap dancing, wanting to be Fred Astaire or Gene Kelly or Donald O'Connor—not Ginger Rogers, as the feminist joke goes, doing the same steps backward and in heels. When his mother signed him up for ballet lessons he balked and did not like it. The others were girls. It pulled him. *No.*

He watched his mother pluck her eyebrows with tweezers and whisk mascara onto her lashes with a little square brush. Like the ladies' room in Schraft's and the women in their slips in Filene's Basement, the memory hung there like a moon, meaningless. Donald shrugged and returned to being a boy.

He was normal, happy, bookish, an only child until adolescence. He stuttered always, making the rounds of speech therapists into high school. There's no cure for stuttering, or none that he persisted in. Stuttering either goes away or it doesn't. His didn't. But otherwise he was studious and obedient and cheerful—no worry, said his mother later. I've never worried about you, she said. He played with toy soldiers in Sammy's basement in Holden Green and read books on astronomy until he discovered that it was applied physics and required a lot of math. He read boys' books, which were the books he was given—the Hardy Boys, not Nancy Drew. Later he learned from his sister that she was encouraged to read *Little Women,* which Deirdre first read at fifty-five. His father gave Donald *The Three Musketeers,* but he didn't like it as much as his father had when he was a boy, the dreams of courage on the page.

Not that Donald had girlish dreams of love. True, he played with string puppets as though with dolls, because it was Howdy Doody time. But it's not as simple as that, Deirdre would explain. I was not effeminate, if that's your theory. I behaved like a boy, dreamed like a boy, *was* a boy. There's nothing plain in such histories. Some male-to-female gender crossers were effeminate boys, but many were not. Effeminate boys most often become ordinary nongay men, less commonly gay men, but rarely gender crossers. A tiny share of noneffeminate boys like Donald wish in time to become women. You can't tell. It takes time to know oneself. There will be surprises.

And in any case, now that we're talking about how to treat people, Deirdre would say, effeminate boys, and tomboy girls, are human too. You ought to see the Belgian movie *My Life in Pink,* about a little boy who shames his family by wanting to be a girl. Deirdre saw it alone in a theater near Southern Methodist in Dallas. The movie was not her boyhood, but it was her desire, which sprang to life as boyhood ended.

So Donald had been a normal boy, though never a thrusting, macho one. He never fought, though teased about his stutter. His mother told how he came home crying at being teased by a cross-eyed playmate named Frankie.

"You didn't tease Frankie back for his crossed eyes, did you?"

"Oh, Mommy, no. That would be a *terrible* thing to do. I'll get over my stuttering someday" (Donald's optimism), "but Frankie will always be cross-eyed."

■

He was eleven years old. They had moved from Cambridge out to the wooded Boston suburb of Wakefield the year before. Eisenhower had won the election, and Donald had to explain to the Republican girls next door why his mother and father had voted for Stevenson. Stevenson's the best, that's all. He played occasionally with the girls, but at football, tussling in the scrum with girls at that age larger than the boys.

On a day in December 1953 he was home sick from school. His mother was downstairs in the kitchen with his new baby sister. He was having the first wet dreams of maleness. Oddly, his dreams were of femaleness, of having it, of being. Upstairs in the bathroom he took a pair of his mother panties from the laundry basket, put them on, and

found a rush of sexual pleasure—not joyous or satisfying, merely
There. It was a mild ache, pleasant and alluring, mixing memory and
desire: the women half-dressed in Filene's, the little ballerinas, his
mother. There was nothing of male lust in it except the outcome. It
was not curiosity about what lay underneath women's clothing. It was
curiosity about being.

He kept the panties on and put on his pajamas over them, and his
robe too, for security, and went downstairs.

"Hello, honey," his mother said, "How are you feeling? Better?"

"Uh, yeah. Y-y-yes. B-b-better."

"You look very handsome in your robe!" A Christmas gift last year.
He didn't wear it much.

■

As Donald aged thirteen or fourteen waited for sleep in his bed in
Wakefield he would fantasize about two things. ***Please, God, please.***
As a little boy Donald had been holy for a while, listening every week
to a radio show about Jesus, *The Greatest Story Ever Told,* and thrill-
ing at rehearsals to his mother singing *The Messiah.* By adolescence
he was not religious—something of a village atheist, actually, and
starting to read Emma Goldman in the Carnegie library downtown.
But the God-draped scenery of his culture remained for times of long-
ing. ***Whoever: Please. Tomorrow when I wake up:***

***I won't stutter. I'll just talk like people do. It'll be easy for
me, like flying in the stories. Sam Small the flying Yorkshire-
man.***

***And I'll be a girl. A girl. It's easy. Samantha Small the flying
Yorkshire WOMAN.***

Deirdre later used the memory to introduce talks, to put people at
ease about both her stuttering and her crossing in one story. She
would joke, "I f-f-f-finally got *one* of m-m-my two wishes!" and the audience would laugh.

Donald crossdressed when he could. Whenever he was sure he was
alone in his own house he would dress in his mother's clothes or in
clothes he had gotten out of the trash. He outgrew his mother's shoes
at age fifteen or so. He once tried on the shoes of his friend Louise
next door, when the family was away, but with her he mainly played
chess.

Donald's mother never suspected, she said later, not at all. At first
this astonished Deirdre, though it shouldn't have, thinking back on
the experience of a parent. Donald as a father did not suspect what
was going on in his son's room or his daughter's head. When he was

working for the highway department during summers in college his mother found a girdle he had appropriated from the trash, but she thought it had been left by some girl he'd been entertaining. The thought was natural because he was for the usual reasons heterosexually attracted to girls. His father once nearly caught him crossdressing, at age fifteen, with his mother's clothes strewn around. Donald had been frantically removing them as his father's quick steps approached the room. If he grasped what his son was doing he never mentioned it. Probably he thought it some usual heterosexual fantasy. Or nothing. His father was not watchful in such matters—a private man, willing to grant others their privacy.

The 1950s were the age of crinolines for teenage girls, and he was jealous. *Oddly, now I have a crinoline, for square dancing,* Deirdre thought. As a teenager Donald broke into neighboring houses to wear the crinolines, and shoes that fit, and garter belts and all the equipment of a 1950s girl. He didn't do it much, escaping out back doors as families came in the front, leaving everything undisturbed. He didn't steal things. Maybe a cookie now and then.

He was never caught. Despite heart-thumping expeditions in housebreaking and almost-caughts in his own home, no one suspected, and the crossdressing never became an issue. *Thank goodness,* thought Deirdre. In the 1950s they gave electroshock treatment for homosexuality, to say nothing of gender crossing. In later decades the psychiatrists persisted, and "gender identity disorder," as homosexuality was in the dark ages before 1973, is an item in the *Diagnostic and Statistical Manual of Mental Disorders,* fourth edition, the DSM-IV. The "disorder" did not appear in the DSM until seven years after the psychiatrists had guiltily removed homosexuality.

Daphne Scholinski, who wanted to be a boy, or at any rate not a regular girl, tells in *The Last Time I Wore a Dress* how the psychiatrists tried to force her. In 1981 they locked her up with delusional patients, the only female on a male ward. She was raped twice. The womanly experience of being raped did not change Scholinski's mind about not being a girl.

Thank God I wasn't caught.

■

He decided not to wish to be a girl, though he kept on crossdressing when he could. He began to keep an emotional distance from his beloved mother, as boys do, nothing strange. He grew taller than his father—six feet, a little above average for Donald's generation of men, big boned—and became a regular guy in his private boys' school in

Cambridge. He was elected co-captain of the football team, which meant he could not possibly be a girl. (Unhappily, God does not arrange for every crossgendered person to be small-boned and pretty. Later Deirdre learned of two massive professional football players from two opposing Super Bowl teams who wanted to come to a crossdressing convention in Dallas but refrained in mutual fear of each other and of exposure. And she heard of two gender crossers who had been opposing quarterbacks on their high-school football teams, not knowing about each other until they were postoperative.)

In the 1950s there was nothing to be done. *It's amazing,* Deirdre thought, *how much depended on the mere practical possibility.* As boy and man he desired, ached, knew, though he often kept the knowledge from himself, as people can do with unpleasant truths. If he had believed crossing was practical before the birth year of 1995 he would have gone ahead. *Without question,* thought Deirdre later. *A woman's life.* But he believed he was too big, too masculine. He thought of this often during the 1950s and '60s and '70s and '80s. He wished he was shorter, of slighter build and prettier face. *Still do.* Donald would recall the beautiful younger lad in his boys' school whom one of his classmates used to covet in jest, saying, "If he wore a dress I'd take him to the prom." Donald laughed, but from a false position. *No, no,* he said to himself, *I'm glad I'm not feminine enough for that to work. My size and looks keep me from it. Yes.*

In 1953 the first famous gender crosser, Christine Jorgensen, had come back from Denmark. "GI Becomes Blond Bombshell," the tabloids put it. At eleven or twelve Donald was embarrassed to stand in the magazine store in downtown Wakefield and read the flood of stories, though he did. She seemed unique. Later when he learned to drive he and his pals would go into Boston to see the drag queens, homosexual crossdressers, near Copley Square—not to hassle them or beat them up, as the bad boys did, but to see the unusual. His friend Paul was a social genius and would engage the queens in friendly talk. Still, the queens were Other—homosexual and lower class, unlike the heterosexual Harvard professor's son from a private school. He did not disdain them but could not see himself as one of them. He laughed when Paul and the others did, but he ached.

At age sixteen, when he and his family were living in Camberley near London while his father was on sabbatical, a neighbor described at a lawn party the *travesti* he had seen in an Italian show. They were "*beautiful* women," he said. Donald had no idea such a transformation was possible. *Could I become a woman,* he thought, *with this football body?* When in the late fall of that year he and his mother and little sister and brother went to live in Italy for a few months he learned of Coccinelle (which means ladybug), a French sex-changed female impersonator at the Follies, who was indeed beautiful, to a Brigitte Bardot standard. He was fascinated, though he did nothing but look at her picture in magazines.

In Rome he found a copy of Jean Genet's *Our Lady of the Flowers,* an account of French drag queens in the criminal underworld that Genet inhabited. Again he was fascinated, but again the characters were homosexuals. He was not. He was not afraid of being one. He just wasn't. *As a man I love women.* At one level he was a happy young man, exercising his new manly body and manly duties and privileges, a coat and tie and chino pants for school and college. Only at another, buried level did he wish to be a young woman. *Nothing to be done. You're a man. Report for duty.*

He never went to a drag show when he was young (it's said that "drag" dates from the Shakespearean theater: DRess As Girl). Maybe a pub drag queen during his graduate-school year in England. *Can't remember,* Deirdre thought. The first time he saw a proper show in anything but magazines or his mind's eye was twenty years later, on Bourbon Street in New Orleans. The bar in the middle of the afternoon was uncrowded, and the man/woman danced up on the tiny stage behind the bartender, lip-synching a Patty Page song. Donald didn't stay long for fear that other conventioneers from the American Economic Association would spot him. In his last year as Donald he met a drag queen, a successful lawyer on the East Coast, who had worked her way through school dancing on Bourbon Street. *Maybe that was her.*

In college he once went to a psychiatrist at the Student Health Service to get advice and told him about his crossdressing. The psychiatrist was the only person apart from his wife who knew before 1995. But 1962 was the height of the talking cure, and the psychiatrist listened and suggested another appointment. Donald didn't go. He later thought in a hydraulic metaphor, the river of his life pouring and pouring into a lake behind a dam, from age eleven to age fifty-three.

For a long time he felt guilty about the crossdressing, and into his thirties he would periodically throw out his collected clothing and magazines in a purge. It's easy to stop crossdressing, Mark Twain might have said: I've done it dozens of times. (Remember the crossdressing scene in *Huckleberry Finn;* and persistent crossdressing by

Jo in *Little Women,* and a short story by Alcott about a male-to-female crosser. Something about that Gilded Age.) But in homophobic times he was comforted that he was in other respects "normal" in his sexual drives. It was important to know this, even in the relatively tolerant household he was born into. "Heterosexual crossdresser" is no contradiction in terms. (Even a completed gender crossing does not imply a particular preference. The conventional statistics for male-to-female crossers formerly heterosexual is that a third go on loving women, a third come to love men, and a third are asexual.) Sexual preference and gender preference are not connected, contrary to the simplicities of 1930s psychoanalysis and 1990s homophobia. Who you love is not the same issue as who you are. You can love your dog and still not want to be one. Donald loved girls, and not because he wanted to be one. Though he did.

He learned in graduate school to be a tough-guy economist, as tough as professors get, anxious in America about their masculinity. Later he had a ferocious professional reputation, developed in a dozen years of harsh seminars as a faculty member in economics at the University of Chicago. In his year of hesitation before crossing he read in a magazine about an army colonel who crossdressed: "Though I walk through the valley of the shadow of death I shall fear no evil, because I'm the meanest son of a bitch in the valley." Overcorrection seems common. At his second gender convention in 1995 he met a man who had volunteered for three tours of combat in Vietnam, trying to cure himself. Manly warfare worked no better than Prozac or purging or economics seminars or football up to the Super Bowl.

He had a mild sense of straining at the tough-guy role, as though reading lines from a script he could not see distinctly, worrying he might accidentally say a woman's lines. Three years before the break, his gender-crossing feelings still accumulating behind the dam, he was invited by some of his former colleagues in the Department of History at the University of Chicago to a little conference to plan a big conference on nationalism in the Third World. About this he knew nothing. He was invited as a maid-of- all-work. McCloskey is an economist who can talk about other things as well; smart guy; a little unsteady.

These were professional friends and recent friendly acquaintances. Toward the end they were dividing up the world for possible writing for the conference. Scotland was an early example of imperialism versus nationalism, and Thomas Macaulay, the nineteenth-century English historian, whose father was a Scot, had been an important writer on the matter, suitable for a paper. Donald had long been a Macaulay fan (his father had known by heart the whole of Macaulay's poem *Horatius at the Bridge* and would recite it on the drive from Wakefield to Donald's school). The project fit with work he was planning on the social impact of ethical values, and anyway British history was his academic specialty. He liked Scotland and had vacationed there.

So at what would have been an appropriate time for a woman in a group of other women, he burst out in a campy, self-parodic, enthusiastic style, "Oh, let *me* do Macaulay!" He had not been interacting in a campy way with the group, and it contained only one woman. His remark erupted from a usually macho mouth. He was making fun of his own enthusiasm for the project, as the camp style does and as women do, overstating in a feminine way rather than understating in a masculine way. With the girlish turn he unexpectedly diverged from the male order.

The others looked down at their notes or their fingernails, and Donald blushed. He didn't get to do Macaulay.

2

MARRIAGE

Donald married his wife in 1965, after his first year of graduate school in economics at Harvard. Their marriage had nothing to do with crossdressing or gender crossing. It was not a cover-up. Donald had dammed up his feelings, letting them out in the censored form of closeted crossdressing two or three times a week for a half hour or so each time, for the sake of a finer love. He married his wife because he loved her, stayed married to her because he loved her, parented two children with her because he loved her, supported her education and career because he loved her, and was faithful to her for thirty years because he loved her. The morning of their marriage in a small town in Vermont, as Donald's wife recounted it, amused, her father had said to her, "Don't marry this fellow: there's something wrong with him." Huh? Something wrong with such a catch as a Harvard grad? Yet her father was nobody's fool, if you set aside thirty years.

They lived the first two years in graduate students' housing at Harvard. Three months into the marriage Donald tearfully confessed the crossdressing to her in the tiny bedroom. He was afraid she would leave him, though not too afraid, since they were surely in love. She reacted as a young wife in love might, sympathetic if worried: Does this mean you're homosexual? No, it's not the same thing. Did you marry me because our shoe sizes are the same? Don't be silly, dear.

Do you love me? Yes, yes, of course I do. She decided it was a minor matter. Donald never told her about his dammed-up desire to cross, because it would have frightened her for no reason. It assuredly frightened him. He was a heterosexual crossdresser, tough-guy economist, regular. *Not a transsexual,* he thought, using the frightening, medicalized word. The denial came in spite of the ache, the feeling that something was awry. Three decades later his wife could not for a while accept Donald's desire as a fact. She clung to his self-deception that he was "just" a heterosexual crossdresser. Just sex. Not identity.

During a year in London during the late 1960s while he worked on his economics Ph.D. dissertation, and then in the first years of his job at the University of Chicago (bell-bottoms, the Daley riot at the Democratic National Convention, Milton Friedman before his Nobel), he dressed more openly at home, experimenting with makeup. His young wife was not yet worn down by the weirdness of male sexuality and was still somewhat accepting. That Donald did not use makeup when dressing until his late twenties shows how closeted his crossdressing was, 1950s-style. Decades later his wife denied that the makeup had happened, though Donald for a while would wear it openly if diffidently in the little apartment on Woodlawn Avenue in Chicago. Her denial showed how determined she was to have a regular husband. He got his first wig at age thirty-one, kept it in a bag in the closet, and did not buy another for twenty years. He did what he did privately, having no idea it could be social, in clubs of middle-class people. The sex magazines he occasionally got up the nerve to buy did not make this point. And since he was too big and too male to pass as a woman he was never tempted to try. He thought: *Maybe it's for the best.*

His wife never liked the crossdressing, they never discussed it, and they never mixed the two lives. Yet the young wife was not censorious. Donald went down to Crouch End in London with her once, having persuaded her to buy him a girdle, which she did in a confused and loving indulgence. It didn't fit very well, because they could hardly try it on in the shop. In a wifely way ("All right, go and do your hobbies") she was accustomed to indulging his projects.

On his side he encouraged her education and her career beyond bedside nursing. In the late 1950s in Vermont the smart girls were offered teacher, secretary, or nurse as suitable before marriage. She had chosen nursing and had supported herself through nursing school in New Hampshire and then college in Boston and then marriage. Professing was the McCloskey family business, and it seemed normal for everyone to have a Ph.D. Donald wanted his wife to be able to stand up to the intellectual McCloskeys. He would say, Go to school if you want, dear. Yes.

Yet Donald was nothing like perfection as a husband. He was a standard-issue straight male. The only things he cooked were hamburgers on the grill and popcorn for watching television. He knew how to clean, because he had watched his mother, but he didn't see dirt, as men don't. *Like the feminist complaint of the man as ball and chain,* thought Deirdre. *Take two steps, drag Donald. I was a man of the age, raised in the 1950s with its gender corrals.* He was better prepared for child care, because as an older brother he had been the baby-sitter for a sister eleven years and a brother thirteen years younger.

Their son was born in Chicago in 1969, their daughter in 1975 during another English year of research into economic history. With children around the house it was agreed that Donald better put the cross-dressing farther back into the closet. *A mistake,* thought Deirdre later, *though a mistake we made together.* Donald became cunning at hiding the crossdressing, so that his wife formed a low estimate of how much he dressed, and the children never knew. When a psychiatrist asked her in 1995, his wife estimated he did it maybe once a month, a factor of ten too low, because without much inquiry that's the most she could infer from the evidence of slightly disturbed clothing. Donald got skilled at the furtiveness of replacing clothing just so. Mainly he left her clothing alone; he had accumulated a little of his own. *A trivial thing. Forget it.* Since they never talked about it, his wife had no check on her estimate. It therefore came as a shock to her when he finally came spinning out of the closet, at any rate to club meetings and to an occasional startled citizen at a suburban mall far from home. She thought it was entirely new and that he had gone crazy.

He had been doing it ten times a month through four decades, whenever possible, though in the closet. The quantifying economist made the calculation: *About five thousand episodes.* When he was alone for a term at the Institute for Advanced Study at Princeton in 1983 he did it daily in his apartment, for hours at a time while he worked on revising his book *The Applied Theory of Price* or on papers about the "rhetoric of economics." Had he met other cross-dressers during the Princeton term the dam of his gender-crossing desires would have broken a dozen years before it did. *For the best.*

If Donald had been in fact what he thought he was until August 1995, a heterosexual crossdresser, there would have been another way. At a gathering of crossdressers at a rustic lodge in the Poconos, Donald met one who had dressed at home all his married life. He sat transfixed in the timbered dining room as the man told how he and his wife had handled it. Openly. His children viewed it as Daddy's peculiarity and protected him from outside discovery. It had no effect on the sexuality of the children or the sex life of the parents. Sharing the secret brought the family together. And there was no shattering revelation in the end, no shame or anger or lack of comprehension. But as young parents in 1969 the McCloskeys were not equipped for taking such a course and therefore put Donald firmly in the closet. They were of the closeted decade, the decade of those state secrets, the decade so attractive to the authoritarian personality. *Ob, well. Maybe for the best.*

■

For forty-one years Donald dressed when he could and otherwise lived a normal male life. He was not unhappy. On the contrary, everyone who knew him, himself included, thought of him as reasonably cheerful. Not easygoing, but no sad sack. He didn't mind being a guy too much. He liked stepping out in a three-piece power suit, or playing touch football with the graduate students, or laughing with the guys on a boat trip over a fourth can of beer. He liked playing and watching sports. He was puzzled by women and wary about opening up to them. With gladness he played the roles of son and husband and father and studied the lessons of secular stoicism: *What am I complaining about? I have a wonderful life. Though a man. Shoulder the sky, my lad, and drink your ale.*

In August 1994 his daughter went off to college. No kids now. The fifty-something parents joked about it: "Free at last, free at last—praise God almighty, free at last!" Yet they loved their children and loved raising them, from late-night burping and first words in Chicago through youth soccer and school orchestra in Iowa City. As teenagers the children had enacted the usual high-school ghastliness, but they seemed to be coming out of it. They were lovely children before age thirteen. Donald remembered playing baseball in the twilight with his son in the park across from their row house in Chicago. He remembered playing cricket with his daughter between the two trees in the front yard in Iowa City. But after twenty-five years without a break—the grandparents lived a thousand miles away—it was pleasant to come home to a house where the phone didn't ring much.

What had not occurred to him until it happened was that for the first time in twenty-five years no kids made the house safe for crossdressing. The only person liable to walk in unannounced already knew. So he started dressing more. Back about 1900, when a Tammany Hall politician was caught robbing the people of New York, he was indignant at the charge. "What's the problem? I engage only in *honest* graft. I saw my opportunity and I took it." Donald saw his opportunity and he took it.

By the 1990s he was not ashamed about crossdressing in private. He was not going to exhibit it to the world. Goodness no. But on the other hand he was not racked by the guilt of his teens and twenties and thirties. After all, he was in his fifties. By then, if ever, people have stopped torturing themselves about who they are, by contrast with their twenties, unaware, or their thirties, when youthful optimism wears out, or their forties, when dismay sets in. Self-acceptance is the compensation of age. At fifty-two Donald accepted crossdressing as part of who he was. True, if before the realization that he could cross all the way someone had offered a pill to stop the occasional crossdressing he would have accepted, since it was mildly distracting— though hardly time consuming. Until the spring of 1995 each of the five thousand episodes was associated with quick, male sex. There was no cure for crossdressing, he read. Aversion therapy did not work. Pills did not work. Talking cures did not work. Nothing worked. The many failed stuttering cures had accustomed him to nothing's working.

But so what? he said to himself. *It's a minor matter. I'm just a heterosexual crossdresser.*

3

INTERNET

So in the fall of 1994 he dressed more. Just for fun. Then he discovered the Internet. He had always read about crossdressing and gender crossing. As an adolescent he would scour reference books in the local Carnegie library for descriptions of Julian Eltinge and other showbusiness types (Eltinge, a female impersonator who flourished in the 1910s and 1920s, has a theater on Broadway named after him). In the undergraduate library at Harvard he read for sexual stimulation the part on "eonism" in Havelock Ellis's *Studies in the Psychology of Sex*. The libraries told him he was not utterly alone, though during the 1950s and early 1960s they said it softly. Emma Goldman in *Living My Life* speaks of her daring lectures during World War I on homosexuality. A tortured young lesbian came up to her afterward: "She had never met anyone," wrote Goldman, "who suffered from a similar affliction, nor had she ever read books dealing with the subject. My lecture had set her free; I had given her back her self-respect."

But libraries are public places, and Donald couldn't be caught in the psychology library reading books about gender crossing—he just couldn't. He never withdrew from a library a book that had an obviously crossgender theme, because then the librarian would have known. Not that the librarian would have cared, really, but the moment of acknowledgment, eye-to-eye, would have been too much, just too much to bear. So he had to read the autobiography of Renée Richards, *Second Serve,* in the library itself, because its subtitle was too explicit. He was able to take out Nancy Hunt's autobiography because it was called just *Mirror Image.* Picture books about drag shows and the like were library-only materials, to be read off in some corner. *Replace them, now; don't be a slob.*

Bookstores were no better. Starting in college Donald had been buying crossdressing magazines from adult bookstores, such as the newsstand on Mass. Avenue in Harvard Square around the corner from his undergraduate dorm, though furtively. Decades later he became less furtive about it: *Dammit, that's what they're in business for; and that's what I want.* But reputable bookstores were sites of embarrassment. He did manage to buy *Venus Castina,* a popular history of crossdressing, from O'Gara's early in his dozen years at the University of Chicago. It told among others of the Chevalier d'Éon, whom Donald had encountered already in the pages of Havelock Ellis (thus "eonism," crossdressing). This French spy and courtier had lived the last decades of his life about 1800 as a woman. The most affecting book was one he found in a bookstore while visiting Stanford for six months as a young assistant professor of economics, age thirty-one: Geoff Brown's novel *I Want What I Want: To Be a Woman* (1966). He bought it timorously, took it home to the rented house in Portola Valley, and read it in one sitting, fascinated. About a lonely British man who tries to live as a woman, it conveyed the joy and terror of passing. The novel ended with him/her falling down a staircase, presumably dying. Transgression was punished, in the style of the Motion Picture Code. Surprisingly, the book was made into a movie. Donald was disappointed that they chose a genetic girl to play the lead.

Jan Morris's account of her transition, *Conundrum* (1974), which he read in his forties, showed Donald that gender crossing was possible for someone other than a French thief or a pathetic loner. *Conundrum* (the title expresses the futility of asking why) rescued gender crossing from the demimonde. Morris was as James and is as Jan a British journalist and travel writer. The book is beautifully written. If intellectuals have read one book on crossing, Morris's is usually it.

Most women and some men would have noticed a pattern (Donald didn't): he always read disproportionately about gender crossers, or about crossdressers who actually lived as women. When in 1994 he ran across *A Life in High Heels,* an autobiography by Holly Woodlawn, one of Andy Warhol's group, the parts he read and reread and was sexually aroused by were about Woodlawn's living successfully for months at a time as a woman, not her campiness when presenting as a gay genetic man in a dress.

Donald's preoccupation with gender crossing showed up in an ugly fact about the pornographic magazines he used. There are two kinds of crossdressing magazines, those that portray the men in dresses with private parts showing and those that portray them hidden. He could never get aroused by the ones with private parts showing. His fantasy was of complete transformation, not a peek-a-boo, leering masculinity. He wanted what he wanted.

If he had had to rely as before on print, if he had not late in 1994 discovered the Internet, it would have taken him another year to come out, in the modest sense of dressing regularly at home and going to clubs once a month or so. He was now going to come out sometime in his fifties, after raising his family. Nothing public. He saw his opportunity, or came gradually to realize that he had it within reach, and he was going to take it, slowly or quickly. Just a hobby. Foreign travel.

The media paid some attention to crossdressing, and he had formed the habit of using the newspaper indexes at the local public library to dig out stories. He was startled by a piece in the *New Yorker* in January 1995, early in his new, higher level of activity, about a crossdresser who was a well-known businessman in Nashville. The piece, complete with pictures, had that defensive, homophobic air that infects most nongay men writing about gender transgressions, since they are concerned to show that *they* would never think of doing such a thing. "I don't *understand* this," they aver, "but here it is for your amusement." Donald showed the article to his wife to suggest to her that people other than homosexual prostitutes on the old Times Square were crossdressers, in this case a married man with a big business career, but she was just irritated and frightened. When the reporter asked the Nashville businessman why he did it—"doing it" included such pranks as showing up with his wife at a restaurant in a tuxedo jacket, male drag, but with an attractive skirt and heels, female drag, on the bottom—he couldn't get further than declaring it was "fun." *Yes,* Donald thought. *Fun.*

What he discovered when he got onto the Internet is that it differed from libraries and bookstores because it was private. Censors loathe it. When he joined he was looking for bulletin boards on economics and on the English game of cricket. He found that the bulletin board about cricket had five hundred messages a day, with detailed accounts of every first-class match in the world and exchanges about this or that controversy.

Then it occurred to him that he might find something on cross-dressing, and on the local Net he did find an on-line conversation that included it. After some weeks he figured out how to access "alt.sex," which contained materials for his fantasies in an abundance that startled him. It aroused him, too. For weeks of spending a couple of hours a day on the Internet, whenever he could make time in a doubly crowded semester of teaching, he would focus on the pornographic bits. Here was a library expressly designed for sexual arousal of crossdressers, and aroused he was.

After a month or so on this version of his hobby Donald began to get interested in the real-life stories and the technical advice on a crossgendered life. Odd. The sexual part started to fade, something new in his crossdressing, though he didn't notice. The Internet contained a library of information on makeup and shopping. For some months he ignored the files on gender crossing itself, the medical information on going all the way. After all, he had decided that wasn't him, right? But he got gobs and gobs on how to make crossdressing work. Just a hobby.

He then found *Melanie's Autobiography,* the on-line story of Melanie Philips, a video producer in California. She has a tape, "Melanie's Tape," famous among the male-to-female crossgendered, that shows—though not making it easy—how to get a feminine voice by practice. But it wasn't the technical success in her story that gripped Donald. It was the anguish and fear, Melanie's attempt to keep her family together, her conviction that she wanted what she wanted, and finally her getting it. He read the book for hours. Being incompetent at computers, he had difficulty extracting it from the Internet, but he finally printed it out. The fascination was still partly sexual, though less and less so. He didn't realize it, but he was deliberating.

He went beyond silent reading. He joined some computer conversations by telephone link, Bulletin Board Systems (BBSs), and began having on-line discussions with other crossdressers. Among Net surfers the BBSs are known for pornography, but the discussions he took part in were Sunday school innocent. On his BBSs the crossgendered men talked mainly about how to go on living with their wives. *Not a transsexual.* He still used the silly medical word, though by now he had stopped using the Latin for what he thought he was by contrast, "transvestite": *I'm just a plain, English-described "crossdresser." "I'm a lumberjack, and I'm OK."* Donald started with a BBS in Massachusetts run by a crossdresser's organization in Waltham. *Funny,* Deirdre thought later, *my first discussions needed to be with people from home in Massachusetts.* He ended on a BBS out of Chicago and became acquainted in the electronic way with a half dozen or so Chicagoland crossdressers and gender crossers. *And my second discussions needed to be with people from my second home in Chicago. And full coming out with my third in Iowa.*

The Internet is filled with aliases and other shifts of identity. Donald chose "Jane Austen" as his handle, a literary and academic choice. As a teenager back in Massachusetts he had had a crush on a girl named Jane. One of Jane Austen's BBS friends was "Lucy" from Chicago, who came the four hours to Iowa City once for dinner. It was the first time Donald had met another crossdresser in the flesh, though both Lucy and he were in male drag. The trouble Lucy had gone to was affecting. He was just as nervous on meeting as Donald was. For the next few months they leaned on each other. They were at the same stage of wholly closeted crossdressing, both married, both with middle-class jobs, and neither had been to any crossdressing meetings yet. Donald had joined the local club, Iowa Artistry (named in the veiled way for security, but reachable at P.O. box 75, Cedar Rapids), through his own recently acquired post office box—more furtiveness—but the club had skipped a month's meeting and so he hadn't been to one yet.

The telephone bills for spending a couple of hours a day "talking" on line to Lucy and other people were large. Because Donald never could figure out how to do it right, the bills started to show an extra few hundred dollars every month. The right way was to take off all the messages quickly, read and reply to them off-line, then stick them back on-line all at once, instead of staying connected to long distance for hours at a time. But he could hardly call in a computer expert to show him how to do it, since then he would be known. It was like the library.

The bills infuriated his wife and added to her conviction that he was going crazy. He replied that it was therapy, considering what the BBSers talked about. She didn't believe him. She wouldn't look at the messages or talk about the crossdressing. He replied that he was spending less on phone bills than some people do on therapy, for the same purpose. He was spending less in total at the height of his crossdressing that year, he explained, ever the rational economist, than many people spend on hobbies. Model trains can be expensive; classic cars, very. She was angry, unappeased. She was the one who routinely worried about money, though they were comfortable. She used the ritual of complaining about his extra spending to express the undiscussable, her fears about gender crossing. Donald remained convinced that he was merely a heterosexual crossdresser who finally was going to indulge his hobby a little more. Relax, dear. During the months of unconscious deliberation his wife knew there was something deeper, and even at the time he could see that it terrified her. Don't worry.

Donald was blithe, exploring a part of himself long dammed up, letting the water dribble unchecked through a widening crack. He became determined to have some of this fun. It was a male project like many, like studying Latin with a passion at age forty or spending a summer month reading all fifteen of Patrick O'Brien's Aubrey-Maturin novels, lengthy dreams of courage in Nelson's navy. He would sweep the kitchen or make the bed while pretending he was swabbing the decks or reefing a topsail.

His wife couldn't stand the new project, and they agreed for a while that he would not dress in front of her. But she was around a lot, since their home was close to her job in the College of Nursing. Donald was home only in the evenings, because of the heavy teaching load that spring. To get more time for dressing and yet not offend his wife's eyes he started sleeping less. He would get up at 3:30 A.M. and dress as a woman. In the wee hours he would prepare lectures and then surf the Internet. He loved these dawns, this fun.

His sister later wove the episode of abbreviated sleep, which lasted a few months, into a tale of "mania," claiming it still was happening months after it had stopped. He slept normally when his wife let him dress. Some mania. ***Nothing serious.***

4

PROFESSOR DRESSED

Donald traveled a lot, lurching from conference to conference. It concentrates the intellect to be scheduled to present your scholarly findings to your colleagues in a month. Academic conferences are somber affairs, at any rate in economics and history, not like Shriners' conventions. But Donald started to use them to pursue his expanded hobby, like a Shriner safely far from home.

The first was a spring conference in California about "postmodernism" in economics. The subject was part of Donald's intellectual crossdressing, though his focus this time was literal crossdressing. He had learned from the Internet the address of a crossdressers' shop near the conference in Riverside, so at the Los Angeles airport he rented a car and set off through the snarl of freeways to find the place. He was frightened as he parked the car and walked unsteadily in the dark across to the shop. Once inside he was the least furtive of the customers. Relief. Delight.

He delighted in trying on shoes in big sizes and found two pairs on sale that Deirdre later found usable for a woman's life. He delighted in trying on the waist cinchers and strapless bras. Deirdre didn't use them. They are not designed for a normal woman's life, and she was not into pain. Besides, the clothes at such shops are low quality in matters like stitching. Better to buy your underwear at J. C. Penney's or Marks and Spencer's.

Most of all Donald delighted in trying on the wigs. If your hair looks good, you look good. *It's something hard-wired,* Deirdre thought later, *this human attention to the details of a woman's hair.* Donald had the ratty old wig, decades old, that served for quick sex. By this stage he was interested in longer illusions, without the sex. (Crossdressing without the sex: What?) With the help of the woman who owned the shop he tried on wig after wig and bought one, synthetic curls, copper colored.

He still had a beard, an Amish style he had worn for about ten years, started as a full beard back when his son was giving adolescent grief. Donald thought the beard might make a more impressively masculine display to his son and bring him into line. The Amish touch came later, when he got tired of getting his mustache wet with wine or soup.

So there he was trying on wigs with a luxuriant growth of red facial hair. The woman said, "You know, the wigs would look a lot better without the beard!" He laughed and agreed, and the next week at home in Iowa he shaved it off. The act frightened his wife, as another sign of something deeper in his hobby. Don't worry, dear. Just crossdressing.

■

He was to give a speech at Lafayette College in eastern Pennsylvania, but first he drove the rental car from Newark Airport to visit Lee's Marti Gras, a crossdressing store in a dangerous neighborhood on the Lower West Side of Manhattan, where the *New Yorker* had described the businessman from Nashville as going. The store had a protective system of ringing you up on the elevator. On a street thronged with tough-looking men stands little you timorously waiting for the elevator to open, self-identified as a crossdresser to those who know what the store sells. Once inside Donald was again bumptious, buying makeup, nightgowns, garter belts, camisoles, hip-padded panties, and what Lee claimed was a little black dress (all at high prices: these people are not in business for love). That night in the guest bedroom at the home of an economist friend, Donald secretly tried on his new nightgown, a slinky ivory-colored satin number redolent of 1930s movies, and was thrilled. In that thing, beardless, he *did* look a little bit like Greta Garbo. In dim light.

■

About two conferences a month. He went for a conference in Philadelphia on English composition, sponsored by his friend Herb, a communication theorist at Temple University. Deirdre made new friends among women, but her men friends came mostly from the earlier life. They were the men Donald liked as a man himself, men who seemed to understand themselves and could therefore handle it. "In touch with their feelings" is the California phrase. As a woman Deirdre liked them too, as most women do. Women call them good men and reckon them rare.

Donald's interest in composition was more intellectual crossdressing (he had once published a book on writing for economists and was happy when it came out in a new edition under Deirdre's name). One of the papers at the conference was called "Writing on the Bias." The woman was arguing that writing could be learned in effect by analogy with other tasks, and she used as an example her mother's gifted dressmaking. As any woman knows, "on the bias" describes the drape of cloth. Her mother's particular skill was using the drape to give the dress special movement and grace. It was like the draping of words, the author declared. One could take the spirit of one activity and use it in another.

Donald was entranced. It seemed to him that his own mother's way of starting and finishing projects around the house when he was an adolescent had in the same way taught him how to work. His mother did everything, from changing diapers (as fathers in the 1950s did not) to tearing down walls and rebuilding them. "Writing on the Bias" fit Donald's life.

In the discussion after the presentation he asked boldly in Donald fashion, "I admire your argument, but would you tell us men exactly what 'on the bias' means?"

"It's too difficult to explain to men," she replied, and the women laughed. Later he ate lunch at her table in the cafeteria and tried to make contact, but the man-woman gap was too wide. As a woman Deirdre learned something about sewing. *"On the bias" is too difficult to explain to men,* she said to herself, giggling.

At the cocktail party that evening Donald talked for a long time with two young women professors and had better success closing the gap. One of the women gave a course at Temple on gender roles. That caught Donald's attention. She had the students come to one of the classes in some degree of drag. The exercise made vivid in a harmless setting how hard it is to cross gender lines. The trick was emotionally hardest for the young men. The professor noted her pleasure when a young man who had been giving off defensively macho messages all semester was able to bring himself to wear at least a feminine scarf to class. He didn't turn gay, or decide to have The Operation.

At the party the three of them, standing with white wine in hand, started to talk about the position of women academics, which Donald craftily specialized to dress codes. One of the women noted the rule that only secretaries could wear colored nail polish. Female graduate students and female professors have to show their seriousness and their resistance to conventional femininity by wearing, if anything, only pale colors on their nails, nothing bright red. The other woman kicked off her shoe to reveal fire-engine red toenails and said, "But you can get away with *anything* on your feet!" They laughed at the feminine and self-deprecating joke, and Donald was nearly overcome with a comic impulse to pull off his shoe and sock to reveal *his* brightly colored toenails.

The toenails were a recent exception to a rule of not "underdressing"—dressing in female underthings. Unlike some crossgendered people, Donald didn't do it. It is uncomfortable, and dangerous for security. I mean, what if you were hit by a truck and the ambulance came and they cut away your pants and saw the female underthings, and so forth, to paraphrase your mother trying to get you to wear clean underwear? (They've seen dirty underwear, Mom, on the right gender or not.) But the main reason was that he disliked presenting as a man when dressed underneath as a woman. It would be more peek-a-boo. Dressed as a woman he wanted to *be* a woman, not a man with a problem. Though just for fun.

Why now the toenail polish? Or shaving his legs, which he started about then too? Or the beginnings of electrolysis on his hands, which gets hair off permanently? Because these were changes to his body itself, he supposed. That spring and summer he didn't see, as his wife increasingly did, that there was something beyond crossdressing about his form of crossdressing. Not a guy thing.

After the conference in downtown Philadelphia he rented a car and went to visit a wig store in a private house on a normal suburban street. The owner was a motherly woman about his age who had been dealing with crossdressers for years. Donald tried on dozens of wigs, and they agreed on five, each for about $80. They were good wigs, at that price not human hair, though unless you are going to buy an expensive human-hair wig, as Deirdre did later in Holland, the synthetics are fine. One of them became Deirdre's standby when she went full time, before the human-hair fitting, and she amortized the investment in the six synthetic wigs (with the one from the Los Angeles shop) over six months of daily wear. Still an economist: the expenditure on the synthetic wigs was about $2.70 a day of full-time wear. Not imprudent.

Afterward Donald drove down to Baltimore and stayed with a high-school friend, being just Don. When Deirdre came out months later the friend was kind. Old, remote friends must love you for yourself alone, and not your yellow hair, since there is no profit or amusement in the relationship.

On the way to Baltimore he stopped at Wanamaker's, the fancy chain of department stores in the mid-Atlantic region, and with heart pounding went up to a saleslady at the cosmetics counter.

"I'm a crossdresser and need some Dermablend. Is that all right?" he asked. Dermablend is a foundation good for covering beard shadow.

She looked bored. "Of course, sir." She had heard this before and went to work selling him more cosmetics than he needed.

5

CLUBS

The big event of that half week was on the way home from the East Coast to Iowa City. Donald had arranged to stop in a Chicago suburb for Saturday night, going to a motel to meet his crossdressing friend Lucy. Then they planned to navigate the parking lot of the motel next door to attend their very first crossdressing meeting.

The meeting was for the Chicago chapter of Tri Ess, the national crossdressing sorority, which Donald had joined through his Chicago BBS girlfriends. He had been excited for weeks and planned it like a military campaign, lugging from Iowa City to Philadelphia to Baltimore to Chicago a big suitcase filled with his outfit for the evening and his Philadelphia loot. He chose his Marilyn Monroe wig and a black crepe dress inherited from his wife.

Lucy arrived already dressed, and Donald complimented him, as women do: "You look great!"

"I found a cosmetician in my suburb who does makeovers on crossdressers." Lucy looked like a suburban housewife, not a drag-show star. Later Donald bought some dresses at the woman's store and had a makeover himself. The cosmetician's youngest son was a drag queen and competed in beauty contests.

Lucy got anxious and wanted to go, and Donald/Jane agreed as he struggled into the dress, a little small: "I'll come over when I'm ready.

Zip me up, will you?" *Better to go by myself,* he thought. The probability of being read rises with the square of the number of crossdressers in a group. (One is "read" like a book, detected in the wrong gender.) The man on the street reads the least convincing one of a group and then notes that all these women seem large.

Stepping out into the hallway of his motel half an hour later he was frightened, imagining detection and the punishment of scorn. On the stairs going down, avoiding the elevator with its long looks, he walked by a couple coming up, but they didn't appear to read him. Clicking in heels around the back of his own motel, he walked into the open toward the other one. It was Donald's first time out-of-doors as a woman, apart from a very few nighttime walks in empty streets in Princeton and Chicago. It felt natural. He hitched up his skirt and leaped over a little stream between the two motels, scuttling through the other parking lot in full drag in the glare of the late afternoon sun. Still outside, as he approached the entrance to the meeting room he encountered a woman: *Uh, oh; she'll read me. Wait: no.* It was another crossdresser on his way to the meeting. *Easy to read when you're looking for it.*

When Jane came into the meeting room it was filled with crossdressers, and his first impression was, *These women are huge!* They were a third bulkier than a roomful of genetic women. It seemed to him that the average crossdresser was above average in height. *Can't be.* (It can, though. If there is a deficiency of testosterone in adolescence the bones do not close off early in their growth. That's why boys who mature early tend to be short and why the castrati playing women's roles with women's voices in early opera were unusually tall for men. Not that there's any evidence of testosterone deficiency in crossdressers, mind you. Just guys.) Still, the clubs ordinarily do not have really big men in them, which makes one wonder how the bigger crossdressers and gender crossers are able to express themselves. Perhaps in football.

Most everyone was cordial, though some of the prettier ones seemed snooty. Jane later met one of the snooty ones in Atlanta at a conference discussion on gender-crossing life for professionals and found him shy and uncertain about his future. They all had name tags, and Jane spotted and hugged Suzy, one of the BBS friends he had not met in the flesh. Suzy was "Susan Roberts," which is to say that in the convention of choosing feminine names among crossdressers he was "Bob" as a man. He was tall, thin, blond, breaking up with an intolerant wife whom he still loved, and struggling with his identity.

"I went to therapy for two years with my wife," Suzy said.

"Two years. Did it help?"

"In a way. We're getting divorced. The therapist finally said to me, 'Look: your wife is unable to adjust. Some women can handle it, others can't. She has her own reasons.'"

When the official meeting broke up Jane was standing next to a vivacious crossdresser named Robin, a little taller than he was, with a Chicago-accented voice. He was brassy, intelligent, extroverted, complaining knowingly about the administration of Tri Ess. (Jane learned later that it was his first meeting too.) He proposed that he, Jane, Suzy, Jane's friend Lucy, and another crossdresser go out on the town. Lucy demurred, and the remaining four musketettes set out for a lesbian bar.

The tougher straight bars are good places to get killed. Gay bars also have the undercurrent of lethal violence that is the male condition. The lesbians are more civilized and don't mind having crossdressers around, regarding them as harmless. The first place was quiet, though enlivened by the crossdressers (ten of them, with others from the Tri Ess meeting, crowded along a set of bar tables like a typing pool out for an after-work drink) and then by an ineffectual fistfight between two lesbians in a love triangle. Jane danced the way the kids do, by himself, different from the lovely paired regularity of square dancing. A butch dyke paired with Jane for a while on the dance floor, and Jane gave himself over to ecstasy. "Just dance!" the dyke said, "Don't come on to me." When he had to go to the bathroom Jane had the others take a picture of Suzy and him outside the "first ladies' room." Pictures are big among crossdressers. How many crossdressers does it take to go the ladies' room? One hundred: one to go and ninety-nine to take pictures.

They went to a much hotter lesbian bar called Temptations on Grand Avenue in the Chicago suburbs. It was in a strip mall next to a tire store, and when the stars came out it glittered. Robin had been to the place before, as everyone else had too. They regarded Jane as bold to go with the girls barhopping on his first night out. What made Jane run? Square dancer, middle-aged college professor, father of two, thirty years married, pillar of the community shook to the beat of the drum with a hundred others of assorted genders and sexual preferences. The cool dance the kids were performing turned out to be steps that Donald had learned the year before at a square dance in Iowa City. The company was diverting, and each set was long.

Robin introduced Jane to a lesbian sitting at a little table crowded with others. She looked like a suburban woman. Kids. Van. She was in her forties, dressed butch but not too. Acceptable in the mall. *Though women can get away with more.*

"I was married and have grown children," she told Jane. "I only figured this out a few years ago."

"How have they adjusted? I mean your family?" Jane was always interviewing people, gathering data like some sort of anthropologist, an anthropologist who could go native.

"Poorly." It was not unusual news. In the gay and lesbian community, Jane read later, they spoke of 80 percent: 80 percent of your family and friends eventually adjust, perhaps after years of rejection, and go on loving you after a fashion. That leaves 20 percent. As they talked about rejection and acceptance Jane warmed to her, and he found himself flirting as the femme. They danced for a while to the throbbing music, then she bought Jane a beer. In his three later visits to Temptations Jane looked for her, a regular it was said, but never saw her. Jane/Donald was still unclear about his preferences. Gender crossing is a matter of identity, not affectual preferences. *A third of post-op transsexuals go on loving women,* he would remind himself out of his new learning. *Not that I'm a transsexual.*

He went to Temptations only those three more times. Chicago is 240 miles from Iowa City. (Deirdre would explain to Dutch people where Iowa City was: "Near Chicago." Oh, how far? they would ask, supposing she meant 50 kilometers. "It's 500 kilometers due west, as far as Amsterdam is west of Berlin. Not too far.") Donald never did go to similar places closer to home. Fear, security, the closet.

Robin said later that he was struck that first time by Donald's reaction as Jane to the unbuttoned scene. Jane came up to Robin and gushed, "Lord, I just *love* this!" The gushing seemed to Robin significant, signaling more than a guy in a dress. Robin was coming to terms with his own gender crossing and went full time the next month, just before Donald's dam broke. Robin had the operation in Montreal a couple of months after Deirdre had it in Australia. Deirdre called Robin afterwards and they talked about how they just *loved* this.

He got back to the motel room at 3:00 A.M. and had a 10:00 A.M. flight home. That afternoon in Iowa he was teaching business economics in his macho, I'm in charge style. As men brag about their little exploits, he dropped hints to the kids about his wild night at a bar in Chicago. He left out the detail that he had danced through it in a cocktail dress.

■

He went to the first meeting of his local club, Iowa Artistry, thrilled and frightened. The meeting was held in a big motel out by the interstate. He was pleased to drive across town dressed—***This is how it feels to be a woman***—but nervous about coming into the motel as Jane. In fact respectable motels are cordial to crossdressers, because they are good customers. Aside from makeup on the towels, they are no trouble. They don't drink much, and they don't do sex or violence.

Iowa Artistry was forthrightly Iowan. The meeting was like a Kiwanis Club in drag, with reports from the treasurer and mild quarrels about governance. Jane had long, earnest talks about living with crossdressing. His attention was held by a thirty-something gender crosser named Anna who worked as a technician in a corporation south of Iowa City. She had been full time for a year and had finished electrolysis on her beard down in Dallas, which he quizzed her about. She was intelligent and sympathetic, once married, kids. Donald was deliberating, unaware. ***But of course I am a heterosexual crossdresser. Just wondering.***

Donald's wife dreaded people's finding out and was appalled that after the meeting a group of fifteen or so went on to a local bowling alley. Nothing happened, no one found out. One attempt at rolling the ball left Donald/Jane's false thumbnail halfway down the alley, and he had to walk out to retrieve it, amused and embarrassed. He watched closely another crosser, very effeminate. She was there with her male lover, the two making an ordinary husband and wife. Three years later she had her operation and they were legally married. She worked as a telephone operator. The daily practice and her determination had made her voice good. The heterosexual crossdressers, by contrast, were breezily male in their voice and behavior. Jane didn't think much about where he fit in.

There was only one other group in the bowling alley, at the opposite end. Eventually one of them came over to see what was going on, and a crossdresser replied with a smile that they were a "mixed league" of bowlers—a man and a woman in the same body. When crossdressers meet straight people in a group it works fine. Crossdressers call it "gender education."

■

After months of new learning Jane was at another Tri Ess meeting in a Holiday Inn in the western suburbs of Chicago, fifty men in dresses, some of them pretty and passable, many now his acquaintances from the BBS or from the nights out at Temptations. There were also half a dozen or so natural-born women (GGs: genetic girls): wives, hairdressers. It was to be an ice cream social.

Who was preparing the food?

One of the GGs, of course, the wife of a crossdresser who was himself sitting with his fifty buddies trading stories about the Chicago Bears. Jane was silently indignant. *This is silly. Isn't the game to play at being women?* He got up and started helping, woman to woman. No other crossdresser got up (and no other GG for that matter). Jane and the wife became the ladies of the church, preparing and serving the meal to the group. Jane liked it, this we women thing, but was surprised that the other crossdressers stayed sitting to be served. The wife didn't seem to find their behavior peculiar.

Time to clean up. Jane started going around the room with a big trash bag. In a roomful of born women half would have risen to help, and the other half would at least have made cooperative gestures. None of the crossdressers moved. Donald later worked it out: These were men, these 97 percent of crossdressers who are not gender crossers. Like the joke card of comfort to a woman friend who is ill: "Feeling sick? Well, put up your feet and let other people serve you." Open the card: "In other words, act like a man!" Jane plucked empty pop cans out of the men's hands without their noticing. After all, they were onto something important, such as that great pass play just before halftime at Soldier Field, or the merits of dual carburetors in rebuilding a '56 Merc. *Don't these guys want to play the game?* Jane didn't realize yet that he was playing a different and more womanly game.

People sometimes say, "I don't understand crossdressers, who dress as women but don't want to *be* women." What don't you understand, dear? It's a game. A man plays pool and gets satisfaction from pretending for an evening that he's Minnesota Fats. He has no intention of leaving his job as an insurance agent and taking to pool hustling. People do things from flower arranging to politics that satisfy them, amuse them, excite them, as a game for an hour or an afternoon or a weekend. Compared with the bizarre inanities of, say, golf—putting a tiny ball in a distant hole with instruments ill designed for the purpose—this game of dressing in women's clothes seems natural, something that might well occur to someone to try out "just for fun."

In Holland Deirdre became acquainted with a man starting a gender change. He invited Deirdre over to his house, and he and his wife and Deirdre talked for an evening about the Dutchman's feminine yearnings and the tactics of coming out. They were a pleasant, intelligent couple, with the usual Dutch ease in speaking English. But his wife served the refreshments and cleaned up. Deirdre sat uneasy. Maybe the wife was self-conscious because her English was less bold than his and welcomed the refuge in the kitchen. Yet it was notable that the male host who wanted to be a woman never initiated serving or cleaning up or attending to the guest. Deirdre wondered if he quite realized what the deal was, this being a woman. ***Being a woman is what you do,*** she thought, ***not what you wear. Caring, watching, noticing.*** It might be difficult for gender crossers to make the transition with their wives. The male habit of being served persists. "Act like a man."

The rule is to clean up your own messes and to be thoughtful about other people's messes. Scottish friends sent Deirdre a British joke card in a series called "Men: The Truth." A half-dressed man looks in his clothes drawer: "It's like magic! Cleaned, ironed clothes appear in my wardrobe each week!" The Truth about Men (on opening the card): "They believe in the ironing fairy." Some women try to believe too, but most don't, and when the average grown-up woman leaves the table she looks for stray cups to be washed, part of the cleaning, loving, caring that women are always doing half consciously. Deirdre's brother, who had worked a long time with women, agreed: "You're right: men never clean up." It's not that all women are neater or more prudent than all men. But many women are ashamed to make work for others, and they see a lone cup the average man cannot see in his passion for the game.

6

IN THE LADIES' ROOM

At first the loss of weight came from reading and then acting on the new food labels that listed fat content. *Healthy anyway.* Donald weighed 235 pounds on six feet of height, and as he got down to 210 and then by late April to 190 people got worried. Cancer? No, just getting rid of 45 pounds of obesity—still not close to my college weight of 175, he replied reasonably, though it was more than reason.

The loss of weight came to have a goal—to get down to size twelve by the time of the big event in June, his first gender convention. It was the "Be All (You Can Be)" in a Holiday Inn north of Cincinnati, four and a half days of dressing continuously as a woman. Four and a half days. *Wow.* Donald's BBS friend from Chicago, Lucy, agreed to drive down to Cincinnati with him. Early on a Tuesday morning Donald put all the shoes and makeup and clothing and jewelry he owned into the trunk of the big Buick Le Sabre and drove to Chicago to pick up Lucy. Lucy and Jane then tootled down to Cincinnati the same day, dressed in male clothing but happy, oh, so happy.

The convention was good humored. The two hundred cross-dressers took up half the rooms, which left two hundred straight people having a strange experience. The second day Jane was riding down on the elevator with a few other crossdressers in full regalia when a straight family of husband, wife, and two kids got on. They were stunned. They turned to the front as people do in elevators, and a silence settled over the car. Just before the first floor a deep male voice came from the gaggle of crossdressers in the back: "Jeez, I'm never coming to this hotel again. . . . Too many weird people!"

Weird at a glance, the way a camera snaps. Diane Arbus was among the first photographers to take an interest in the crossgendered, but her photos of weird people are glances, staying on the surface, treating the people as objects, the Other. The documentary *Paris Is Burning* is like an Arbus photo collection brought to film. You do not come to know the people doing the drag queen style shows except to find them pathetic and distant, Them. For the straight hotel guests in Cincinnati it probably felt like the camera's glance. But for the participants in the convention it felt like the movie *To Won Foo,* a sympathetic farce about drag queens. The feminine sympathy emanating from a story about people you have come to know is nothing like the voyeuristic experience of the glance, the male gaze.

The hotel staff was courteous. Three of its young women judged a femininity contest for dress, hair, walking, standing, talking. No one took the contest very seriously, though no one played "Hey, I'm really a guy," either. It wasn't comic drag at the Lions Club picnic. The convention organizers suggested that the participants tip the chambermaids for the extra work in cleaning up after people like Jane and Lucy. The crossdressers threw the rooms into chaos daily with quick changes from one outfit to another, staining the towels with the larded makeup for covering beard shadow. In an appropriate Sunday dress on the last day Jane stopped one of the maids, thanked her, and started to give her $20. (Deirdre would have given her $10, rather than brag by the larger amount how rich and powerful Donald was, in the style of Frank Sinatra.) The maid started to take it and reflexively said to the deep voice, "Thank you, sir." Jane snatched back the bill, and corrected her, "If you please! It's 'ma'am'!" The maid laughed and said the magic word.

Jane toured the shops set up temporarily on the ground floor, buying a makeover from one, a glamour photo from another, rings for large hands from a makeup man from Long Beach famous in the drag world, a set of fitted breast prostheses that glued to your chest (by now Jane was shaving his copious chest hair), and a couple of dresses with sequins from the clothing shop. He was still not trying for ordinary women's clothing, and he had draggy tastes. The clothing store let him dress up in a Scarlet O'Hara outfit, complete with green hoop skirt and a fetching bonnet, and he wandered around the convention in it for a while, beaming at compliments. As he had said to Robin in Temptations, "I'm just *loving* this!" There was nothing sexual, no masturbatory climax and then back to work as Don. Just Be All (You Can Be) in Cincinnati.

One of the Chicago crowd whom Jane knew slightly leaped into the motel's pool and lost his wig, which echoed on the BBS for weeks afterward. He was older and had been taking hormones a long time, developing breasts but cycling on and off the hormones to retain his male potency. Jane found this odd, though he heard it was not uncommon. It didn't occur to him to find his own attitude odd—that if you're going to take hormones (he wasn't, but by this time was imagining it and learning about it on the Internet) you took hormones for good and all. By that time the sex was not the point for him, and so losing the ability to have male sex did not seem much of a loss beside the joy of being.

A television executive Jane met at the first cocktail party was further along. He also had been taking hormones for a long time and looked convincing in décolletage. He told of going to Key West for a weekend with another crossdresser, somewhat taller, and demanding that his friend, as the taller one, go in male drag. They presented themselves to the airline as a couple—this before picture IDs became routine—but the "boyfriend" didn't like his role and showed annoyance at check-in. The woman clerk exchanged sympathetic woman-to-woman glances with the "girlfriend." You know how men are, dear.

The television executive knew all the people at the convention famous in the little world of crossdressing and had Jane join them at one of the tables. JoAnn Roberts was there—Jane had seen drag photographs of him in the magazines and in guides to crossdressing but never any in male clothing. Jane had been introduced to JoAnn a couple of hours earlier, before the start, and JoAnn, at that moment in male clothing, with his wife, had been delighted that out of drag Jane had no idea who he was. JoAnn, an industrial chemist by training, operated a store and provided other innocent support and services for the crossgendered out of his Pennsylvania home. He had Jane photograph him together with the Long Beach makeup man in one of his rare appearances in drag himself: the makeup man was gay, but that doesn't mean he liked wearing women's clothing.

The convention took a dinner cruise one late afternoon on a little Ohio riverboat. It was gender education for the crew of college kids. At dinner Jane talked to the wives about how to manage a marriage. He found he liked talking to women as a woman. One of the crossdressers attending with his wife told about coming out to their circle of married friends. The couple had decided that these were friends they could depend on. After he came out the friends threw a party and invited him to come as his femme self. Jane was touched. *Ob, for such loving acceptance.*

After the cruise a few of the party wandered around the tourist areas of Cincinnati near the river and ended up in a straight bar, middle class, not crowded, not too drunken, safe. By the end of the evening there were about a dozen from the convention there. They formed a kick line, and the band played "Hello, Dolly." The straight customers found such antics amusing, these pretty dresses and male voices. A convention of Canadian businessmen was in town, and some of the crossdressers engaged in conversations with them about auto repair and the prospects for the Detroit Red Wings. It didn't interest Jane. He noticed two young couples nearby sneering and laughing, and he sidled up to them for gender education, professor-style. They asked the usual questions, and he gave the usual answers contrary to expectations: yes, we are all married; no, we do not want to be women (as Donald in June still believed about himself); no, it's not sex, it's identity, and it's fun; yes, we think of ourselves as guys; yes, we love women; yes, your dad could be one of us! The young women were curious, the young men worried.

■

Eventually Jane had to go to the bathroom. He walked tipsily to the ladies' room, went straight into a stall and plopped down. The manuals for survival as a crossdresser say, Don't stand in a stall. You'd think that would be obvious. One of the women already there, a little drunk like Jane, talked loudly to a friend from stall to stall, as women do:

"Yuk! The seat is wet!"

"Oh, *yuk!*"

"I'm going to have to stand!" She meant raising her behind up away from contact with the dribbly seat. "I *hate* it when you have to stand to pee!"

Jane wanted to laugh at the irony but couldn't with his male voice, sitting and not standing to do his business. He adjusted his dress and went back to the bar.

Not all Donald's experiences in the ladies' room were amusing. He avoided having to use gendered bathrooms. He had no desire to fool the women and certainly did not want to frighten them. Crossdressing itself is not illegal in any state, but in some places it is a crime for a man to enter a ladies' room, and the test of manhood is the unreasoned one of genital condition, not social presentation. Like many sexually freighted laws, it is not based on evidence (rapists do *not* disguise themselves in women's clothes). But it was no thrill to run the risk. Donald just wanted to go to the bathroom and couldn't safely march into the gents' in full drag. The women might be angry at the intrusion into the ladies' room, but the men in the gents' might kill him. The literary critic Marjorie Garber calls the American obsession with where you go to the bathroom our "urinary segregation." It is invoked against gender crossers by genetic women with gender anxieties, complaining about "him" (a postoperative woman, say) using "our" bathroom. *I merely wish to join,* Deirdre would think, bitter at the insult. *Nothing sexual about it.*

The only time he was read and punished for entering a ladies' room was coming back from a clothes-buying expedition to Des Moines as Jane. At a rest stop on the interstate he imagined he was not being read and waited patiently at the picnic table in his elegant dark green dress until he was sure there were no women in the ladies' room. He just wanted to go to the bathroom, not to alarm women. But when he came out of the empty ladies' room there stood an angry janitor, who had been monitoring him. As Jane walked by, the janitor hailed him: "Fella!"

Jane kept walking, not being a fella.

Louder. "Fella!"

Jane had to respond, so he turned and said in his obviously male voice, "Yes?" The janitor was angry—he had planned to catch the crossdresser before he went in, not after, but the little bastard had eluded him. Violence is dangerous to both sides in the game of men, which is why men use it only when their judgment is impaired by beer or lust or war or youth or sports or pride or honor or driving or ambition or tiredness or vexation or the little woman or the damned brat or a few other things. The janitor was big, but no man can be sure that the other is not in some way even more dangerously violent. For all he knew this weirdo, not small anyway, could be a black belt in karate, or armed. (Donald sent the janitor a letter afterward, apologizing for upsetting him and casually claiming he *was* a black belt in karate; he figured it might restrain him from actual violence against crossdressers.) Iowans are not known for violence. The janitor told Jane in an angry voice to scram, and he did.

Later Jane drove to Chicago dressed for a Tri Ess meeting, and the second cup of coffee got him into trouble. He could not find a bathroom, and on the cultivated plains of northern Illinois there were no bushes to do it behind. Little gas stations required you to ask for the key, but Jane close up was not passable in looks. And the voice. It was summer, so there was no disguising oneself in heavy outerwear.

He thought he'd use the ladies' room at the major rest stop around De Kalb. In such a big place you didn't have to get a key from an attendant. He parked close to the entrance, adjusted his makeup, and flounced across the parking lot. He started into the ladies' room but froze: inside was a long line of women waiting for empty stalls, with nothing better to do than scrutinize the next woman. He retreated abruptly and went back to his car, heart pounding. Ten miles farther on he discovered that the toll booths had Johnny-on-the-spot toilets.

As Deirdre she was able to join the bathroom line without fuss, though usually the tallest woman in it.

■

Evenings at the Cincinnati convention the crossdressers went out to this or that bar. The second night was a gay bar, a tough-looking place with a cage for go-go dancing, which one of the crossdressers, little though not pretty, climbed into. At the lively karaoke bar in the hotel itself late on the last night, half straight and half crossgendered, the crowd was forgiving. Jane sang the only pop song of the 1950s that he knew a complete verse and chorus to, "Lipstick on Your Collar." The girl berates her lover:

> Lipstick on your collar told a tale on you.
> Lipstick on your collar said you were not true.
> Bet my bottom dollar, you and I are through,
> 'Cause lipstick on your collar told a tale on you.

The party ended at 1:00 A.M. with a mixed straight and crossgendered line for the bunny hop snaking through the bar. *Toujours gai, Archie, toujours gai.*

Every night was a sit-down dinner, hotel style. At one of them Jane sat beside a crossdresser about his age, a professional person, strangely simpatico. It felt eerie, how well he knew this person in the little black dress. For security they were using femme names. No one at the conference knew anyone else's male name, first or last, unless they wanted it known.

On a chance, Jane asked: "When did you go to college?" The little black dress answered with the same year as Donald's graduation.

"Where?"

"Uh, Harvard College."

"Good Lord. . . .We're classmates!" They had not known each other in the thousand-man class at the time, but their generational experiences were parallel.

"My male name is Donald McCloskey."

The other crossdresser was astonished. "McCloskey! You mean you're the government professor's son?"

"Yes."

"I had him for Gov One!"

At the talent show the next night Jane's new friend told the story of meeting at this very convention a college classmate who was also the son of a teacher. Donald/Jane/Deirdre and he kept in touch.

The Cincinnati convention had serious sessions during the day, from a husband-and-wife team of psychologists about handling a marriage with crossdressing or from a fashion consultant on how to build an outfit with taste or from various doctors on what to decide on medical matters. Jane didn't go to the session on the operation—after all, he was a heterosexual crossdresser, not a gender crosser. He had found by this time from repeated experience that with his face he did not pass as a woman. He wanted to pass, so *just for the hell of it,* as he said to himself, he went to hear a surgeon, Douglas Ousterhout (pronounced as in its Dutch spelling: OH-ster-hout), speak on "Feminization of the Transsexual." Jane was entranced. Ousterhout told about his inquiry into what makes a feminine as against a masculine face and how a cut here, some bone grinding there, a new nose can make it work. The bone ridge under the eyebrows is how archaeologists distinguish a male skull from a female one. Men do not get water in their eyes from a shower because the browridge makes it drip beyond their eyelashes. (Deirdre was delighted after her facial operations that she could no longer keep her eyes open under a shower.) The grindings and shapings and prostheses make a man look younger.

Ousterhout was engaging and convincing. Jane judged him as one judges an academic, for wit, insight, fluency, intelligence. Jane was impressed, as he often was too easily impressed by such qualities, and for some reason touched. Deirdre later learned that the impression was right. Ousterhout was well known as a facial bone surgeon and had written a textbook. He worked mainly on severely deformed children, acquiring his small practice in gender crossers by accident, trying to help one who had been in a car crash. He considered them courageous.

A year later Deirdre was standing at the reception after the inaugural address for her professorship in Holland, bearing Ousterhout's work. A plastic surgeon from the university hospital started chatting with her. When Deirdre learned his occupation she asked,

"Do you know Dr. Ousterhout in San Francisco?"

"Doug Ousterhout? Why of course I know him! We're conference friends."

"He's my surgeon."

"How remarkable! You know he was offered a professorship in Holland at the University of Leiden?"

"Yes, he told me. I sent him a postcard last month from Oosterhout in the South."

"You know, his family has been misspelling it for generations."

Jane toyed at Cincinnati with the idea of having facial surgery. It would not of course be acceptable to his wife for him to have surgery to make him look more womanly. That was decisive, among the things that could not be talked about. But he kept deliberating. *A man's face could be feminized. Could be. Could.*

■

That night at the last dinner Jane persuaded one of the crossdressers to dance with him. The other took the male role and was a good dancer. *Wow, what a feeling, being swept around by a man— even if a man in an evening gown. Could be.*

■

The following morning, Sunday, the last day, Jane went with a big, anguished crossdresser, a carpenter by trade, to the Christian services for the conventioneers. Though Jane was in his Sunday best, he thought he was not religious and viewed himself merely as cross-dressing—in church even. He took a seat at the front of the little meeting room. The minister was a lesbian and spoke eloquently about inclusion. Jane was touched and cried and cried, as he never did. He thought he was grieving for his marriage. It is Deirdre you mourn for.

7

BOLDNESS

After talking with the crossdressers' wives at Cincinnati, Donald was optimistic about saving his marriage. His wife was angry and depressed and unwilling to talk. But the reaction of his sister when he told her in early June fed his optimism.

His sister was eleven years younger, a professor of psychology at the University of Arizona, a liberal woman with liberal views on gay rights and South Africa. Only later did Deirdre learn that her liberalism had limits. When his sister came through Iowa City on her way east from Arizona to a sabbatical term in Boston, visiting without academic appointment at the Harvard School of Public Health, it seemed a splendid idea to tell all. Donald's diary was ecstatic:

> It proved to be the second best thing I've done this week (the first best was going to Be All). I said to her, "There's a piece of the puzzle of your older brother that you're missing." She's the second to know outside The Community and this or that care provider. I was pleased beyond measure by her reaction.

Oh, Donald, Donald. Later his sister told Deirdre that she had sobbed for miles as she drove her car away from Iowa City. She decided, "he's crazy," the only reason her big brother would want to play at being her big sister.

The next day he went to Chicago. One occasion was a Tri Ess meeting in the evening at a suburban motel, with instruction in modeling. The big occasion, though, was an outing the afternoon before with a pre-op named Carole. They ate at a restaurant in the mall of a northwest suburb, and were "ma'am'd" by the help, though read by everyone, as Jane could see in the smiles and giggles and startled looks. His gender-crossing friend was short but had not had much electrolysis, and he had dark beard stubble difficult to cover with makeup; Jane was six feet tall and male-featured. A large proportion of the help at the restaurant found an excuse to turn up in the vicinity of their table. The waiter wrote on the bill in the tip-soliciting style of America, "Have a good day, ladies. Carl." Jane was pleased. They went to Carson's, the anchor in the mall, where Jane bought some hair clips and costume jewelry and Carole tried on clothes. Carole wanted to be treated the way she regarded herself, so when she saw something she liked she would take it to a store clerk and ask, "Is there a place I can try these on?" Asking permission was supposed to insulate her from later complaint about "a man in the women's changing room." She just wanted to see if the clothes fit and looked good, not test the law or peek at women.

Donald slept at Carole's apartment and then drove back the four hours to Iowa, this time in male clothing, out of boredom. Just a little fun.

■

It's easy to tell if you've passed, Deirdre would explain. You randomly check people shortly after the first look. If they've gone on to something else you can assume they haven't read you, because a man in a dress is very interesting to go on looking at, hard even for Deirdre to resist. It has nothing to do with politeness or toleration, except perhaps in gender-crossing centers like the Castro district in San Francisco. Everyone stares at a guy in a gown.

And at the initial meeting of looks you can watch for changes in expression as the thought dawns. You've been read if you see amusement in men, anger and suspicion in women.

The trouble is that the tests sometimes give false positives. People's looks sometimes linger quite innocently. A woman could be looking at Deirdre and thinking, "Hmm. That skirt doesn't go very well with her blouse" or "Hmm. Attractive hair. What *has* she done?" Or a man could just be thinking, "Hmm." Smiling or scowling having nothing to do with you, or nothing to do with being read, happens naturally. The man smiling could be thinking of a joke he heard at the office, or the woman scowling could have just then remembered she forgot her shopping list. Testing for being read is a paranoid style of life.

Some women resist such an analysis. They cannot imagine themselves being misidentified as to gender and say things like, "The instinct is to turn away from a man dressed in women's clothes" or "People are being polite in not looking twice." No. When Jane early on or Deirdre later was read, it was obvious. When she was not read it was obvious too. There's no way of mistaking the reaction to a man in a dress, if you are in the dress and watching.

■

He wanted to pass. So he started electrolysis, first at a discreet local beauty parlor and then at the specialized Clinic of Electrology in Iowa. He was bold, but he did not notice or ask himself why. *Just fun.* He had electrolysis done only on his body, not his face, where it mattered most but also showed most. First hands, then arms; then as the weeks added up on a male schedule of completion, working out how many scores of hours it would take to do the entire body, he had it done on back and legs and stomach. A few thousand dollars. *I can afford it.*

Doing it on the beard hairs would show. In the summer he called up Electrology 2000 in Carrollton, Texas, north of Dallas, which removed beards in four-day sessions, first clearance, with local anesthetic to mask the pain. Donald had read about it in the crossdressing magazine he had started to subscribe to that spring. You go to Electrology 2000 if you have a serious problem with superfluous hair. A male beard is serious, 150,000 hairs to be zapped with electricity one by one and then extracted. He made an appointment, devising a dishonest scheme to come back early from a conference in Europe and do it without his wife's knowing. But then he thought better of it and contented himself with slower local procedures.

His electrologists in Iowa, a mother and daughter, spoke pleasantly to him over the dozens of hours they treated him, dressed as a male. For a crossdresser, they said, he was unusually open. They showed him a sewing video, and hour upon hour the womanly talk would flow.

Later, after the dam broke and Donald was to change gender, he called up Electrology 2000 again. *Let's see,* as his hands trembled, *972-416-3390.*

"How are you, sweetie?" said Bren, one of the owners, a dentist by training and the dispenser of anesthetic. Bren remembered the canceled arrangements to visit Dallas a couple of months before.

"Fine, I guess. I've decided to go ahead. I've decided I am transsexual."

"We have all kinds: crossdressers, transsexuals, people with bothersome hairiness. Can't get you in 'til November."

"Fine. I'll go before an academic conference in Austin."

Electrology works. Nothing else does (except it seems—too late for Deirdre—the new laser method or the Epilight just starting, if your hair is dark enough). Electrology was developed a century and a half ago to prevent blindness from ingrown eyelashes. It kills the hair follicle with an electric pulse, which causes heat and a chemical reaction deep in the follicle, the electricity coming through a "probe," or needle. It hurts a little in some places and a lot in others. Roxanne, one of Deirdre's electrologists at Electrology 2000, came in one day angry at a lineman for her Dallas Cowboys. "That ole boy lost the game on Sunday," she declared. "I'm gonna bring him in and do his nose hairs without anesthetic!" But under local anesthetic you just sit and watch movies while Roxanne or Ruthann or Cari or Dana or Jacki zaps one hair follicle after another painlessly. The only pain is the unavoidable one when Bren gives you the local anesthetic by injection. The longest single treatment at Electrology 2000 was a beard so dense that the first stripping took seven straight days of eight or nine hours a day, with two electrologists working simultaneously.

It needs to be done expertly or it can scar the patient. Jane was told by a drag queen in Cincinnati that she knew someone whose face had been scarred in the pattern of her male beard by incompetent electrolysis. Maybe the story was an urban myth. The more usual incompetence, quite common, is merely to pluck the hairs instead of killing them. This does nothing. A lot of incompetent electrologists work endlessly, because they pluck without realizing it. Even good electrolysis seems at first like it's not doing much, because only about 40 percent of the hairs treated are at a stage when they can be killed. You can't tell from the outside whether a follicle is "active" and therefore killable. So at each successive stripping of an area you would later get what looked like "regrowth" of 60 percent, then at the next stripping (.60) times (.60), or 36 percent of the original 100 percent of your beard, and so forth. *It's like the money multiplier,* thought Donald the economist. The third stripping leaves (.36) times (.60), or 21.7 percent, the fourth 13.0, the fifth 7.8, the sixth 4.7 percent, then 2.8, 1.7, 1.0, 0.6, 0.4, 0.2, . . . percent. So it takes twelve sessions of complete stripping (the later ones very brief) to go from 100 percent beard-covered to one-fifth of 1 percent beard covered. For each ten thousand of the original hairs, one-fifteenth of the area of face and neck with hair, only two or three hairs would survive, often in light form not noticeable. The math fit Deirdre's later experience at Electrology 2000, which she was still visiting in shorter and shorter sessions two years into full-time as a woman. And then rarely, an occasional cleanup of fine hairs when she could get to Dallas on business, nothing unusual for a woman in her fifties.

It costs about $10,000 to get rid of a male beard by electrolysis. The beard has to be extirpated. Female hormones don't stop it from growing, and any trace of beard is a strong male cue. That's why females-to-males have it easy, Deirdre would explain. As soon as they start testosterone their voices break and their beards grow. Deirdre later realized that if you're taking estrogen and no longer are producing testosterone, then electrolysis on the body is silly (except, she said, on her hands, which show all the time; she had her local electrologist work on those for a year or two after returning from Holland; and later she had some of the laser treatment). Within two or three years on female hormones the hair stops regrowing anyway, and the body hair off the face takes on a female pattern. But not the beard.

In the summer of 1995, as he started the electrolysis, before the breaking of the dam, Donald had none of this in mind. Just cross-dressing.

8

EPIPHANY

All through the summer Donald and his wife quarreled about Jane. "Learn about it," he would say, angry or pleading. His cure for everything was book learning. He would press books and articles on her. She wouldn't read them.

"I can't handle it," she would say. "I'm tired. No, no, *no.*"

"I'm just a heterosexual crossdresser," he would reply, convinced and argumentative, guy-style, professor-style. "No problem. We can work it out. Let's talk."

"No, no. I don't want to talk now."

"Call up the women I met at Cincinnati, the wives who have adjusted. Mrs. Realtor, Mrs. Chair of the National Crossdressing Group, Mrs. Endocrinologist."

"I can't handle it." Donald realized she was ashamed to face another woman. What kind of woman am I, she would think, that my husband dresses in women's clothes? Ugh.

"Come on, dear, call them up. Come on."

After weeks of hectoring she called up Mrs. Endocrinologist, who at the convention had been kind to Jane. It turned out to be a consultation with an anti-crossdresser. According to Donald's wife's report Mrs. Endocrinologist sneered at the silly little crossdressers buying "Melanie's Tape" and trying to achieve a female voice. Hopeless. They would never be women. Ha! Donald imagined that the sneers reflected her negotiated relationship with her own husband, in which he was "permitted" to come to such conventions and dress, so long as it was understood that gender crossing all the way was out. Donald was reminded of a little man at a Tri Ess meeting in Chicago dressed in a skirt and blouse, the visit a birthday present from his wife, who accompanied him, the first time he had been allowed to dress in five years.

The conversation with Mrs. Endocrinologist hardened his wife's attitude. In June, while Donald was away at the convention in Cincinnati, his wife had gone to the medical library and did her only reading about crossgender, some psychoanalytic papers redolent of the 1950s and its homophobia. Then Mrs. Endocrinologist, then no more Mrs. Nice Gal, until a brief softening, and back.

■

He and his wife went on a cruise up the Inner Passage from Seattle to Juneau. He still believed himself to be a heterosexual crossdresser. For a few days they forgot and wondered at seals and glaciers and a bear slaughtering salmon on the beach. His wife believed this was typical: that he could be distracted; that he didn't really crossdress very much. In Juneau they shopped and Donald bought Jane a cheap hematite necklace. His wife was angry, disappointed that Jane was back. That night in the motel she said, "You've got to stop this."

"No, leave me alone." And they quarreled loudly in the thin-walled room.

■

About noon on August 20, 1995, Donald had started the drive back from Aurora, Illinois, to Iowa City. He had spent the night at a pajama party at dear Robin's apartment, then a few hours of sleep after greeting the dawn in Aurora. Robin had just decided to go full time as a woman. They had come home from partying through lesbian bars with Nikki from Milwaukee, Nikki the computer programmer, four years on hormones, Nikki with the lovely long, brown hair. Nikki had taught him how to hold a bottle of beer as a woman: "Not by the neck, dear. Delicately, around the body."

As the car pulled out of the parking lot Donald thought,

I am a fifty-three-year-old heterosexual crossdresser, married thirty years, two grown children, a professor of economics and history. I don't want to be a woman.

Of course not. Just a hobby. Relax.

Let's see: East-West Tollway. He thought he knew the road well. *What a night. The last dance at Temptations at 4:00 A.M. The staff at the grocery store spotting us in drag. It's so easy to tell: the smiles, the startled looks. Getting read was my fault, mainly, since Robin is passable and Nikki even more so. Then the chatter until dawn at Robin's apartment. Crazy, harmless fun.*

Just try it on, he said, as the car carried him west toward the Mississippi. *How would it feel to actually* be *a woman?*

A mental exercise. I'm in male drag now, of course, no women's clothes. Appropriate: heterosexual crossdresser. Not a transsexual! Not me.

Go ahead: think about it. I've spent eight months January to August dealing intensely with this stuff. A convention, a few crazy fun nights at Temptations, coming out to clubs of crossdressers after forty-two years entirely in the closet. Oh, yeah: and that mall in the northern suburbs. And the trip to Des Moines and the angry janitor at the rest stop.

Just a guy who gets off dressing occasionally as a woman. No one knows in Iowa City. No problem.

Maybe one guy in a hundred does crossdressing, otherwise straight and married. Or gay. Women, too—though they can crossdress without anyone caring, like that wife of a colleague who wears men's shoes. None of them want to be in the other gender for real. Out of a hundred crossdressers maybe three do want to change. Three in a hundred out of one in a hundred. Hey, a different thing, very rare. Not me. It makes crossdressing look conventional.

I'm not transsexual. I don't want to cross permanently, be a woman. I don't want to become a Venetian. In the past eight months I've spoken to lots of transsexuals, though. Just out of interest.

Wife, grown kids. Me still Tarzan, not Jane. We can work it out. If my wife will be reasonable. Just reasonable.

But let's see.

Try it on. A mental experiment.

Just thinking.

Near De Kalb, the only town between the outskirts of Chicago and the Mississippi, after twenty miles of just thinking, he said,

Wait:

Good Lord.

I can *become a woman.*

I have always wanted *to. I have learned by accident that I* can.

I am not a heterosexual crossdresser. All this time. I am *a transsexual.*

I can be a woman, he said. And he wept in relief, as the car drove itself. *I am a woman,* he said. *Yes!*

She said again, *I am a woman,* and wept.

■

That's what the crossdressing since age eleven had been about, closeted over four decades, confined within marriage. And the open dressing in clubs and at home during the eight months past, more and more. The womanhood was there beneath the surface and yearned to take form.

Later in an interview with the student newspaper he described the feeling on the toll road as an "epiphany," which was a dangerous choice of words. It is a religious word, evoking Saul on the road to Damascus. "And suddenly there shined round about him a light from heaven, and he fell to the earth, and heard a voice." Donald was not then religious, Deirdre later was noncharismatically so, and the experience was not spiritual. No light, no presence of God, no voice. The danger is that newspapers and psychiatrists treat religious experiences as madness. Donald's epiphany was merely a moment of personal insight, a realization on the toll road near De Kalb. This "epiphany": people have moments like that, Deirdre would say, moments when self-knowledge becomes more than a swirl of facts. A singular truth of character stands in front of you, as clear as a crucifix. *Watch it: more religious talk in an irreligious world.* Secularly speaking, understand, it is knowing yourself instead of knowing about yourself. He knew the dam. On the twentieth day of August 1995 a little after noon the dam broke and the water of his life swirled out onto the plain. He knew himself. Herself.

That's it, she said: *I am a woman.*

And later in the crossing from man to woman Donald/Deirdre never doubted. He and then she didn't "decide," though an economist would like to think this way, in terms of cost and benefit and a decision. Donald's son's letters of protest later in the year were that way: How can you want to be a woman? It's stupid. Let's see: adding up the convenience for career of being a man, the inconvenience of hair and panty hose, the cost of clothing—but its benefit in prettiness and variety. . . .

A few months before, Donald had actually done such a calculation, a man's way of thinking and an economist's:

The Costs and Benefits of Womanhood
At the limits of my fantasies is transsexuality—but I believe
it's only a fantasy, stimulating in the mind but not something

I want. As a literal woman, gender reassignment surgery and all that:

My wife would leave me. This would be the loss of my best friend.

My daughter would reject me, though my son I think would continue to love me.

My birth family would be appalled. My mother in particular would be unable to handle it. Though my sister would be fine. Cousins—no way. Granny likewise.

I'd lose all my more casual friends, essentially—think of Dick! Or many, many of my professional friends, whom I really do value highly: Joel, Dick Z., Bob H. Jesus! None of these people could handle it.

The transition is impossible in my occupation.

A woman would not be allowed to have the intellectual style I have.

I couldn't possibly just drop out and go get a job as a clerk. At fifty-five I would not be a hot property for development in the business world.

The hormones do nothing like the job in your fifties that they do in your twenties.

On the positive side, I get to be pretty—ho, ho. I would make a not very attractive woman, certainly *very* tall and *very* broad shouldered, things that nothing whatever can be done about. A plain face, though not hideous.

I could—here's a wild one—get the love of a man, maybe. But it's not anything I want now. I am determinedly heterosexual. Maybe I would fall for a man, as a woman. I'm not repulsed by the idea. Just uninterested.

Silly, he said to himself as he recalled the calculation. (And later Deirdre learned that the judgments about almost every person mentioned were wrong, the opposite of what happened.) *It's identity, stupid. Not cost and benefit.* She merely was.

As he crossed the Mississippi into Iowa the old uneasiness dropped away. The question since age eleven was answered. He knew: another life.

An hour later he pulled into the driveway at home in Iowa City and smiled.

"You're home," said his wife, who was watering flowers by the driveway.

"Yeah. I had fun."

Angry. "'Fun.' I'll bet." He didn't tell her.

■

Donald and his wife went briefly to a square dance in a small town Saturday night but came away early because they didn't like the caller. They crept through the parking lot giggling to get to the car without offending the hosts. Donald played the manly role but daydreamed at the dance about what it would feel like to be a woman. He watched a woman across the school gym talking animatedly to other women, with the self-deprecating style women use when charming others of their tribe. *Unlike the boasting of my tribe,* he thought. As they drove home he could feel himself resist telling his wife about his new conviction. *It would only upset her. Without medical backing she will scorn it. She feels that scorn is her only protection, her only hope. I've got to talk to the psychologist.* Donald practiced feminine ways of holding the steering wheel. For the past two months he had never sat down without crossing his legs. The unaccustomed pressure on the nerves around his knees made his feet partly numb. *Or maybe it's walking in heels that don't fit very well.*

■

A few days later he told his wife about his epiphany, and she cried and raged.

Who wouldn't? She couldn't talk to Donald about her feelings, but Deirdre later speculated: *Women tell a story of connection, and Donald's wife's was a connection to Donald, not Deirdre. The story of her life was being shredded. Who am I, she would ask, a woman who lived thirty years with . . . a woman?*

Is that right? Is that how she feels? Oh, God, I could help. I could show her that she is mistaken about our past. I wish she would talk. Talking cures do sometimes work. She wants to be strong. Oh, dear one, please, please.

■

Donald went to the year's first faculty meeting in the Department of History and found himself playing his usual role as smart aleck, pushily male, presuming to take up emotional space the way men do. He found he still liked doing it, or maybe by now it was automatic. He was angry at himself: *Jesus, what a stupid performance. I don't deserve to be a woman. Could I absorb the "dose of humility" for a woman's role?*

Yes, by recovering the character I had as a child. He did not mean being childish, but being as he had been before putting on manhood like a football uniform. Deirdre was later something like the boy Donald, less stupidly assertive or smart-mouthed than Donald the man, less joking—though still it was there, the trick practiced since high school of searching for double meanings and topical references to set off laughter. The lessening desire to practice the trick came from his new aversion toward the "*io, io,*" the "me, me" of men's conversation, as he began to think of it. In a marketplace in Italy Donald had once seen a little boy, three years old, furious at not being allowed to have an ice cream. The boy filled the market with his cry of egotism thwarted: "*Io, io, io,*" Me, me, me. The *io,* the me, became less important to Deirdre. She would say to herself of some potential story or remark, after the moment had passed: ***Let it go.***

■

He woke at 3:00 A.M. and called J. C. Penney's catalog number and ordered a set of underwear for his new, weight-reduced body. First time buying lingerie from a regular store. He had spent some time the day before preparing the order, reflecting on bra sizes. On the phone to Penney's the woman was not contemptuous and acted as though it was natural for someone with the name Donald McCloskey on the credit card to specify a post office box address for "Jane Austen" for receiving four half-slips, three bras, and so forth. Actually, it is not rare. Men order for women and women for men. Maybe not to a post office box. Maybe not in the name of the first big female voice in English literature. They were good pieces of clothing, and Deirdre wore them out.

■

He wondered: ***Is it significant that this crisis has come near the anniversary of my father's fatal coronary, at age fifty-three, which I become next month?*** His wife later told a psychiatrist, according to notes in a legal record, that "Donald did not expect to live beyond age fifty-three," and the psychiatrist in the tendentious style of his profession wove it into the story of "a danger to himself" that he wanted to tell.

No. It was the end of a summer free for tacit and then explicit deliberation.

■

A certain amount of underdressing now seemed appropriate, trying on his gender crossing, a token of sincerity. After a while he gave it up. It was not presenting as a woman. It was continuing forty-one years as a male with a secret vice.

■

After he had told her about the epiphany he and his wife visited their psychologist, Frank, whom they had seen a few times to try to save their dissolving marriage, first about crossdressing. His wife seemed comforted by the visit that morning, and when she got home she hugged Donald and said she loved him. He wept, as he hardly ever did. He wanted to stay married to this woman, or to stay close.

Donald, though, was still going to electrolysis, two hours that same day, and his own hour with the psychologist.

About the gender crossing, Frank said,

"You get to decide."

"What do you mean?"

"I mean that you are a free, sane, adult person. You get to decide about whether to transition or not." Frank did not like to make his patients into children.

"I agree, Frank. I think it's political."

"Political or not, you get to decide. It's not to be forbidden by the fears of outsiders." Grow up: take responsibility for yourself.

Frank suggested Donald make an appointment with a psychiatrist in town, to check for major mental illness. Donald's wife and sister were demanding that he be "treated" for "mania." Their notion was that he had gone crazy, and that if treated for the craziness he would drop the silliness about becoming a woman. ***Maybe it would satisfy them.*** The appointment was made for Donald's fifty-third birthday.

He told his wife what Frank had said and about the appointment with the psychiatrist; she wept in turn, and he held her.

$$\boxed{9}$$

LOSING A FAMILY

An odd-numbered day of the month, so Donald was up early, a little past 4:00 A.M., to dress as Jane. The agreement was odd days, a little joke. On the even-numbered days he ached for the day to end. His wife had been gracious the evening before about the next day's being a Jane day, but at 6:30 A.M. Donald as Jane was on a BBS at the computer and his wife burst in and "caught" him. It was like a mother bursting in on her son smoking pot in his room. She was playing gender cop. But nothing more happened. His wife went to the Nursing College and Jane finished a review essay. Donald was on leave that fall.

■

A few days later Donald's mother called.

"I'm out in Michigan seeing Granny." She was in Saint Joseph, Michigan, two hours east of Chicago, five or six hours from Iowa City.

"That's nice."

"I'm coming out to Iowa City."

"Mother?"

"Yes. I need to come." She was worried. Donald's sister had been hinting to her.

Five hours later his mother arrived. As he came out to meet her at the car she said, "Oh, Donald. What is it?"

"What do you mean?"

"You've lost so much weight! Is it AIDS?" She hadn't seen him for a year.

"No, mother, it's eating less fat. The little labels on the boxes? Stay below 5 percent and you get back to a sensible weight."

"Oh, thank God! I thought you had AIDS."

"Turned gay and gotten AIDS in a few months?"

"Oh, thank God!" Seeing his wife, she said, "Hello, dear."

Sullen. "Hello."

They went inside. His mother grew calm as she listened to her son tell her that he wanted to become her daughter. Donald was amazed and moved and thought back to his economist's balance sheet of costs and benefits: his mother would not be able to take it, he had calculated. Here she was, taking it. He had expected her to be scornful, to disbelieve him, to treat him as a patient, to act like his wife and sister. Those two had been having conversations on the phone, trading anxieties and schemes for forced treatment. What to do about him? They were developing their theory that Donald was not actually a gender crosser; no, nothing of the kind. A pill, his wife hoped. A month or two in the madhouse, his sister proposed.

His mother, though appalled and worried, as she later told Deirdre, offered advice at the time from one who loves in Aristotle's third sense, respect as much as absorption, love for the loved one's own sake. Be careful, she said. Choose your doctors carefully. Move to New York if you can: the Midwest is not tolerant, she declared, out of her experience of growing up in Michigan in the 1930s. Will it hurt your career? Are you *sure* it won't?

"You know," she said, revealing the memory that was frightening her, "there was someone at Christ Church, Cambridge, in the 1950s who wore his wife's hat to Easter service. No one took him seriously again."

"I understand, Mom. Times are different." *I hope,* he thought.

"No they're not."

His wife stayed through the first hour but then grew angry and went off to bed. She had told Donald, "I expect your mother to support us," support in the gender cop and psychiatric nurse approach.

"What do you mean 'us'?"

"Last night I talked to your sister again. I'd like you to take pills for your mania. She wants to commit you as mentally incompetent."

"Jesus! How stupid can you get?" He scorned the notion of a commitment, inflamed by imaginings a thousand miles from the events. His sister sitting appalled in Boston seized on the diagnosis of mania as soon as Donald started talking openly about gender crossing. Cross-dressing's one thing. She never did visit Donald to test her hypothesis. She spent the autumn in faraway Boston trying to confirm it.

■

The next day when Donald came downstairs he found his mother scrutinizing the stock quotations in the newspaper over a cup of coffee.

He said, "Mom, would you mind if I dressed? It's an odd day of the month."

She looked up, the thought of Home Depot's stock quotation disappearing from her face. "Son, of course I wouldn't mind. Don't be afraid of me."

"I didn't want to offend."

"No offense!" and went back to the stock quotations.

He went upstairs and showered, put on makeup, and dressed in Jane's denim skirt, a white formal blouse, heels. He came back to the TV room.

"Goodness!" His mother seemed startled by the change. "But you shouldn't wear rings on every finger!" Jane agreed and took some off, though he loved rings.

They spent the day talking about intellectual things as they always did, mother-son talk in the McCloskey family about art and politics. But they also talked in a mother-daughter way about life and relationships, the inexhaustible subject. Jane found it riveting to talk as a woman. Donald would have been bored or embarrassed once the talk moved beyond exchanges of salient fact and lofty opinion and What I Just Accomplished. He had been puzzled as men are by the endless gossip of women. "Gossip," the male jibe. How do they find things to talk about? I mean, without sports.

Donald's wife came home from work, clattering at the back door, and looked into the sunroom, where Jane was sitting with his mother. She smiled sarcastically as she threw down her purse and said, "Why, hello 'Jane,'" and went upstairs to change.

"I don't know why she can't control her anger," Jane said to his mother. "It's September, and she's been angry for months and months, wearing me down with lack of love."

"It's hard."

His wife went out with her friends to eat and didn't return until late, with a friend. Jane changed to male clothing, though by this time the friend knew. A lot of his wife's friends knew.

■

An even day of the month.

"You know," Donald's mother said to the husband and wife standing in the kitchen, "yesterday I talked easily with Jane. Today I've talked easily with Donald."

"What's your point?" said his wife, irritated.

The next day, an odd day, Jane's mother drove back to Michigan. Her visit seemed to have calmed the house. Donald's wife and Jane cleared shelves in their daughter's room for painting. Jane thought, ***Doesn't she notice our calm as two women?***

■

Donald came out by e-mail to his Dutch friend Arjo (ARR-yoh) Klamer, the first person he told outside his family. They had been closer than most men for years, visiting, talking, collaborating on projects. At a conference in Holland earlier that year Arjo and his wife Marijke (marr-EYE-kuh) had been worried by Donald's loss of weight and a certain oddness of manner, and Marijke, a clinical psychologist, had gone down the list of possibilities with Arjo: Transsexuality? No, they agreed, that would be absurd for macho Don.

When in August Donald confessed, Arjo rapidly started discussion about his coming to Erasmus University of Rotterdam to visit for a while, perhaps a year or even two.

"Do I need to know Dutch?"

"Not in Holland." Donald clutched at the idea. ***It would lessen the strain on my wife, with me away for a long while, starting in a few months. And Holland is tolerant.*** Or tolerant enough. Slowly it emerged that Donald was to be the Visiting Tinbergen Professor of Economics, Philosophy, and Art and Cultural Studies, starting that very January. Maybe. It needed to be approved. October. November. As a woman.

■

Donald spoke on the phone to his sister in Boston.

"Donny, you aren't going to attend the meetings of the Economic History Association as a woman, are you?"

"Jesus, what are you talking about?"

"You think you're a woman."

"I don't think I'm a woman: I want to be one. I'm not imprudent."

"You go to class in drag."

"For Lord's sake, of course I don't." A small misstatement, because when teaching the spring before he had sometimes underdressed.

"For one thing, I'm on sabbatical this term, so I'm not going to class. But I've told no one except you and Mom and Arjo, and I won't go full time until January at the earliest, if I go to Holland. I crossdress in public 240 miles from here, if at all. I go to entirely private meetings of my club. Get this: I'm not crazy; I'm crossgendered. You ought to come out here and get a reality check."

"You're planning to show up at the meetings in Chicago in women's clothing."

"Where do you get these ideas?"

"Donny, I think you should go to a psychiatrist." She wanted him to be crazy. Treatably crazy.

"I am, on September 11."

"Can I have his phone number?"

"Sister *dear,* you shouldn't get involved." Donald had not yet worked out that her attitude had shifted since their pleasant talk in June.

"Your wife told me she's been to a lawyer about a divorce."

That was news. "I repeat: you shouldn't interfere. You don't know us well enough. You don't know me at all: our conversations are about your academic career and have been for twenty years. You don't know me or my wife or the situation. Be my sister, not my jailer."

"But I love you."

"I know that." He thought later: *A love like ownership.*

■

In bed that night Donald asked his wife, annoyed, "Did you go to a lawyer? My sister told me on the phone tonight that you went to a lawyer."

"As usual she got it a little wrong," she replied in a weary tone. "Tomorrow I will. Just to see my options."

"Lawyers!"

"It's *just* to see my options."

"Why can't we work on the marriage?" He was indignant, his wife silent. "Why can't *you* work on it? Going to law! What a stupid idea."

"What am I supposed to do, help you become a transsexual?"

He raised his voice. "Not to *become.* I *am,* and always have been. Can't you grasp that? And why *wouldn't* you go on loving me and helping me?"

"Don't shout: the neighbors will hear. I love *Donald,* not '*Jane,*'" she said with as much venom as she could get into the word.

"What do you mean? I'm me, the person you say you've loved for a third of a century." She lay silent. "Do you know what love means?"

he continued, relentless, feeling the betrayal—though he could not feel her loss of a husband. "It's not about fun or convenience. It's about Aristotle's third and highest kind of friendship, for the friend's own sake."

"You and your books. That's what *you* know about love. Anyway, the best thing for your own sake is to stop you. I think you're manic."

"'Manic.' Good Lord, you're getting that from my sister. It's silly."

"I don't think so." Donald did not see the danger in her reply. Manic = crazy = disloyalty = men in white coats.

"You and she are medicalizing the situation. You, the nurse, demand pills. She, the psychologist, demands compulsory confinement."

"You *should* try some Prozac." Now she too was shouting. They were standing now in the bedroom. "Slow down and try the pills. For your own good, and your family's."

Donald was angry, because he half believed her, worrying for a moment that he was mistaken, and because he felt betrayed. "You are a failure as a wife."

She looked at him startled. "What . . . what did you say?"

"I said you're a pathetic failure as a wife. You don't know what love means. I can't imagine not being willing to help *you* in your considered dreams." She stared at him open-mouthed. ***No going back now,*** he thought. He would say what he felt. Usually it was she who raised the stakes sharply in a quarrel, hurting in ways that could not be taken back. Men fight fair. ***The dopes.*** "In fact, I have helped you, dear, for thirty years. You've done nothing but complain to protect your convenience. Someone to escort you to square dances. Or what the neighbors will think. As you get older you get worse. The crossdressing and the transsexuality just test it. You know what? You've failed the test." He twisted the emotional knife as it went in.

She rushed out into the hall and back into their daughter's empty room in the corner of the house, slamming doors as she went. ***She'll be crying,*** he thought as he stood in the middle of the bedroom, his heart throbbing, fight or flight. He could hear her yet behind three doors. Husbandly pity and remorse rose in him, and he went and knocked.

"Go away!"

He went back and got into bed. His red-painted toenails comforted him. Her.

■

His wife wept to their son on the phone, and the son, stouthearted, drove from Chicago to help. He had no idea. He arrived in the early afternoon, and Donald in men's clothing sat down to tell him every-thing. He reacted with amazement but with the sort of toleration Don-ald expected from him. *Good. My loving son. Man of the world. It's going to be fine. No sides. Support both parents in their troubles.* Later, while Donald was doing chores, his wife got her time with him, and by dinner the son was primed to urge slowing down. The wife and son viewed it as a passing mania. They couldn't credit Donald as a potential woman, this masculine man. His son had never seen him dressed as a woman. They were frightened he would do something to show it to the world. The shame, the shame.

Donald replied to them—to his wife again—that nothing to be done was irrevocable. The irrevocable step was publicity, and by telling her friends his wife had done more to cause publicity than Donald had. "Slowing down is not what I need to do," he continued, warming to his theme. "I need to learn about transsexuality and about being a woman and about the futures I can or cannot have. Jogging in place is not sensible. You, my dear wife, have had eight months and have shown no signs—zero, nada—of adjusting even to more open crossdressing than the sort I've been practicing all our married life. You resist learning anything about transsexuality, as though ignorance would make it go away. You declare you will never adjust. I have to believe you." The professorial speech did not comfort them.

His son started driving home to Chicago late that evening, after hugging them both. But in a divorce the children normally side with the mother, and a son especially would want to protect her. If she claims hurt and demands a choice he would have to take her side. Donald didn't realize as his son drove off in the dark that he had lost him, his firstborn child.

His wife touched a psychological truth when she complained about Donald's "going too fast." He did and would go fast. Many went slower and saved their families. Kate Cummings, who offered to try going back to being a husband for a year, to not dress at all in that time, kept one loving daughter out of three. Susan Marshall kept both her daugh-ters and remained a friend to her wife. Jan Morris kept everyone, and they kept her. Yet many went slowly and did not in the end save any-thing. Suzy Roberts's two years of therapy did no good. In Donald's family the refusal to go to therapy or to read books or to see Jane or to talk about the problem except to urge secrecy and slowing down made the outlook poor.

Yes, Jane/Donald went fast. The same Suzy, who was with Jane the first night she went to a Tri Ess meeting and then to Temptations, had been out and active in the crossdressing community for two years and thought herself transsexual. She was divorced, on her own, and able to do what she wanted. She was more experienced and more passable than Jane. Yet by the time Jane/Donald decided he was Deirdre, Suzy had still not bought clothes in drag. A few months after the first Tri Ess meeting that last spring Jane had shopped a mall with another gender crosser in drag, had gone to Truly Talls in Des Moines by himself in drag, had shopped a resale store in Chicago for a couple of hours in drag. Suzy started electrolysis, did it for a few hours, then stopped on financial grounds. Full-beard electrolysis for an average male costs about the same as a low-end American automobile. It and the operation are the two essentials. People manage car payments. Two small cars or one full size. By the time of his epiphany Jane/Donald had already done sixty hours of electrolysis in a month.

Yes. Fast. That was the truth that his wife's fear had spotted. She said, Go slowly, slowly. Please. Stop. No. No. I will divorce you.

10

ACADEMIC DRAG

Donald drove three of his graduate students to the Chicago meetings of the Economic History Association. No one knew. The Association is a little group of academic economists and historians, Donald's crowd since graduate school. No one knew. Underneath his manly front he was miserable. He and his students had a guys' dorm room in the hotel on North Michigan Avenue. He felt like he was faking in the man's role, though to the brother of his student Steve he showed off his prowess in football, dropping to a three-point stance in the lobby, guy-style. *Women don't do that kind of thing,* he thought as he did it.

He bumped into Betsy checking in, a dean at Iowa State, an economist and historian. She was as tall as he was. *Hmm.*

"Hi, Betsy."

"Hi, Don. How are you? You look so thin."

"Dieting: low fat. No illness. I've not lost any weight since getting down this far in June."

"Oh, good: we are so worried about you." Womanly kind.

"Thanks, Betsy." A thought was forming in his head. "Say, do you mind if I ask an impertinent question?" He was thinking: *She's my height, good looking, professional; if I could get to her weight.*

"Sure."

"How much do you weigh?" As soon as he asked it he realized how crazy the question sounded. *It* is *crazy. What a stupid thing to ask.*

Pause. "Uh, let's just say: more than you might think!"

When months later Deirdre came out, Betsy did tell Deirdre her weight, woman-to-woman. Greater love hath no woman. The figure was depressing. *How am I going to get down to that? Exercise, and eat less, dear.*

■

Between sessions at the conference Donald sneaked over to Borders Books on the other side of Michigan Avenue and stood at the shelves reading babies' name books. *Silly to be furtive.* He could explain it innocently, a grandfather speculating on the name of his granddaughter. Yet he was guilty with anticipation. He had half decided to keep the *D*. The vain professor thought, *It will help the librarians catalog my numerous books.* The earnest man, *It is a loyalty to my parents and past.* "Diana" was the name of an aunt, who though dead would not be honored by the choice. "Dorothy," God's gift. *No.* "Dora," the same. "Donna," from "Don." *Too cute by half.* "Dawn," pronounced almost like "Don." *Good Lord, no.*

Then he saw "Deirdre," which he did not know how to pronounce or spell. The received pronunciation was "DEER-druh." *It's lovely. And it's Irish, like "Donald," which means "world ruler." What does this "Deirdre" mean? Hmm! In that spelling in Old Irish it's "wanderer." Perfect!* He scrutinized the femininity scores in another of the half dozen name books, noting that by popular opinion "Deirdre" was among the highest. Later he found the romantic story fifteen centuries old of Deirdre of the Sorrows, made into plays by Yeats and Synge. Deirdre was "of the Sorrows" because it was prophesied at her birth that her beauty would cause the death of many warriors, an Irish Helen of Troy. When grown up she fled to Scotland with her lover and his brothers, the sons of Usnach. Seven years later the High King lured them back, and after much slaughter, fulfilling the prophecy, he had her lover murdered and took her as his queen. She did not smile for a year, and in disgust the High King gave Deirdre to her lover's murderer. But she cast herself out of the chariot delivering her, dying gloriously for love. Aside from the masculine ending, it's a woman's story. Deirdre learned that in Holland a version of the story written in poetic Dutch in 1920 by Roland Horst became a school text that most educated Dutch people of a certain age know well, *Deirdre en de zonen van Usnach*—Deirdre and the sons of Usnach. *Just perfect.*

Well, not in every way. The Irish spelling runs against the English rule of "*i* before *e* except after *c*." Someone told her that in Northern Ireland, where the other half, "McCloskey," comes from, the Protestants spell and pronounce it without the first *r*: "DEE-druh." It's another of the divisions in the six counties. In England they say "DEER-dree," "dree" instead of "druh" on the end. It doesn't sound so pretty, and it makes the spelling still more mysterious. On mailing envelopes it comes out Dierdre, Diedra, Derida, Deidre, Deidra, Derideru, a little test of care.

Later in Australia she met a lifelong Deirdre, a lecturer in English.

"You've had this name longer than I have. Do they ever learn to spell it?"

"No, but it helps to mention the word 'wEIRD'!"

A year later back in Iowa City at the Hy Vee grocery store she took to calling herself the old "Jane" when the clerk asked for a name for the drive-up. Simpler, though by no means so romantic, and she didn't stutter on *J* as she often did on *D*.

And so it would be "Deirdre." Her colleagues called her "Dee," which was comfortable: Donald-Don-D-Dee-Deirdre. She herself preferred the full, lush, Irish, and antique name, Deirdre the Wanderer and, when spelled "Deirdriu," of the Sorrows. Or something. She learned later that the etymologies are doubtful.

∎

As the convention in Chicago came to an end Donald drank coffee with an old friend from Israel, who was worried, as everyone was, about Donald's weight.

"Don't worry. It's just dieting. I'm still twenty pounds above my college weight. Look at you: I'll bet you haven't gained an ounce since the '67 war!"

"Well. . . ."

"But there's something else. My wife and I are probably getting divorced."

"Oh, I'm sorry to hear that."

"And something else." He wanted to tell this gentle, intelligent man, willing to listen as few men are. ***But, no.***

∎

On Saturday night Donald skipped the conference banquet and instead went excitedly in male drag out to Irving Park Road in Chicago, to a social of the Chicago Gender Society. The bar was almost empty when he arrived. ***Must be early. More people will come.*** He had brought along a garment bag with his cocktail dress, and he changed into it and put on makeup in the tiny ladies' room. When he came out there was still no one from the Society there. Jane took a stool at the bar and nursed a beer, doing what a lady would do: *Drink slowly; back straight; don't look at the men; move with grace.* After a while a middle-aged man came over.

"Mind if I join you?"

"Uh, no; fine." *One never knows how naïve people can be,* he thought, *but he* **must** *read me. Still, as long as he treats me with courtesy.*

"Name's Ashworth. Call me Charlie. I'm a printer." In the tradition of printers he read a lot and had opinions, which he poured out. Charlie needed a woman to listen, and Jane was willing to play the role. When Jane offered an opinion Charlie would shut him up. Just listen.

In a rare moment of reciprocity Charlie asked, "What's your line of work?"

Jane answered, proud, as if to punish the man for his male *io, io:* "I'm a college professor." As soon as he said it he knew it was stupid. He should have said "secretary," or whatever would protect Smith's ego. For a while the answer slowed Charlie's torrent of opinion, but soon he was back at it.

Charlie went to the men's room, and the bartender came over and said, "I'm sorry, ma'am. Charlie's a real pain."

"Oh, no pain!" Jane thought, *I can learn to just be pretty and listen. I'd better.* She meant that men expect attention, not that they deserve it. *Io, io.* Peggy Seeger sings bitterly, "Just stay mum, pretend you're dumb, / That's how you come to be a lady today."

Only Robin from the nights at Temptations, and Carole, the gender crosser with whom Jane had gone shopping in the mall the spring before, showed up at the social. *Some social.* It was disappointing not to meet the many earnest gender crossers he had hoped for, to learn how it's done, though Robin and the other woman were gender crossers all right, and earnest enough. (He was beginning to use the nonmedicalized term "gender crosser.") So they went to Temptations. Jane danced some, though he didn't get into it as during the three other visits. *It will become boring soon,* he thought. *I've never liked nightlife.* It proved to be the last visit. A tall crossdresser, six feet five, sat at the bar in the middle sipping a beer, an engineer from another city in the Midwest who frequently came through O'Hare a few miles from Temptations. The engineer admitted to gender-crossing desires.

"But I'm too damned tall to do anything permanent," he said with a strained smile. "I just do this when it works out. I have a little bag with clothes and stuff."

Jane thought about his own height, six feet, which he worried was the upper end of the possible. If he'd been the height of the engineer he would not have allowed himself to hope. He would have stuck to the little bag, as he'd done through four decades. *With a feminine face by surgery,* he thought, *and a feminine voice I'll be OK. Plenty of women are as tall as I am. Well, some. Please, dear God.* For years afterward Deirdre was gratified when she encountered a woman as tall or taller.

Temptations was closing. Jane went to the ladies' room and then went to the men's to change back into Donald. The owner, a gay man, knew Deirdre by this time but was surprised to see Donald.

"Oh, honey, you look *cute* as a guy!"

"Thanks. But *this* feels like drag now."

"I understand, dear, I understand."

A DAY YOU FEEL PRETTY

At 10:00 on Monday morning, September 11, 1995, Donald's fifty-third birthday, he went to his appointment with the psychiatrist Frank had recommended. It was odd to sit talking about gender crossing in the conventional office near Mercy Hospital in Iowa City. It reminded him of his doctor-rich childhood, with its accidents and the round of speech therapists, though he had never told anyone, and later only that psychoanalyst at the Harvard Health Service. And once in a psychologist's office in Iowa City, when the whole family went for therapy in his son's most stress-provoking teens, Donald was filling out one of their forms containing hundreds of questions. For the hell of it he answered truthfully the item, "True or false: I sometimes have fantasies of being a woman." The psychologist took no note of the strange response buried in normality.

By custom though not by law or scientific evidence, one set of gatekeepers are the psychiatrists, M.D.'s who specialize in major mental illnesses. The psychiatrists certify competence for the gender crosser to decide to cross. But there is no evidence, Deirdre came to say, that people want to cross gender because they are manic or depressed or delusional. Clinical depression causes people to jump off bridges, and schizophrenia causes them to hear voices. None of the mental illnesses cause people to think they were assigned to the wrong gender.

It doesn't happen. No need for psychiatrists, Deirdre said, especially since the psychiatrists so often are ignorant about crossgendered people. You might as well have priests or police or cab drivers involved. The custom of involving psychiatrists satisfies the gender anxieties of society, not the good of the "patient." ***More like the prisoner.*** Culture determines the rules, not medical reason. Thus in Japan until 1998 it was illegal to perform gender reassignment surgery, and thereafter it was in the hands of crossphobic psychiatrists who seldom approved.

Donald and the doctor had a quiet talk, Donald taking care not to be too passionate or to express political opinions about compulsory psychiatry. His sister's and his wife's nutty diagnosis of "mania" had to be offset, though a woman psychiatrist he knew had told him on the phone that his behavior didn't sound like mania, and that mania is unmistakable. Donald had not told her what the matter was:

"Suppose someone had . . . well . . . a model train set in the basement and was so excited that he spent a fair amount of a large income on it, and would sometimes get up very early to play with it. Would that be mania?"

"It depends what his affect is," she replied. "Manic behavior is hard to miss. It often involves grandiose feelings."

"What do you mean?"

"If the man with the train set knows it's just a toy, no worries."

"An expensive toy, quite a few thousand a year," he said, testing his wife's insistence that he was spending crazy, manic amounts on electrolysis.

"But lots of people spend that much on hobbies," she noted.

"Yes. Especially men."

She laughed. "Yes, especially men. But you would know manic behavior in a half hour of conversation. For example, if our model train enthusiast starts telling you that his toy will change the transport system of the nation. . . ."

"Then you start worrying."

"Yes, then you start worrying."

He came to the point: "Do you think I'm manic?" They had known each other slightly for a long time, belonging to the same eating club. She was a successful research psychiatrist, who had gone back to medical school after a Ph.D. in English. A small, ambitious woman, she was tough for the male world of medicine, glinty intelligent.

"I've never seen signs of it. You're enthusiastic, optimistic, I'd say. Real mania is usually pretty evident. Understand, this isn't a professional opinion, since I've not examined you with care."

"I understand. I'm just looking for friendly advice. How about manic depression?"

"Have you ever had a depressive episode?"

"No, not clinical depression. I've been sad."

"Sad doesn't count," she said.

"I understand."

"It would be very unusual for what we call 'bipolar' illness, manic depression, ups and downs, to start at your age."

"Thanks. Thanks very much."

"That's all right, Don. I hope it works out."

A good conversation. Later, when she and everyone else found out what the model train in the basement was, and her Department of Psychiatry at Iowa fumbled its dealings with Donald, she closed ranks with her colleagues. She wouldn't return Donald's calls, and when he wrote she responded with a letter suggesting he move anonymously to another town and start his life over. It was the policy psychiatrists had favored in 1965. Psychiatrists don't know now, and never have.

At this appointment on his birthday the psychiatrist was to look for indications that Donald was clinically crazy. The psychiatric exam was part of the "[Dr. Harry] Benjamin Standards of Care," formulated in the 1970s when even less was known about gender crossing than the little known now, and accepted since then as protecting the caregivers, though not from legal test. The Benjamin Standards set up psychiatrists and psychologists as gatekeepers and require two years of full-time life as a woman before the operation. Two years as an unconvincing and indeed illegal woman is a long and dangerous time. *That the crossers are free adults,* Deirdre reflected later, *is not deemed pertinent.* Another gender crosser put it so: "When you want surgery on your nose, it's called a nose job. When you want surgery on your boobs, it's called a boob job. When you want surgery on your genitals . . . you're crazy!" And another noted that no surgical procedure has more than a two-day waiting period except *the* operation, which requires a wait of two years. *Let's see,* said the economist, *the exchange rate is two days against . . . 730 days. Something is going on. It's not so special that the operation should be made unique among medical procedures.* Deirdre collected adjectives that in her hardening opinion described the Benjamin Standards, well intentioned when devised so long ago: antique, outdated, unscientific, silly, hilarious, contemptible, unfair, unconstitutional, inconsistent, crossphobic, terrifying, cruel, illiberal, lawyer-driven, psychologist-enriching. The self-appointed committee that had issued them tried in 1997 to make them worse, with no scientific evidence and no representation from gender crossers.

The psychiatrist in Iowa City concluded in effect that Donald was not "doing this" because he thought he was Marie Antoinette. He said, "You are not manic. You are transsexual." A doctor would use the medicalized word. "With present techniques transsexuality cannot be changed. There is nothing I can do for you." Donald was pleased by the sober words and paid at the desk.

When he got home and told his wife, she wept. She had hoped.

"Your sister and your mother tried to have you committed yesterday," she said after blowing her nose.

"What are you talking about?"

"Your sister briefly convinced your mother you were manic, a danger to yourself. There's a procedure, 'civil commitment.' I wouldn't do it."

"Thank you." It was a husband's thanks: **Of course *she will protect me, as I her, though hell should bar the way.*** "I'll call them both," he said, and went upstairs to his office phone.

His sister was furious when he talked to her, though as always calm on the surface. She habitually played her cards close to the chest. It was her main gift for secular stoicism.

"Attempting to commit me was a stupid thing to do," Donald said. He still didn't realize how close she had come. It still felt like one of her occasional panics about her brother or mother, a lot of telephonic sound and fury, never candid, manipulating for control.

"I talked to your psychiatrist. He's an idiot," she said emphatically.

"I don't think so, dear. He's a board-certified psychiatrist, recommended by my very good psychologist. And he seemed quite sensible to me."

"In your mania, you *would* think so." It was the catch-22 of the mental health nut: If you don't agree with my diagnosis, that just shows you're crazy.

"I don't have 'mania,'" he said with rising annoyance.

"Of course you do." Her airy confidence was irritating. "Your wife thinks so."

"Not any more. Not after the psychiatrist."

"I told you: he's an idiot."

"For God's sake stay out of this. You're so damned sure. What can you know from Boston?" He was angry and loud. He didn't know she was taking notes, writing down things like, "Irrationally angry, protective of the psychiatrist who approved him." After all, catch-22 was an invention of psychologists, and she was professor of psychology.

"I want my brother to be treated for his mania."

"You want your brother to remain your brother, and the psychiatrist wouldn't cooperate with your conspiracy to stop him from becoming your sister."

"That's not so. I love you. I want to help you."

"Yeah. As in 'I'm from the government, and I want to help you.'"

Then he called his mother.

"What's this about your conspiring with my sister to get me committed?"

"I didn't 'conspire' with anyone, son. She had me frightened. It lasted about half an hour."

"What do you mean?"

"I had agreed to cosign the papers. She was going ahead. But I realized it was wrong and called her up and changed my vote. I've been sick again. She took advantage of my state. I hate it when you kids get into these quarrels."

"Oh. I thought you were on her side."

"There's no 'side' here. I love all three of my children and want what's best for them. You're not crazy. You're transsexual."

"So the psychiatrist and the psychologist think. Even my wife."

"I *wish* your sister would have more sense. But just remember: it may wreck your career."

"I don't care."

"That's a terrible thing to say."

"I wouldn't have said it two months ago. I was looking at costs and benefits, not who I am."

"Remember the man in his wife's hat on Easter Sunday."

She's not listening. He didn't care about his blessed career. But he would comfort her, dutiful child. "Times change."

"I don't think so."

■

On the day of the psychiatrist, the day after his sister's attempt to have him committed, his wife left a birthday card on the kitchen counter. It showed a photograph of a girl of about twelve staring wistfully into a mirror. Inside the card it read, "I hope this is one of the days you feel pretty." Donald cried. His wife said again that she would divorce him. She was determined by then to leave if the gates could not be closed. But she promised to help him achieve what he wanted. For the beloved's own sake. She was keeping her promise by not cooperating with his sister. She had stopped believing in this way of closing the gate. "No, he's not crazy. He's transsexual." A brave thing to say, against the more hopeful if manic diagnosis of mania.

■

It was the second night that his wife and Donald had slept apart. Donald wanted them to stay together, for support, but she couldn't. Donald now slept in the room across the hall. It was a new life, and a woman's nightgown ever after. When he woke the next morning it was an even day of the month. But he felt entitled, so he put on a skirt and blouse and went down to make breakfast.

"What's this?" his wife asked, indignant. "It's an even day."

"Things have changed, haven't they? The nonsense about 'mania' is dead. We don't sleep together."

"I think it's very inconsiderate."

"All right. All right. It's back to Donald drag. But I think it's unfair."

That day he went for the last time to the psychologist, who sent a letter to an endocrinologist at the university hospital. The endocrinology appointment was to be a week later.

12

PREMARIN

At a little weekend in the Poconos, Jane and two other crossdressers went to a distant mall to see *To Won Foo,* in which three drag queens have car trouble in a small town on their way to Hollywood and fame. You are on their side, as are all the townsfolk except one gender cop. Gender education.

Jane was as usual the least passable, being the tallest, and they were read by the dense crowd, heads jerking around to get a second look, stunned expressions, people nudging each other as the trio strode up to the multiplex ticket booth. Jane put down a $20 bill in front of a startled young man selling tickets.

"Three, please."

"Uh, um . . . to which show?"

Jane spotted the gag. Waving his hands campily, "You get one guess, dear!"

"Oh . . . yes . . . um . . . *To Won Foo?*"

"That's right: three."

They went in and found their places in the dark. When the movie ended and the crowd had been gender educated, the three rose slowly and walked out smiling.

Tuesday, September 19: My sister sent an e-mail to my wife saying in its entirety, "My brother does have the illness of manic depression, you know it, and I shall never forgive you for doing nothing to ensure my brother receives appropriate evaluation and treatment, for blocking our attempts to help him." This is a tendentious reading of my "symptoms" and a fraudulent use of "our," since she is the only one who believes her diagnosis. My sister has reported falsehoods about my behavior ("He hardly sleeps"; "His mind races") to psychiatrists whom she has boldly called on the telephone, getting them to confirm her predecided notion that I am in the manic stage of manic depression. I gather that she has had run-ins with my psychiatrist and my psychologist, who refused to talk to her without my permission. She is furious at them, as at anyone who stands against her will.

Donald had expected the appointment with his endocrinologist to be one of many, pleading and pushing to open the gate. But the doctor did not view himself as a gatekeeper. He said: that's for the psych guys. So he prescribed some estrogen.

As Donald walked away from the hospital pharmacy clutching his Premarin, he felt reborn. Later the doctor also prescribed spironolactone, the antitestosterone medication permitted in the United States. Still later, when Deirdre was living in Holland, she got the Androcur permitted there, which blocks the effects of testosterone better, and joked with girlfriends about the solution to the problem of men: Lace the water supply with Androcur.

When he got back to his house, a couple of blocks from the hospital, his wife was there, depressed. He could not be unhappy.

"I got the hormones!"

She was sour. "The endocrinologist should be sued for malpractice."

■

He was going briefly to France for a conference. The night before he left he got a call from his brother, the youngest of the three McCloskey children, by now in his forties, who had been alarmed by their sister. After a few minutes his brother turned calm and loving.

"You do what you need to, Donny. I'm behind you."

"Thank you, brother, thank you very much." Donald remembered how he had expected his brother to have difficulties. He was having no more difficulties than his mother.

"Don't let our sister interfere."

"I won't."

"She's dangerous." His brother spoke from experience with her medical and manipulating style. Donald remembered with shame his own part in it, financing an aggression of "helping" his brother many years before: $5,000. Someone else always financed her family violence. "I repeat: you should watch out. She's determined."

"Yeah." But Donald did not watch out.

> September 27: A week of a conference in France. On the plane over I read Deborah Tannen on men and women in conversation, *You Just Don't Understand.* I took a nightgown. Conference in Montpellier. I tried to be like a woman in my interactions. At the formal dinner I was seated with five women around me and fell into womanly conversation with them. I think I succeeded, using the Tannen rule: women are egalitarian. They look to an apparent man for the lead because men are always seizing the conversational initiative, establishing hierarchies. I tried not to. After an informal dinner on the last night in Montpellier, at a gathering for a drink with three British couples, I noticed my fluency in the male style of interaction, with its kidding and pushing and objective-information-laden character. The conversation broke naturally into girl talk and guy talk. I kept trying to join the girl talk but didn't succeed as well as I had the previous night.
>
> At the airport flying out of Paris I overheard a man, apparently a technician for Boeing, talking endlessly to another man about airplane facts. The victim had no great interest in the matter, but men are willing to bore each other if it establishes dominance: you shut up and listen; I know the game.

13

SWEET OCTOBER

October 2: I'm back from the "Southern Comfort" convention in Atlanta, which I decided to attend when I realized it had a full program on gender crossing. The event itself was not as exciting as my trip in June to Be All in Cincinnati. Only one first time.

On Sunday morning a couple reaffirmed their marriage vows, he in a fancy wedding dress, she in a simple one. They looked out of place on the patio around the pool with a dozen amateurs wild for shots and a German TV crew and Mariette Pathy Allen the photographer who wrote *Transformations: Crossdressers and Those Who Love Them.* The ceremony was performed by a crossdressing Presbyterian minister, himself recently and disastrously outed. He did an ecumenical service, and I often got teary, as I do.

I noticed a line of civilians standing some distance away, stunned by what was going on, and I walked over to them professor-style with gender education in mind. (Would a woman think of doing such a thing?) The main talker was a woman about my age who was amazed to discover that in fact all these people were men, except the other bride, and that it had nothing to do with homosexuality. People merge all sexual abnormalities into one weirdness—any deviation from the missionary position between man and wife on Saturday night is thrown in with rape, child molestation, and mass murder. Anything weird is weird and just like all the other weirds.

It's hard to get people to admit that they have elements of both male and female in them. The woman turned to a grizzled older man and asked with ironic intent, "Joe, you got any female in you?" It was tempting for her to enforce the gender rules this way, for reasons of her own.

One of the men said, "I used to drive a busload of them from San Francisco all over once a year. Not a real woman among them." I took a chance and asked him whether they were clean, honest, polite, upright, courteous, reverent, and so forth, and he said, yes, they were all of these. It wasn't much of a chance, because he wouldn't have remained the driver of the bus year after year if the crossdressers hadn't been all right.

On the way to the airport from the convention I met Stephan Thorne, a female-to-male police sergeant in San Francisco. I had heard his presentation the day before to the ABC *20-20* cameras describing his recent outing as a gender crosser (he transitioned on the job a year or so ago). The female-to-males are going up the status hierarchy, which I think is less threatening to the born men. Men seem worried about holding it together, staying men, as though they were threatened with slipping down into womanhood. They do regard it as "down."

Stephan told of his epiphany, similar to mine. When he was she, she was with her lover saying to herself, "I am a lesbian and a San Francisco policewoman. Cool!" Then he said, "like glass breaking," the conviction came, "Wait a minute. I'm not a lesbian. I'm a *man.*" And that was it. She became one. So like De Kalb.

There seem to be two patterns: either you've always known you were of the wrong gender or you've constructed a psychological dam against the realization, which suddenly breaks, usually in mature adulthood. The categories correspond to Richard Docter's of primary and secondary gender crossers; Docter, a psychologist, has written on gender crossing; I must get his book.

October 4: At home now, I made dinner for us both, and my wife and I had a peaceful evening. She said, "You're treating me nicely." I replied, "If you accept what I'm doing and respect me, we'll have no problems." I don't understand why she can't grasp this. She really does think that I gratuitously attack her, because she views the dressing itself as an attack. That I do not intend it so, and that on the contrary I would like to keep her love, and that in other ways I treat her with love and respect, is not relevant in this way of thinking. It sounds like people who view homosexual behavior or liberal politics or Catholic religion itself, without any actual damage to be cataloged, as an "attack" on their values.

Of course it's horrible for her, painful, a shocking revision of the story she had of her life. She seems to reason so: "I am hurt by his behavior. Therefore he is to blame. Therefore his behavior is bad, to be punished." The notion that two people in a relationship can hurt each other without intent or blame, because they feel they must be themselves, is not a notion she's ready for. Maybe she will be later. For now it's his bad behavior, and blame and punishment, because she is hurt. I guess.

On a Sunday Donald went to his eating club, university men and women he had known for years. At dinner he was sitting at the end of the table, with men on either side. He applied Tannen again. Without changing his tone he adopted women's rules for conversation: Listen, do not interrupt, support the speaker, maintain eye contact, do not gratuitously change the subject. Tannen explains that it is a cooperative rather than competitive theory of what a conversation is for. Not *io, io.* Whether or not this blithe view of womanly interaction is wholly correct, within a few minutes the two other men were treating Donald as a woman. They were going on with their ping-pong of competition, not looking, interrupting, not listening to him. He was out of it, as women are in men's eyes. Later he did the same thing in a group of women, and again within minutes the women's rules had led them to treat him as another woman. He went home in the dark elated.

■

Donald as Jane went to an Iowa Artistry meeting at a crowded motel in Cedar Rapids, dressed for a party. The motel clerk gave him a second, startled look. ***Irritating not to pass.*** A wedding group sent a representative over to the Iowa Artistry room to ask someone to come over and speak. Just thought it would be fun. As the professor and professional talker in the group, Donald did it, the usual gender education: We crossdressers are harmless. It's not about sex. Notice that we have real jobs and families. No, we are not homosexual. Notice that most of us are married. No, we do not want to become women. *Though I do,* he added mentally.

■

One evening that sweet October Donald and his wife watched *Pride of the Yankees,* the Lou Gehrig story with Gary Cooper, and Donald found himself reacting to it as a woman might. It was not a matter of following page 35 of a manual on *How to Be a Girl.* Without effort he listened as a woman. The sporting scenes now bored him. (He would click past baseball and football games on the TV that a couple of month's earlier he would have seen it as his duty to study briefly.) The love scenes in the movie entranced him. The sentiment about the crippled kid Gehrig hit two home runs for made him choke up. He thought, *I expect the same will be true of every piece of fiction I have read or seen enacted. I will see King Lear not from his point of view but from his youngest daughter's. It's a new pair of glasses, and the world is differently focused and colored. If it's true of fiction it would be true of poetry, song lyrics, epic: I see myself weeping for Queen Dido abandoned by Aeneas instead of thinking, "For Lord's sake, he's got to get on with the founding of Rome."*

October 10, Monday night: My wife came home and as usual was visibly disappointed to see me as Jane. The odd-even rule has been dropped, and she's increasingly depressed. She's still not adjusted to the reality, still hopes that by giving me dirty looks or by sneering or by talking in some magical way she can stop it. It's the impulse I heard about from a female-to-male whose mother continued to use "Cindy" when everyone else had adjusted to calling him "Ralph."

My wife bitched at me about not stripping the second bed that was occupied by one of two house guests: she is trying to show me that I do not know how to be a woman. I had given and cleaned up a party, buying and cooking everything for it; had stripped the *other* bed; had just finished ironing a pile of clothes, half hers, and so on. She asked if I had taken the trash out to the street, and when I said yes she snapped, "I didn't see it there." Her patience is gone.

The last bit of male behavior she can evoke in Donald is angry shouting. At least at the top of his lungs Donald is behaving like a man, which is what she bargained for. I know I am disappointing her, not slowing down—as perhaps I could, and as she deserves, my loving wife of thirty years. But can someone ask you for their continued routine of life to give up who you are? Oh, Lord, peace, peace.

I forgot to tell her that I went to the speech therapist and had a wonderful experience (she would have sneered). The professor who handled it was unfazed when I told her what was up; and within hours had found someone to try to teach me to speak like a woman.

"Loft" the voice, they said, in a series of sessions over the next month. Make it come from the top of your throat, not from your chest like a man. Stress the sibilant quality of *ssssss*. Vary your pitch within the sentence.

October 15: Called the surgeons, one for voice and the other for face. I had met them both at Southern Comfort in Atlanta. The voice surgeon's office had given me a weeklong runaround. I do not know where surgeons, much less secretaries, get the idea they should prevent people from getting harmless procedures. I called the face guy in San Francisco, Douglas Ousterhout and his excellent office manager Mira, and it was from night to day. They are private and considerate. And enormously expensive.

■

Donald had a conversation with himself about whether what he was doing was unusual. On the one hand, *I wonder why more people aren't doing this.* But then, *You don't get it, do you, Donald? Most people don't want to change gender.*

Puzzled in return: *Oh. You don't say. That's funny.*

October 23: My wife comes back from her (male) divorce lawyer always with fresh aggressions. This time she shouts that she will make the divorce painful and expensive unless I let her stay in our house in the spring at a greatly reduced rent—she suggests a figure of zero, as penance.

She has become the masculine force in the house, brimming with aggression, unwilling to talk. Yesterday she was yelling at me about some silly issue that neither of us really thought was important, and I said, "I have a tape recorder in my pocket." A stupid, challenging thing to say, when what she needs is sympathy. She attacked me. We struggled for a while. I fended her off, trying not to hurt her and to keep her from hurting me. War of the Roses.

I came out by e-mail to my two oldest friends in economic history, Joel Mokyr of Northwestern and Richard Sutch of Berkeley. I wept when Joel sent back his reply: "I admired you from the first time I met you. It matters not what your gender is."

■

On Halloween, two and half months after the epiphany, a month and a half after starting hormones, no physical effects yet (those took months and years), Donald was alone in the house. His wife was out of town on business, and he was in male clothing. Three little children with their father came to the door demanding treats. Before the new role Donald would have offered conventional praise for their costumes and gone back to watching the football game on TV. But without intending it he/she went nuts over the children. They were *so* cute, the little girl of six, who will be plain but doesn't yet know it; the boy of four, much prettier; and the tiny girl in tow who did not grasp Halloween. Donald wanted to adopt them. He wanted their father to leave forever. It was a grandmotherly reaction. *A month and a half and the hormones are working,* he thought at first. *Or was it merely that the real person could now stand up?* Was he stripping away the accretion of maleness, settling into the calmness, the warmth of womanhood? Biology or core identity?

Deirdre later would correct herself: *That way of putting it naturalizes a difference in gender, putting it "deep" within the individual, whether in mind or in biology. At one level, I have found, gender is "deeply" superficial, a performance, something that must be studied and learned. We are our masks.* The third and nonessentialist possibility explaining Dee the grandmother at Halloween, then, was "doing gender," a way of being in the world learned over decades even by the other gender: just do the opposite of "being a man." We make ourselves with our habits, as William James said a century ago, speaking in a tradition going back to Aristotle. Doing gender can be viewed as an accretion of learned habits, learned so well that they feel like external conditions, merely the way things are. It is a shell made by the snail and then confining it. The reaction to the children at the front door felt "natural." But society is involved in shaping such a nature, a second nature.

Nature, nurture? One can't be sure. Even I, inside the experiment. Yet what does it matter? she asked herself, with a philosophical pragmatism she knew would annoy both sides, who insist on one or the other as a test of ideology. *Gender must be enacted daily in a hundred ways, but to be enacted it must be felt, too, "from the inside." Like method acting. Pretend you're an orange.* Be *an orange.* Be *a woman of the 1990s. I feel like one.*

PART TWO

DEE

NANCY, BUSINESS COLLEGE FRIEND

GARY FETHKE, DEAN

SHARON, LAWYER

DAVID GALENSON OF CHICAGO

MARTY OLNEY

JOEL MOKYR, RICHARD SUTCH

DR. OUSTERHOUT, PLASTIC SURGEON IN SAN FRANCISCO

ESTHER

GARY, FIRST DATE

DR. SATALOFF, VOICE SURGEON IN PHILADELPHIA

MARIJKE IN HOLLAND

EUGENIA, VISITING ROTTERDAM

14

OUTED

On a mellow evening in late October Donald's wife came home pan-icked: "It's all over campus."

"Good Lord. I wanted it to be confidential until I left for Holland in January."

"Well, that's not what's happening. My dean in the College of Nurs-ing told me she knows. She heard it from someone in the Iowa Foun-dation." The Foundation was the fund-raising arm of the university.

"You've been telling some of your colleagues in nursing. They have connections with the Foundation."

"That can't be. It must have leaked through you."

Dee was later told by officials of the university's administration that someone in the Foundation had been telling it as juicy gossip. The of-ficials were annoyed. "This person is notorious for getting position by telling tales," one of them declared. Quite a tale.

■

When the news broke Dee decided to spread it himself to as many people as he could. *It would be better to appeal to their best sen-timent, their love, rather than letting it spread through their worst, glee at another's discomfort.* Later that was Deirdre's ad-vice to gender crossers: get ahead of the news. Tell people yourself before they hear of it. So Dee sent a letter out to all her colleagues, men and women, at Iowa and in economic history:

Dear Colleague,

I want to tell you something as directly as I can. You should hear it from me, not from a grapevine—though the news has spread quickly and I worry I'm too late.

I am a gender crosser. That is to say, I am one of those few people (it surprises me always when I see the statistics of how few) who wish very strongly to live in the opposite gender. Only one out of 3000 men wish to cross the line. "Transsexuality"—the desire to cross permanently—is less common than crossdressing—occasional dressing as the other gender for sexual or other pleasure. As many as 1 percent of men cross-dress, often with stable marriages. The men who wish to *be* women are a tiny minority of those who wish occasionally to *dress* as women. Of course.

My past behavior, I realize, has not prepared you for such bizarre news. It will seem strange, but I was not miserable in my male life—on the contrary, you knew me correctly as an essentially cheerful person. Such evidently happily masculine people as the British journalist and war correspondent James Morris (now Jan; see her book *Conundrum*) and thousands of policemen, marines, businessmen, together with a handful of that most masculine category of all, the top macho occupation, college professors, have had gender dysphoria and have spent part of a lifetime concealing it, mainly from themselves.

Until relatively recently, of course, it has been impractical to do much about it. The Chevalier d'Éon, internationally acclaimed spy and swordsman/woman was discovered after his death in 1810 to be a biological man in a dress. Dr. James Barry, Inspector General of the Medical Department of the British Army, was discovered on his death in 1865 to be an unaltered she. Modern surgery and therapy—not just The Operation (I can see the men crossing their legs), but facial surgery and voice surgery, speech therapy and so forth—can do a little more. No one can "become" a woman in Aristotelian essence: XX and XY genes are different. More important, one's history is different; one cannot be a woman 100 percent without a girlhood. History matters. But for practical purposes we do not perform genetic or background checks on a man or woman functioning in a social role. I can be a 97 percent woman. I think.

In 1949 Simone de Beauvoir wrote in *The Second Sex,* "A man is in the right in being a man; it is the woman who is in the wrong." I'm doing "the wrong" because my lifelong identity has been split, and is more fundamentally female than male. I learned the male presentation with difficulty, against my character. (I know the many victims of Don's male aggression will smile at this news!) You cannot imagine the relief in adopting my correct gender. Imagine if you felt French but had been raised in Minnesota.

I am not ashamed. For one thing I do not regard being a woman as shameful. And for another I do not see that gender borders should be any more uncrossable than national or cultural or disciplinary borders.

You can't change your gender in private, so I can't stay discreetly in a closet. If I don't want to abandon being a teacher and scholar I have to do this in the open, alas. By the way, if I *had* to hide I would gladly move to Spokane and get a job as a secretary in a grain elevator ("My husband just died: that's why I don't have an employment history"). I want you to feel how amazing such a statement is in someone as career-driven as Donald was.

My marriage family is having a terrible time. My wife is distraught, and who wouldn't be? We will part shortly, as amicably as we can. So far she and my grown son and daughter have had a hard time moving beyond their love of Donald. If you know them I ask you to help them. There is nothing false in my love for my family, then or now. That I was deceiving myself about my gender identity does not have to do with my love for them. I wish they could accept this.

I won't be appalled if you "can't handle it." Some people can't, and in my male mode having failed often enough to visit a friend in the hospital (Deirdre will do better), I can understand the embarrassment. Give it a try, please, but don't be mortified if you can't.

Love,

Deirdre Nansen McCloskey

She sent it by e-mail, and it echoed round the Web.

On the same theory—appealing to their best side, not being ashamed, no closet, ever again—he spoke openly to newspapers, though it infuriated his wife, who believed Dee could stop the stories from appearing. The newspapers first learned through rumors in the university and then a copy of the letter, so the newspaper stories were going to appear regardless of whether Dee cooperated to make them accurate. His wife raged at the reporter from the Des Moines *Register* who called to check facts in a story his editors were intent on printing. She wouldn't let Dee talk to the reporter at home, shouting and grabbing the receiver. He had to go out and call back from a phone booth so that the story to appear the next day on the front page of the state's main newspaper would not be about a shameful secret badly understood. The result of speaking to the reporters from the *Register* and from the students' *Daily Iowan* and then later to other journalists was that the newspapers told of an unusual personal decision instead of a scandal. Deirdre was thereafter willing to talk to the respectable press. *I am not ashamed of this and am not going to let people treat it as shameful. For myself and for the politics I am not going to be put back into a closet, ever.*

15

"WELCOME"

To women he included another letter with the first:

Dear W,

I'm sending this letter to some of my women friends. I enclose what I sent to the men, explaining what is going on.

In brief: I've always felt more female than male. What you have observed in my tough-guy mode was acted, though not recognized very clearly by the person doing the performance. I think most women can understand this better than most men.

As I asked the men I ask you with greater urgency: to love me. It's what I need. At this juncture I need women friends very much. A woman can do without men, of course, but not without other women.

I do not ask for special treatment, as some privileged woman who has been a man—it would mortify me to take up extra emotional space on that account (I already take up more physical space than most women, and do not like it). I am aware that operations will not make me a 100 percent woman; and I am aware that a school of radical feminism is hostile to the idea of gender crossing anyway. I do not dismiss these points of view, though I hope that in practical terms they do not stand in the way of amicable conversation. Someday we can talk about them. You'll find me less implacable!

This has been awful for my wife, and I hope you'll support her. For myself I feel I am in a Comedy, in the technical, English-department sense of a story with a happy ending. We'll see.

Love,

Deirdre Nansen McCloskey

■

Before the rumors and letters, Dee had come out to a luncheon group he belonged to. The half dozen men and women had sat stunned in the booth in Givanni's restaurant. Lola, an experimental psychologist and a colleague at the College of Business, had to leave for another meeting.

"I have only one thing to say to you, Don."

"What's that, Lola?" They were friendly anyway.

"Welcome."

"Welcome," the women said. A woman sociologist joked to Dee that what made the women so gracious was their amazement that a man would want to join them. Dee knew Alice, a biochemist, from committees. Alice wrote a note observing, on the contrary, that a woman's life just has "more." Yes, more, though getting it was not the impetus for changing gender. It was a matter of identity, to say it again, not cost and benefit. Yet. In *Cool Memories* the French sociologist Jean Baudrillard writes as a man envious of women: "We [men] have dreamt of every woman there is, and dreamt of the miracle that would bring us the pleasure of being a woman, for women have all the qualities—courage, passion, the capacity to love, cunning, whereas all our [male] imaginations can do is naively pile up the illusion of courage." When Deirdre came back from Holland she and Alice lunched monthly at what they called Alice's Restaurant.

■

Nancy, the university ombudsperson and a specialist in employment law, an associate of Dee's in the College of Business, worked to find precedents for how to handle the transition, and at a meeting with the vice president for university relations she announced she had found one.

"There's a case in a business south of here. I've spoken to the person involved and to the bosses."

"That's wonderful, Nancy. Thank you very much."

"Not at all. I can put you in touch with her."

"Uh, yes, thank you. Is her name Anna?"

Nancy looked startled. "Yes. How did you know?"

"She's a member of my Iowa Artistry club here in town."

"Goodness! Well. . . . I guess then you're already in touch with her."

"Yes. But thank you, thank you very much." What mattered was the loving and womanly effort to do justice.

■

And some men. The first administrator Dee had come out to was his dean in the College of Business. Dee was standing outside the dean's office on another matter. Dean Gary Fethke wandered through on his way to his office and noticed McCloskey's ear studs, small, but both ears. McCloskey and Fethke had known each other since 1980 and were on man-to-man terms. Fethke thought he knew that McCloskey was straight, even macho. In the gender policing way that straight men have with each other, he smiled and said jocularly, "What's this, Don! The earrings. Have you turned gay?"

Dee decided then. It had not been in his mind.

"You want to know, Gary?"

"Uh . . . yes. Come into my office." He shut the door.

Dee spoke with his ironic, tough-guy demeanor, the last defenses of masculinity. He admitted to being terrified at how the university community might react.

Gary sat stunned for a moment. They were both economists, conservatives by academic standards, free-market enthusiasts. Then:

"Thank God. . . . I thought for a moment you were going to confess to converting to *socialism!*"

Dee laughed, relieved. The dean was going to act like a friend.

"And this is *great* for our affirmative action program—one more woman, one less man!" More laughter, more relief.

"And wait a minute—it's even better: as a woman I can cut your salary to seventy cents on the dollar!" Not so funny.

And then seriously he said: "That's a strange thing to do."

"Yes, it is."

"How can I help?" The month of hormones was working, but even without the hormones Dee would have felt like crying.

Gary kept his word, acting to the administration and the faculty as advocate for Dee and his strange thing to do. Later Deirdre would advise other gender crossers: Get support at the top. Never approach through channels, from the bottom. Personnel departments are not at present equipped to handle gender crossing with common sense, the common sense of "one more woman, one less man." The lower people will discriminate in fear of imagined gender anxieties at the top and will indulge their own. But the top people have fewer anxieties, not more. Later when a male-to-female professor of chemistry came out at the University of Tennessee the president was impatient with the anxieties of his subordinates: "Grow up," he said. "This is not a big deal." Stephan Thorne tells of going to the chief of the San Francisco Police Department, telling him that she was to become a he. The chief was "professional and compassionate" and supported him without fuss.

The University of Iowa is known in the crossgendered community as having the best protection of any university: "The University of Iowa prohibits discrimination in employment and in educational programs and activities on the basis of . . . gender identity." Harvard and Princeton have refused to add gender identity to their lists, though Harvard in practice was calm about a female-to-male freshman on a men's floor in a dorm. Iowa City, to Dee's amazement, passed an ordinance just as he was coming out, having nothing to do with his case, that forbade housing and employment discrimination against gender crossers. You would expect it in San Francisco, Seattle, Evanston, New Orleans, Minneapolis (and the state of Minnesota), Houston (a strange one, caused by a tough litigator in town who is a new woman herself). But Iowa City, population fifty-five thousand? Iowa City is a progressive little place, and contrary to coastie prejudices the state of Iowa is not the Bible Belt. When a reporter asked the conservative Republican governor what he thought about the gender-crossing professor at the state university, the governor replied, "That's a personal decision, and no business of mine." Gentle Iowa.

And gentle Holland. It was by then fixed that Dee would come and teach for a year at Erasmus University of Rotterdam, starting in January, in a couple of months. When Arjo Klamer had first raised the possibility Dee was Donald, and no one in Holland knew except Arjo. "Arjo, you *have* to tell them!" "Yes, yes, I know. Later."

Klamer described the chat he finally had with the *rector magnificus,* a sort of college president.

"Do you remember this Donald McCloskey who is coming as Tinbergen Professor?"

"Certainly."

"Uh . . . he's actually coming as 'Deirdre.'"

The rector did not seem surprised. "Fine. I understand. Why are you telling me this? What does it matter?"

Arjo thought the rector must not be grasping that "Deirdre" is a woman's name. "I mean 'he' is coming as 'she.' He's going to change gender."

The rector grew impatient. "Yes, Arjo, as I said, I understand. And I repeat: Why are you telling me this? What does it matter?"

Toleration in Holland is the civic religion the way freedom is in the United States. Deirdre would tell the story and draw the moral: "I could have shown up as a palomino horse and the rector would have said, 'What does it matter? Can the horse lecture? Does the horse have the same publications?'" The rector later told Deirdre that Arjo had warned him beforehand that there was "a personal problem," and since homosexuality could not possibly be a "problem," the rector had guessed it must be this odder thing. Oddness is not a bar to university employment in Holland's second golden age.

From the women, "welcome." From the men, "what does it matter?" Praise the Lord.

16

THE CUCKOO'S NEST

*O*n November 2, 1995, about noon Dee was sitting in his sunlit living room, in jeans and rumpled shirt and unshaven face for a day as a man at home, giving an interview to a reporter from the Cedar Rapids *Gazette.* Dee had taken pity on the reporter when he had whined about being scooped by the Des Moines *Register*'s story the day before. Anyway, Dee knew the reporter, who had asked him from time to time about economic stories. All right, fine. Come over to my house.

They had just started when someone knocked hard on the door. The schnauzers barked hysterically as always, and his wife answered it. **Probably some delivery,** thought Dee. But he saw two uniformed men and got up. **What's this?** In came two sheriff's deputies in brown uniforms.

"Sir, you have to come with us. We have a warrant."

"A what!"

"A warrant for arrest for mental examination."

Good Lord, my sister's done it. Dee turned to the reporter. "Please, please don't print this!" The reporter was confused and said he wouldn't. But reporters report. The next day the *Gazette* recovered from being scooped a couple of days before, printing its own scoop on the front page: "Professor Seized by Police." Donald McCloskey, the University of Iowa professor of economics who has declared that he wants to be a woman was taken in handcuffs yesterday by Johnson County sheriff's deputies to the University of Iowa Hospital's mental ward to be tested for insanity.

His sister and a former colleague of Dee's at the University of Chicago named David Galenson had used the civil commitment procedures designed to stop people from jumping off bridges. The bridge this otherwise normal-seeming man was jumping off was the series of operations in San Francisco scheduled a month later. A nose job; a smaller voice box. His sister and Galenson wanted to save him from himself. He's gotta be crazy. Danger to himself. Stop him.

Dee offered no resistance to the sheriff's deputies and was cooperative. Libertarians like Dee appreciate that the core of state power is lethal violence. As a concession to his cooperative attitude and his social class, the deputies agreed to cuff him with his hands in front instead of behind. They did it in his front yard, on the lawn where the squad car had pulled up, stuffed him gently in, and drove the two blocks to the emergency room. After some delays the deputy who was to stay with the "danger to himself and others" marched him through the crowded hospital to the adult psychiatry unit. Dee sat with the deputy and a psychiatric nurse for an hour waiting for the admitting psychiatrist, talking peaceably.

Dee thought he was going to be given a chance to explain, and to show on the spot that he was not crazy. *The craziness is my sister's and Galenson's,* he thought. *Surely this is all silliness, and a competent doctor will see it immediately. Gender crossing is not illegal or evidence of craziness. I am going to have a nose job. There is no "danger to myself," that elastic cover for psychiatric thuggery. Surely the psychiatrist will let me go home after this.*

He did not realize that the doctor who was about to see him had been talking with Dee's sister and was probably cowed by her self-confident presentation as a "Harvard" professor of psychology. Dee did not realize that in such a civil commitment the psychiatrists seldom let the victim go, regardless of how reasonable he or she proves to be. The ceremony of examination is empty, a cover against liability. It's not the liability from false confinement that really worries the psychiatrists, but the other side: I mean, what if he walks out of our hospital and shoots himself? In Iowa and many other states (it's harder in California, and impossible in Holland) the law provides that someone seized in this manner can be held three days for observation—it works out usually to five days, because the courts that can free the victim are not open on weekends. In Dee's case the psychiatrists decided without telling him that they wanted him held for eight days. The feelings or condition or evidence or convenience or reputation of the victim are given no weight.

Psychiatrists do not like civil commitment. It is messy and is often employed by abusive husbands to keep their wives in line—if the wife acquires a "mental record" in this way the husband can plausibly threaten to get the kids taken from her by social services if she misbehaves, like not getting up quickly enough to get him another cold one. Sometimes it works the other way. In one case a woman divorcing her husband had him committed for three days, and in his absence she sold the furniture and moved to Illinois. The treatment protocols, Dee would summarize with bitter exaggeration, appear to be these: the victim has no civil rights, especially if poor and unable to hire a vigorous lawyer; nothing he says is to be credited; no penalty of perjury or civil liability or even court costs attaches to the people initiating the seizure if their testimony proves to be false; and the psychiatrists do everything to avoid the liability from letting the victim free, are cowardly about taking the responsibility to do so and in effect are exempted from liability for the consequences of a false seizure and an unreasonable detention. In Iowa, as in many states, any two people who claim to know the victim can have him committed for observation if they can lie successfully to a judge. Dee's sister was willing to do anything to save her much-beloved brother. Anything. Love and courage.

The interview had the planned result. By all means, hold him for three, five, eight days. When the psychiatrist, who had a twitch in his eye, announced this judgment, Dee protested angrily, and the twitch intensified. But Dee's protest was of course more evidence of the madness, that he did not eagerly accept treatment. The psychiatrists have a word for it: "insight." A patient who does not accept an opinion a psychiatrist articulates is said to exhibit "little insight." Catch-22.

■

And so he was held in the locked ward. The room had a telephone. He called his divorce lawyer, Sharon, and explained his situation.

"Do not sign any papers," she said. "Do you understand?"

"All right, but why not?"

"If you sign an agreement to be 'treated' they can hold you indefinitely. I mean six months. A year. Three."

"Good Lord."

"And be as calm as you can. Do nothing unusual."

"Yes. I see."

A few minutes later a nurse brought in a form for him to sign. He looked at it and declined. She seemed surprised. Dee strolled around the unit, exuding normality, and discovered an acquaintance who was in it voluntarily for manic depression. Dee chatted with him for a while, then went back to his room, which was next door to the conspicuously locked front entrance.

He told himself: ***Keep calm. Lack of calmness in a madhouse is not a good idea.*** The day dragged on. He called his mother, and she was shocked. He called his business school dean, who said he would help, and others.

In the evening it occurred to him that he needed clothes for the hearing the next morning. Hospital clothes, being dressed as the patient, would be bad for a hearing on mental competency. He had only the casual clothes he'd been wearing at home. Anyway, hoping for love, he wanted an excuse to call his wife, who had not wanted to be involved. They lived together because neither would agree to move out. "You should leave," she had said, to which he replied, "I'm not an adulterous husband. I've done nothing wrong. I'm staying." This day, phoning from the madhouse, he said,

"Hi, love," a supposition on three decades of love and marriage. A good marriage.

"Hello."

"I'm frightened here. But I guess it will be all right."

Silence.

"Would you do me a favor?"

"What is it? I don't want to be involved." Dee resisted saying what he was thinking: ***She does not want to be involved, she who could stop it at any time, saving me, as I certainly would save her. She could say, "This is ridiculous. This is my husband. He is perfectly sane. He is going to have a nose job. None of what his sister claims to have heard from me is true. Lay off!" The case against me would collapse.***

He composed himself. "I know. You don't want to be involved. But I need professor-type clothes for the hearing tomorrow morning. Could you bring some over?"

Silence.

"A clean shirt. Dress pants. Tie. Dress shoes. Shaving stuff. Comb. Can you do that?"

Silence.

"Are you there?"

"Yes. . . . Well. . . . All right."

"Thanks very much. My lawyer says that everything's going to be all right."

Silence.

"So, bye."

"Good-bye."

Click.

He expected her in a half hour or so, walking from their house a couple of blocks from the hospital. He watched TV for a while, then walked down the hall to his depressed acquaintance. After a conversation of forced cheer he came back to the room, closed the door, and looked at some magazines.

An hour and half later he was wondering where she was. To the nurse on duty: "Do you know anything about my clothes? My wife was going to bring some over."

"Clothes? Oh, yes. The clothes. Your wife and son came over an hour ago. They left that paper bag."

He stopped breathing.

"You mean they came over . . . and dropped off the clothes . . . and left?"

She hesitated. "Yes."

You mean. He stuttered in thinking. *You mean. She came. Into. The ward. The clothes in a bag. Left. Without knocking. Wife. Son.*

Later it returned and returned. He would think, astonished: Them, these two, my son of twenty-seven, my wife of thirty years, they both, twenty feet away. They came to the madhouse and left, ashamed.

■

Later that evening Dee was interviewed by numerous psychiatrists, students and faculty, all curious to see the gender-crossing professor. He saw that none of them knew anything about gender crossing, though all confidently claimed to be expert, which frightened him. *They can hold me forever but they don't know what they are talking about.* The legal question was whether he was competent to sign the surgical permissions in a month to have his nose job. The psychiatrists seemed to be confused about this, and inquired irrelevantly into his sexual practices. *Huh? What do my gender crossing or sexual practices have to do with the major mental illness that would make me incompetent to sign?* He noticed that the psychiatrists were humorless. His little jokes about the absurdity of the situation got nowhere, so he stopped making them.

He slept uneasily that night, but hid it, pretending to sleep when awake, because the psychiatric nurses check for sleeping disturbances every hour. In the cuckoo's nest you develop a protective paranoia, if you have your wits about you.

HEARING?

In the morning he got dressed in his professor clothes, and the orderly
came to take him to the hearing. The orderly treated him as though
he were an independent person, but he knew what would happen if
he took a step toward the outside door.

He came into the hearing room with counselor Sharon. It was too
small, a seminar room. His endocrinologist was there. *That's gallant
of him,* he thought. And Frank, his psychologist, took a day off at the
cost of patient income to be there and support Dee. Lola, she of "Welcome," and the business school dean, Gary Fethke, he of "Thank God
not socialism," were also there, to testify to his sanity on the job. It
was helpful that Fethke had long before worked part time as a medical orderly in the same madhouse where his faculty member was now
confined. So, oddly, had Sharon, the lawyer. The admitting psychiatrist, the one with the twitch, was there, and the doctor in charge the
night before, now jolly as though at a golf outing, along with another
doctor and also the chair of the Department of Psychiatry, who
seemed to have nothing better to do.

Dee was surprised to see his son sitting in a corner looking grim.
He must have driven straight from Chicago the day before to arrive in
time to leave the bag of clothes and not to see his father in the madhouse.

"Hi, Son."

"Hi, Dad." No warmth. **Odd.** Dee's wife was not there. Not involved.

The judge took a seat, and around him sat a secretary and Dee's sister and the assistant district attorney Anne Lahey, who was to prosecute him. As Dee found a seat a few feet away, his sister spoke.

"You know, Donny, I'm doing this for love."

"Yes, dear. And Hitler loved Germany."

Dee's lawyer loved that crack and afterward congratulated him. As men are, he was stupidly pleased to amuse a woman. Grace under pressure, his father used to say, in the words of Saint Hemingway of Key West. Later Deirdre would plod forward with the Hitler thought: Love, after all, is not an excuse for everything. Deirdre was studying the history of ethics that year and saw her own situation in tomes by Aristotle, Aquinas, Adam Smith, and modern theorists of the virtues. If the love is exercised without prudence or temperance or justice, she wrote, it is dangerous and productive of evil. Years afterward her sister could not get the point. She repeated as a talisman: "You know, Dee, I did it for love. For love." Yes, dear, I know.

The admitting psychiatrist was questioned by the prosecutor. In committing Dee he had relied, Deirdre later realized, on what Dee's sister had written in a declaration to the judge to get the emergency order: about Dee's alleged "manic" behavior, arousal of the fear of the operation.

Manic depression, the doctor testified, runs in families. His sister had not at first revealed to the court that she was herself depressive since adolescence, with major symptoms absent from the immediate family members she routinely accused also of being mentally ill (her mother, her younger brother, and now the big prize), or that she was exhibiting manic behavior in her attempt to get Dee declared manic, spending large sums of money, obsessing on it, telling lies to get evidence or to get influence before judges. The eighteenth-century way of defining just that, "mania," would be purest love and courage with no prudence or temperance or justice. But all this was hidden. So it was important to the admitting psychiatrist's testimony that a maternal cousin did in fact suffer from manic depression, bipolar illness. It runs in families, you see. Even if Dee's behavior seems normal, the illness runs in families. Yet the disease appeared to have more to do with an uncle by marriage. There was no such disease on Dee's father's side, or for that matter on the mother's except brought in by the uncle: his child by a previous marriage also was manic depressive. Such fine points were not explored. Is there any chance Dee is suffering from the disease, any chance at all? Value at zero the damage from mis-diagnosing him.

The psychiatrist read out his report on the interview the day before. The patient had showed in the interview no signs of mental illness, the doctor admitted. None, that is, except for a very significant one.

"And what was that, Doctor?" asked the prosecutor.

"He became angry at the end of the interview, after I told him that nonetheless I had decided to hold him."

Dee's lawyer cross-examined. Dee thought, *I am being prosecuted and defended by women. Welcome.*

"Doctor, did Professor McCloskey shout or weep or throw chairs or anything?"

The psychiatrist's twitch grew more pronounced. "No, but he said he was angry, and spoke in an angry tone." Lack of insight.

"Was it an unusually angry tone? I mean unusually loud or abusive?"

"Uh. . . . No." He looked miserable.

"Doctor, suppose someone had just interviewed you and had concluded that you showed at the time no signs of mental illness, but nonetheless suggested you be kept for observation in a locked ward for many days. Would you be angry?"

The twitch intensified. Dee felt like laughing. The scene with the twitching psychiatrist was like Dr. Strangelove in the War Room, unable to control a Nazi salute. Psychiatry: Vee have vays. *Don't laugh, for God's sake.*

"Yes, I suppose I would be a little angry."

"And so being angry at such a suggestion would be normal, would it not, and no sign of mental illness? Rather the contrary?"

He sat silent for a while, unable to see a way out. *The poor man,* Dee thought bitterly. *He is trying to prove that a sane person is insane, and he himself is insane. Well, be fair; not "insane." But on this showing lacking in the judgment and human insight necessary for his profession. The poor man. Really.*

"I repeat, was it unreasonable or indicative of mental illness for Professor McCloskey to be angry?"

"Uh, no . . . I . . . I suppose not."

"No more questions, Your Honor."

Then his sister testified, the old claims about mania, quasi facts skillfully exaggerated and undated. She worried that Dee was going to have irreversible operations: voice, a nose job. "Irreversible operations" in this context evokes the gender reassignment operation and terrifies people. Two years later Deirdre extracted the notes the psychiatrists had made out of the sister's tales and out of an article in the student newspaper. The notes accounted for thirty pages of Donald's and then Deirdre's file over the years at the University of Iowa Hospital. Digestive upset, knee trouble. Then seized and judged crazy by psychiatrists, in a Marx Brothers scene. The examining psychiatrist wrote in notes of October 30, as he discussed the action with Dee's sister, of "the impending sex-change surgery," a month away, which will do "irreversible damage to himself." He repeated the phrase in notes on the day he helped to have Dee seized: "The impending sex change surgery." He was not listening to Dee, who told him it was a nose job, not "sex change surgery." One does not listen to crazy people. Even on discharge, even after hearing the evidence to the contrary, the psychiatrists kept writing down what Dee's sister had induced them to believe. The other doctors declared that "he has . . . scheduled sex change surgery for approximately one month from now." Again and again Dee had explained: nose job, reversible voice operation. No sex change. Get it? The operation you so fear is months or years off, maybe never. But his sister had fooled them, playing on their anxiety, which was her own.

Dee was indignant as his sister told her loving lies, and he kept passing notes to his lawyer. His sister testified on oath that her mother and brother had bipolar affective disorder: "She's wrong," Dee scribbled. That her mother and brother had in fact been hospitalized for it: "That's not so." That Dee had previous episodes of depression: "Nonsense." These statements were all consistent with what his sister had told the judge to get the commitment in the first place, but no one had shown Dee the written declaration. After all, crazy people are too crazy to defend themselves, and so the University of Iowa Hospitals and Clinics was casual about showing the "patient" the claims made to get him committed. The psychiatrist Thomas Szasz at the State University of New York Health Science Center at Syracuse has long angered his colleagues by arguing that "if the persons called 'patients' break no law, they have a right to liberty." Szasz traces the antilibertarian practices of psychiatry to Freud's alliance with a Swiss psychiatrist named Eugen Bleuler. Bleuler adopted Freudianism in his large state hospital and in return Freud dropped his principled insistence that patients volunteer for treatment.

It occurred to Dee later that his sister, the professor of psychology intent on making such a case, must have researched the question whether there was scientific evidence that manic depression shows itself in gender-crossing delusions. The psychological-psychiatric literature has been keyworded and indexed for decades, as Dee knew from surreptitious reading of articles about gender crossing in psychology and medical libraries. Yet his sister did not claim in court that there was any such evidence of a connection between mental illness and gender crossing. She left it to the untutored imagination of the psychiatrists. ***Hmm. She must have known she had no scientific case.*** Yet there she had sat in her best suit at the hearing, a professor who knew that her case was a scientific fantasy, arguing it, playing the anxieties. For love. For pride. For her conviction.

Two years later, in the sunroom of Deirdre's house on a first visit of reconciliation, her sister claimed she had at the time found an article.

"Why didn't you cite it, dear?"

"I don't know: Why should I?" The little girl had been caught cheating on a test.

"You were using every piece of your status as a professor of psychology to get me locked up, yet you didn't use the smoking gun?"

"So?" Teenage defiance.

"I see. Send me the article, will you?"

"Certainly."

■

On a speakerphone the district attorney interviewed David Galenson from the University of Chicago, cosigner with his sister of the commitment request. Galenson testified that Dee was above all cautious as a scholar, and that his present resolve was therefore a sign of madness. Yet Dee was notoriously bold as a scholar—sometimes people would say "stupid" or "foolhardy," and sometimes just "bold." No one else said "cautious."

Dee passed notes to his lawyer, and made indignant faces of scorn and disbelief. This was not effective, his lawyer said at a recess: stop it. We must match the accusers' calm in the cuckoo's nest.

Galenson's aged Aunt Eleanor, a retired psychoanalyst in New York, was brought onto the speakerphone to testify. Dee sat dazed. When she had called Dee at home a few days before, Dr. Galenson had claimed that she intended to help him, and she said at the end of a long chat that she would put him in touch with a colleague in New York who actually knew something about gender crossing. ***Good idea, Doctor.*** Now at the hearing she said that her call to Dee was in fact for gathering evidence for her testimony, based on psychoanalytic principles from the 1950s, when people were put in jails or madhouses for, say, homosexuality. That was of course her conclusion:

latent and suppressed homosexuality. Psychoanalysts of a certain vintage believed that everything indicated latent and suppressed homosexuality. Dee remembered his smile at the diagnosis, when he had extracted it from her at the end of their phone conversation: "Well, Dr. Galenson, what do you conclude?" Dee had had decades of anxiety about gender, but never any anxiety about homosexuality. He had been offered homosexual love, as boys are from time to time, but had said politely, No thank you. He wasn't gay. He loved gals, not guys. He would rather have been gay than a gender crosser: it was less bother, at least after the homophobia of professional psychiatry had died. He thought it funny that this old lady was reviving the homophobia thirty years after its death.

At the hearing it was not so funny, and he was again indignant. Dr. Galenson said on cross-examination that she thought Dee's stuttering was a sign of his "mania," apparently not aware that he had always stuttered. Just as well, since for a while in the early 1950s the psychoanalysts believed that stuttering indicated . . . latent homosexuality. Thus Winston Churchill and Jimmy Stewart and Daniel Patrick Moynihan.

■

Then they did something that felt like torture. They called his son to testify. *That's why he's here,* he realized, startled. Legally the testimony was harmless, as Dee's lawyer told him afterward, since all his son said at length was that he loved his father and didn't want to lose him. But as the nondamaging words of love poured from his son, the thought flashed and flashed: *If you don't want to lose him, keep him, Son. For God's sake don't testify against him in court.*

Dee could not stay indignant long. His son was in his testimony the loving boy, passionate, who had a hard time judging coolly. He thought he was doing the right thing for his father. Lahey the prosecutor appeared to become embarrassed that the testimony was not relevant—after all, his son could know nothing firsthand of his father's recent behavior. Dee's son lived in far-off Chicago. Yet he testified, in words that sounded as if they were provided by the prosecutor herself, that to his own, nonhearsay knowledge his father was likely to flee if released on his own recognizance, a knowledge the son had no way of acquiring. The court shifted uneasily. Lahey tried to cut it short. Perhaps it indicated mere preparing of the witness. Overpreparing. State-sponsored lying. For love, for love. Whatever it was, it was embarrassing and was showing.

No damage. Yet it disturbed Dee for months and years afterward, on his son's account. *What would the son/man do with this fact now standing in his life, that he had once testified against his father? Could he ever admit he had done wrong, and would the inability to admit it freeze his emotions, and poison their relationship, and his life?* Dee thought of Euthyphro, on his way to testify against his father in an Athenian court, whom Socrates stops to question about piety. *On that occasion the father had been accused of murder,* Dee would think angrily, *not of wanting a nose job.* His sister and Lahey the assistant district attorney had brought his son to the little quasi court in the hospital to say favorable things about the father he imagined he loved, yet still to testify against him. *Lahey and my sister her manipulating mistress are evil people,* he thought bitterly, *the one motivated by ambition, the other by love, both of them stupid and imprudent.*

Two years later, talking about it at last, the sister denied that she was responsible for the son's testimony. It was hard to distinguish the denial from her other claims of nonresponsibility. Some were truths, some untruths, some self-deceptions, some irritations with Deirdre's wearying insistence that under the rules of secular stoicism she, Deirdre's little sister now grown up, must take responsibility for having done something wicked.

"I had nothing to do with that . . . ," she said.

"Except starting the business in the first place."

" . . . and I was as surprised by your son's testimony as you were. I think it was a doctor at the hospital who enticed him into testifying."

"More incompetence by the Department of Psychiatry at Iowa?"

"Yes."

"Their usual abuse of crossgendered people?"

"Yes."

"Their fault?"

"Yes, their fault. Not mine. I did it for love. For love."

18

THEN WHY ARE YOU DOING THIS?

The competency hearing droned on into the afternoon. The judge complained that it was the longest he had experienced. Usually it is obvious that the person is in fact a danger to himself or others.

Suddenly it ended. The judge appeared to lose patience with the arguments and counterarguments of the lawyers locked in the dialogue set in motion by Dee's sister and Galenson. He pronounced abruptly that the immediate danger justifying further loss of freedom had not been proved and that the attempt to show that Dee was likely to flee if released was also unpersuasive. But the defendant was to stay in Johnson County for further examination to decide once and for all if he was competent to sign medical consent forms for the operations. The assistant district attorney had lost, but for some reason she kept at it, opposing release, working, working. Perhaps she was cowed by the sister's threats. The district attorney's office pursued with full vigor and at taxpayer expense this college professor planning a nose job. Next year the same office refused to indict a policeman who had violated procedures about firearms and had shot an artist dead in his studio one night.

Dee walked the two blocks home. His wife was there, unhappy at his release, it seemed. Didn't want to be involved.

He went up to his study and for the first time looked closely at his sister's written declaration to the judge, the one that had got him seized and that he had not been shown until the hearing started. The errors began with the first sentence, and he sat reading it angrily, turning over a reply professor-style to each of twenty-five assertions delivered in its short paragraph. *Good Lord,* he thought, *they could have saved themselves a lot of trouble by respecting my legal rights and asking me earnestly about my sister's claims and then listening with some intelligence to what I said. I would not have ended up in the madhouse, $3,000 poorer from legal fees.*

And yet, as May Sarton points out, "Every middle-class 'safe' person should have to go to prison at some point to find out what that the locked world is like." Or to a madhouse.

■

A week after the commitment Dee went over to the hospital, as the court had ordered, to be interviewed by a young psychologist who had had some experience at the program for gender crossers at the University of Minnesota. *Uh-oh,* Dee thought, *one of the American university programs following Johns Hopkins.* His opinion of Johns Hopkins's program was low. It had once been a help for gender crossers, he believed, but long ago had been taken over by psychiatrists who wanted to "cure" them. Medicine and surgery could help the gender crosser by carrying out his or her harmless desire. Dee had heard of no gender crosser cured by psychiatry. About as many as the religious right has cured of homosexuality. Yet, as he put it, the Johns Hopkins psychiatrists kept on racking their patients. *Help or medieval cure,* he thought indignantly. Both the good and the bad approaches to gender crossing, the help and the rack, suppose that it is a "disease," but the choice between the two depends on which metaphor of disease you use. Is help for a gender crosser like plastic surgery after a disfiguring auto accident? Or would giving such "help" be an unprofessional indulgence, an approval for insane and immoral cosmetic surgery, and should one therefore help the patient by hurting him, jailing him, delivering a painful cure for a silly delusion? The Johns Hopkins way. *Vee have vays of "curing" dat.*

The young psychologist was apparently amiable, and better informed than his colleagues. *Watch it,* Dee reminded himself. *Amiable or not, he's not your friend.* But then in a feminine way, or maybe just the self-involvement of a man, he forgot his caution and talked too openly. After Dee had been talking to the psychologist for an hour or so they were joined by the psychologist's boss, the chair of the Department of Psychiatry. For some reason, probably his M.D. degree in the doctor-mad environment of a big hospital, he was to be involved. The Department of Psychiatry appeared to be terrified by the case.

The psychiatrist swept into the little room with the air of a man cutting through all the nonsense to get to the core.

"Are you a homosexual?" he demanded, without sitting down.

"Uh, no." *Good Lord,* Dee thought, astonished, *doesn't he know the difference between homosexuality and transsexuality, who you love and who you are?* Yiddish syntax: *This is a* psychiatrist? *Not so funny. Watch out.*

"Have you ever had a homosexual experience?"

"No." *Sweet Jesus, what's he leading up to?*

"Do you wish to become one?" *Holy Mary, he's got a category Them in his mind, containing all sorts of threats to maleness. The chair of the Department of Psychiatry doesn't know anything at all even about as common a thing as homosexuality. I might as well be "diagnosed" by the average homophobe drinking boilermakers at the American Legion. Watch out. Be careful. Remember: these are not your friends. Jailers rather than healers. Don't say any of this. Don't get indignant that he doesn't appear to know his job and can ruin your life with his ignorance. Don't. Keep your temper.*

"No, I've never wished to become a homosexual," replied Dee as nonchalantly as he could manage.

The doctor stood astonished. "Well, then, *Why are you doing this?" Good God in heaven. Can it possibly be true that the chair of psychiatry has the religious right's theory of homosexuality, as something you decide like style in clothing? That gender crossing is that sort of thing too? It looks worse: he appears to think that homosexuality and gender crossing are the same thing—that homosexuals want to be women and that gender crossers are in it for the sex. Don't say any of this. Don't.*

Dee looked up with alarm but did not reply. The young psychologist, seeming embarrassed by this showing of his boss's ignorance, changed the subject. The two of them wrote a finding for the court, which admitted that Dee was competent to have the surgeries, the only legal point at issue. And then gratuitously they expressed disapproval of his longer-range plans to become a woman, urging the judge stop him for a year. By force. Policing gender.

19

CHICAGO

*I*n the middle of November, two weeks after the cuckoo's nest in Iowa, Dee was to go to the annual meetings of the Social Science History Association at the Palmer House in Chicago, and then to the Speech Communications Association meetings in San Antonio, living conference to conference. At both he was giving papers, and in Chicago he also wanted to show off his graduate students. He had dates to go out with his new e-mail girlfriend and fellow economic historian Martha (Marty) Olney and her friend Esther on Friday night and then with a larger women's group on Saturday night, in drag.

At the last moment the judge allowed him to leave Johnson County, ordering him to return for a final hearing the next Wednesday, in which the assistant district attorney would try one last time to stop this citizen from crossing genders. A colleague in the College of Law had warned Dee that not showing up at the crazy hearing was a crazy idea, so Dee intended to be there. Quite early on Thursday morning Dee rode from Iowa City to Chicago in a university van with his male and female graduate students. They talked about economic history and men and women and gender.

The news from the e-mail messages buzzed in the convention. Dee was dressed conservatively as a man, in an old three-piece, pinstriped suit from twenty years before that fit him now, though he wore small studs in his pierced ears. Nothing else womanly. His bag contained clothes for the two evenings of dressing. In the registration line people came up to him and asked about his health, assuring themselves he was sober and sane. The women were welcoming. One of them was a history professor at UCLA, married to the movie actor John Lithgow. They had once had Donald over to eat at their house in Westwood. Dee said to her now, "Tell John that I think his portrayal of the gender-crossing ex–football player in *The World according to Garp* is the best adoption of womanhood I have ever seen. Except maybe for John What's-his-name as the Latin drag queen in *To Won Foo.*"

It was time for the first session of the afternoon, honoring Dee's recent work in the "rhetoric" of economic history, three papers of praise. Dee sat uncomfortably and tried to think of what he could say at the end. Shortly into an encomium by Joel Mokyr, the Dutch-Israeli-American colleague from Northwestern who had said, "It matters not what your gender is," a hotel employee hurried into the room.

"Professor McCloskey, you are urgently needed outside. A phone call."

"What? What's happening?" As he got up: ***My God, my son here in Chicago has been hurt in an car accident. My wife is deathly ill. My daughter.*** He rushed out into the hallway.

And there was his sister, with two big Chicago policemen. ***Oh, my God, not again.***

"I don't suppose you informed the new judge that you've tried this once already in Iowa?"

Ignoring him, she ordered one of the policemen: "That's him. Seize him."

"This is so stupid," Dee said, exasperated. To the policeman who stepped forward: "I want to cooperate and will offer no resistance." Libertarian theory in practice again. "But will you let me make a call, to get my lawyer?" Dee went over to a pay phone and agitatedly punched in his mother's number and his AT&T calling code. In the next day he would use the code forty times.

"Hello, Son, what is it? I thought you were in Chicago."

"I am. She's done it again: had me seized. I guess it's another jurisdiction, and she's convinced another judge."

"My goodness, that's terrible!"

"Yes. Would you call my lawyer in Iowa City?"

"Certainly. This is outrageous. She's gone too far."

The policeman tapped Dee on the shoulder.

"I have to go. The police are taking me."

"Oh, Donald!"

By this time Joel Mokyr was out of the session and arguing heatedly with Dee's sister. He said emphatically to Dee, "Don't worry: we'll take care of this."

"Thank you, Joel." He was among friends. Later that afternoon they contacted a big-time lawyer in town.

The two policemen took him downstairs and out to State Street. All they had was a paddy wagon. "You'll have to go in the back," one of the policemen said. They could see he was not insane. "Regulations. I'm sorry."

"Where are we headed?"

"The University of Chicago Hospital." *My sister's snobbery,* Dee thought. *Cook County's not good enough.* In the paddy wagon he sat amazed. It must have been used recently to bring in prostitutes: from the floor of the paddy wagon Dee picked up a bright red broken acrylic nail and smiled. *About as much harm from that victim-less crime.* He could just see out the tiny window the familiar scene of the drive from the Loop down the lakefront to Hyde Park. He took out his ear studs. Remembering his picture in drag in his wallet, he removed it and tore it up. *Anything else? I want to present as normally as possible to the shrinks.* Dee had witnessed the craziness that gender straddling brought out in medical people. Despite his precautions, the medical record at the University of Chicago Hospital asserted that Professor McCloskey presented that afternoon dressed entirely in women's clothing. His Chicago lawyer later told him about this and other errors in the record, smiling: "It makes me salivate for a trial." Dee thought, *Gender change terrifies them, so they go crazy and write down nonsense.*

When they got to the rambling hospital the policemen were uncertain where to take Dee. He knew the hospital from his time at the university, and the three of them consulted here and there, Dee talking amiably to the policemen. No cuffs. That way? No, I don't think so. Must be down here. Look, there's a sign. The emergency room. When they were to leave him, after he had been searched and put in a locked room—a danger to himself—one of the policemen asked Dee, "Is this about money?" He meant: You obviously are not crazy; is your sister trying to get you declared crazy in order to take over some inheritance?

"No," said Dee, "It's about love." The policeman looked puzzled and left with his partner.

A wait of six or seven hours in the room began. Dee's friends back at the convention had gotten him the best of Chicago's mental health bar and were helping the argument before the judge. During a recess the lawyer called Dee on the phone in the emergency room and said,

"Don't sign anything."

"Yeah, I know."

"Don't argue about anything."

"Yeah, I know."

"Don't make jokes."

"Yeah, I know."

Marty Olney and Esther came to see him, with his students and some of his other friends from the convention downtown. The nurses in the emergency room had noted after an hour or so that the danger to himself was in fact sane, so they left the door of his room open and let him wander out to chat with supporters over the admitting desk. His sister was out in the waiting room, and Dee watched his students quarreling with her.

A series of psychiatrists came in. The psychiatric nurses, who spend all day with the patients, are in a better position than the psychiatrists to judge sanity. But the hierarchy of medicine leaves them out, and their word is weightless. Mania is easy to diagnose, but the gender transgression confused the psychiatrists. The best was a Polish woman psychiatrist with blond hair and apparent sense. She sympathized. *Watch out, Dee.* But the doctor in charge, who in the evening settled the matter, was a short, bossy man, unhappy with himself, Dee thought. *He's never going to let any patient out, and he knows nothing of gender crossing.* The Polish psychiatrist came back. Dee said, "I'm terrified of your colleague. Save me from him, please, please." She didn't answer. The boss came back and declared he was going to keep Dee. *Maybe forever.* With a show of taking care the doctor insisted that Dee ride up to the locked psychiatric ward in a wheelchair. The doctor loves his patients. *A creepy little man,* Dee thought, *dangerous, ignorant, a jailer. Don't show this feeling.*

And there he was again, in the cuckoo's nest, the locked ward with the other cuckoos, two weeks since the last time.

■

More psychiatrists. One woman psychiatrist asked Dee when he expected his voice would rise, with the female hormones. He thought, *She did not pay attention in her course on endocrinology.* He explained that male vocal cords do not shrink, any more than the male body shrinks. She seemed surprised. *These are the people "assessing" me.* He went to sleep about 10:00 P.M.

An hour later the same woman psychiatrist woke him up. "I'm sorry: we forgot to do some tests." *More incompetence.* "This medical student will do them. I hope you don't mind." *You bet,* he thought, *I show signs of "minding," "lack of insight," and you get to lock me up forever.*

They took him to a little room with a gooseneck lamp and sat him down police-style. He wanted to laugh at the mishandling of his rights, as in some film noir of police torture circa 1948. *No laughing in the madhouse.*

The medical student was nervous. "I'm going to tell you three words, which I'd like you to repeat. I'll ask you to repeat them again in a few minutes, and then a third time at the end of the interview."

"All r-r-right."

"Chair. Love. Orange."

"Ch-ch-chair. L-l-love. Orange."

His stutter had returned in the turmoil of the past two weeks. *Irritating,* he reflected. *The psychiatrists will interpret it as a sign of conflict. They know as much about stuttering as they know about gender crossing.* The medical student asked Dee to count backward from ninety by sevens, to touch his fingertips together, and to do various other tests of mental coherence and central nervous system function. Then:

"I want you to repeat the three words I told you."

"Chair. Love. Orange."

And more tests. Then it was time to go. The medical student and the woman psychiatrist were evidently embarrassed about having had to roust their sane "patient" out of bed.

"Well, good-bye," the medical student said.

"Good-bye," said Dee, smiling. "You've forgotten something."

"Huh?"

"Chair. Love. Orange."

The pair retreated. *A costly witticism. Doesn't show insight.* Dee went to sleep without having to pretend for the psychiatric nurses.

■

Marty Olney spent much of the next day cheering up Dee in the madhouse. One nurse gave them trouble, and Dee and Marty took to calling her Nurse Cratchet, after the nurse in *One Flew over the Cuckoo's Nest.* Marty stayed during the lunch hour — no visiting hours then, but she stayed anyway and the other nurses weren't worried. Marty was sitting on the bed in the little room, Dee at the other end, when Nurse

Cratchet burst in and said, "None of that for visitors—no sitting on the bed." She didn't get it, and when in conversation Dee touched her lightly on the arm, as women do, she told Dee off. Nurse Cratchet had sex on the brain, but the matter was identity.

His sister had hired the second-best lawyer in the mental health bar of Chicago, using $10,000 she had lied to get out of their aged grandmother: "Donny's sick, Granny. Mom won't help. You have to give me the money to help." Joel Mokyr, Jewish and a student of Irish history, was amused that this second-best lawyer was Jewish and that the first best, defending Dee, was Irish. The two lawyers fought it out at last in a long hearing the day after Dee was seized, in front of a judge in his eighties who had recently been overturned on an appeal made by Dee's lawyer. A case of lesbians adopting a child, which the judge had tried to stop. *Swell,* Dee thought. *My case is to be settled by an aged judge unsympathetic with harmless acts—in this case, helpful acts—by sexual minorities. My sister did a good job in her judge shopping.* Dee's students and friends went to the courtroom, passing notes to his lawyer, which they later collected and gave to Dee as a memento. The judge said he had seen nothing like it. Usually these cases are about some nut.

The Social Science History Association passed a resolution condemning the seizure of their former president, gave it to the judge, then rescheduled the session honoring Dee's work. This was unusual. Academic associations are usually timid, which is better illustrated by the Speech Communications Association, meeting in San Antonio, to which Dee was scheduled to fly on Sunday. The Communications people heard about his commitment and canceled his participation.

The psychiatrist in charge at Chicago seemed intelligent, and Dee fell for him. Dee put altogether too much weight on IQ, an occupational hazard of professors. Dee's lawyer argued all afternoon with the judge, who finally in vexation threw the case into the hands of the psychiatrist. You decide.

But the doctor didn't want to decide. *Psychiatrists don't,* Dee concluded, thinking as an economist about the incentives they face. *Psychiatrists want to wait. A month, a year. What does it matter? The patient has no right to freedom. We need to be careful. We'll see. They have every incentive,* Dee reflected, *to act as professional cowards.* Dee's lawyer worked and worked at hundreds of dollars an hour on the psychiatrist and finally persuaded him. *Probably out of fear of suit,* Dee imagined. *What if I were poor?* He was released the evening of the day after he had been seized.

His legal bills to fight the commitments in Iowa and Illinois came to $8,000. ***Thank God for an upper-middle-class income.*** Not for the last time in his transition the conservative, Chicago School economist, recovering his youthful days as a Joan Baez socialist, asked himself, ***What justice for the poor in the mental health system?*** Dee had encountered a woman in the Chicago madhouse who had been committed for crying about losing a lover of seven years. She stayed the full five days: no money to object. Later the university hospitals of Iowa and Chicago sent Deirdre bills for $3,000 each to pay for the overnight commitments. It seemed odd and insulting, considering that in both madhouse episodes and two other times in that psychiatric autumn Dee was judged sane enough to sign the surgical releases. Four times the psychiatrists had admitted officially and in writing that they were wrong to believe Dee's sister. But because Dee had declined on legal advice to sign a permission to be "treated" by the madhouse psychiatrists, Blue Cross would not pay his hospital bills. The natural assumption that his sister would therefore have to pay them turned out to be false, in practice and in law. She would not pay when Dee asked, and the law unwisely said she did not have to. ***Wrong incentives,*** thought the economist. In Iowa and Illinois you can accuse anyone of madness, and if you are negligently wrong nothing happens to you, considering the high cost of proving negligence.

After a year of dunning letters, which would arrive monthly in the rain of Holland, the university hospitals stopped pursuing their past and present faculty member. At Chicago an administrator intervened and stopped it; at Iowa the Department of Psychiatry finally responded to threats of legal action. This nut's upper middle class. We better watch out.

■

After being released, Dee dressed and went out late with Marty and Esther as promised, and the next night, a Saturday, he went to a party with Claudia and Elyce and Marty and Esther and others, with balloons declaring "It's a Girl!" The group of women then went out to a restaurant, and afterward Dee was brought in triumph to Joel Mokyr's house up in Evanston. The party gathered. Richard Sutch, another knightly protector, arrived, and stood dominating the conversation in the center of the room. Dee sat on a couch with some other women. Richard held the floor, the prime male. Dee curled his legs under him on the couch, arms folded, smiling indulgently, and listened, happy.

20

CHANGING

On November 13 he dressed as Deirdre to go to court to change his name. Ten o'clock. It was the first time he had appeared as a woman outside of ironic adventures in drag, and he dressed with care. A conservative suit, a hand-me-down from his wife (she would sometimes give in love, but then in anger send other wearable clothing to Goodwill). He applied nondraggy makeup, though it was hard to cover the beard shadow.

He looked at himself in the mirror. ***Unconvincing,*** he thought, ***easy to spot as a man in a dress. But serious, conservative, appropriate for driving the few blocks to the county courthouse.*** Nancy, his lawyer colleague at the College of Business, the ombudsperson who had found Anna, was waiting on the steps. She knew courthouses. More: she gave Dee a card of congratulations. It showed a cartoon woman in the lotus position, smiling goofily and saying, "Some Eastern religions believe that you move to a higher level of being." Open the card: "In other words, all the men are becoming women!" Deirdre later found twelve copies of the card in the airport shop in Minneapolis and bought them up for distribution to other gender crossers.

After waiting out in the big Victorian lobby of the courthouse, Nancy talking in an amused and comforting way, Dee was called before the judge, back in an ordinary office. He was no black-robed presence on the bench. Thirty days earlier, as required, Dee had filed a petition in his own words that said, "The petitioner is 6' [alas!], weighs 170 pounds [well . . . 185], has brown hair, yellow-green eyes, is white, now female."

You say, "Not 'now female'"? (Thus Deirdre later when challenging officials.) What's female? How do you know? Why wouldn't an earnest and harmless desire to act as one be enough? Why should the operation define it? The answer is not obvious, and since no financial fraud is involved the government has no interest in stopping someone from claiming female gender. The question should be Why not? It's harmless. The only purpose of the procedure for legal name change is to prevent financial fraud. No one who registers in this official and recorded way to change a name is intending to use the name or identity to pass bad checks. There's no public interest in refusing whatever gender the person so earnestly and seriously proposes to adopt.

No fair just sneering indignantly, as though it were *obvious* why in the official records Mr. X should not become Ms. Y. (Deirdre was, after all, a professor and was not easily stopped once she began an argument: fifty-minute lectures.) This is a time for reasons. If you are inclined to doubt, and especially if you are a judge or other official of the state, make yourself be fair, as you would wish to be, holding yourself to the minimal standard of reason in a free society of adults. No fair not giving reasons. Ask the freedom question: Why not? In slave societies the answer is, Because it is my whim and wish as master that you do not. In free societies there has to be more reason. Is anyone else's freedom curtailed by this act?

The judge in the Iowa courthouse, getting no such harangue that morning and himself engaging in no inquisition, smiled pleasantly from behind his desk and signed the document, wishing Dee good luck. In the year of Our Lord nineteen hundred and ninety-five he had seen this before. Nancy and Dee got someone to take a snapshot on the courthouse steps.

A few days later Donald's wife sat before the same judge in the divorce proceedings against now Deirdre. She was enraged that she had to divorce someone with a woman's name and believed that Dee had scheduled the name change to achieve this. She later claimed that the judge had thought Dee was a divorced, completed, operated-on new woman and that that was why he granted the petition. Or perhaps he saw no state priority in stopping people who wish to change identities without criminal intent. Perhaps he asked, Why not?

Dee drove straight to the bureau of drivers' licenses in Iowa City and sat for a new photo ID and a license with the crucial identification "female": F.

■

Donald's former wife would not let Dee stay for Thanksgiving. "Let the children and me have time together." It seemed wise, though later the time stretched. A year and half later it was still, Let me be alone with them. Two years later: They decide for themselves. Three years.

Marty Olney was offering a room in the house she shared with Esther, so that Dee could stay close to San Francisco for the surgeries, starting just after Thanksgiving. The surgeries would go on for three or four weeks. The offer was high charity, as in faith, hope, and charity, *caritas, agape.* Richard Sutch and Susan Carter, both colleagues in economic history, he at Berkeley, she at Riverside, and Richard also an old friend from graduate school thirty years before, proffered an invitation to stay with them in Berkeley for the holiday itself. And on Tuesday and Wednesday before Thanksgiving Dee was going to Dallas for more electrolysis.

Dee thought, ***If you leave town for Thanksgiving and the operations extend over weeks, why wait until January to go full time?***

No reason.

Now.

■

On the Monday before Thanksgiving Dee packed femme clothing in the two largest suitcases, put on butch blue jeans and a man's shirt, and left Iowa City as Dee in male mode for the last time. In darkness at Dallas–Fort Worth airport Bren the partner in Electrology 2000 was there with a car to meet Dee and another patient. Bren introduced Dee to the other, a lean man handling his suitcase with quick, masculine motions like a cowboy handling a saddle. Dee asked his name again, apologizing.

"I'm Kate Bornstein," the other replied, as he slung the suitcase into Bren's trunk. Kate Bornstein was the name of the writer of *Gender Outlaw,* which Dee had read avidly a couple of months before.

"Oh, sure! That's cute! I was 'Jane Austen' for a while." The cowboy looked puzzled, then smiled and closed the trunk.

"No, you don't understand. I *am* Kate Bornstein. Really. I had to let my beard grow out a few days to give them something to pull at here, so I decided to come from Seattle in male drag."

"Good Lord, you're not saying you're *Kate Bornstein?*" Kate smiled back indulgently. "Why, I *loved* your book!" Remembering authors and their wishes. "It had a massive effect on me." But it did, in its cheeky courage.

"I'm glad. Thank you. The royalties from the book made electrolysis possible—I've not had much."

Dee could not recover from the presence of fame. "Wow! I can't believe this! Here I am with Kate Bornstein!" Kate looked amused and then a little impatient, and they got into Bren's car and drove to the motel.

■

With a face puffed and blue like a fighter's Dee rushed from Electrology 2000 to the airport and flew to Denver and then San Francisco. Dee used the men's room in the Denver airport, standing up at the urinal in a line with the others, assertive. Turning away and zipping, the thought came, *The last time.* In the airport and plane Dee felt furtive and slept in starts as the plane plunged toward San Francisco. Richard and Susan met Dee and hugged, then drove across the Bay Bridge in the dark to Berkeley.

Dee slept exhausted, only to wake toward dawn sweating, stomach tight, expecting sister and her police. Back to sleep.

Then it was light and late. Dee could hear Richard downstairs clattering over the breakfast. It was time.

Dee dressed carefully in blouse and women's blue jeans, earrings, the reddish wig, with makeup to cover the worst damage from the electrolysis. Down the stairs and into the kitchen, a woman. She.

Every twenty-third day of the month in her appointment diary for 1996 she marked "five months full time," "ten months full time." She would celebrate the full-time birthday on Thanksgiving, another reason to love that most lovable of American holidays.

After Thanksgiving she moved to Marty and Esther's house, though no one knew. They were trying to keep the knowledge from Dee's sister. Dee's sleep was disturbed by fears of her sister's arriving suddenly with her state power, her police and psychiatrists and locks. Dee talked to a lawyer in San Francisco over the phone and prepared legally for renewed assaults, but in California the laws of commitment are not so easily manipulated as in Iowa or Illinois. If the police came to the front door of the house Dee planned to slip out the back, through Marty's study into the garden. *Maybe.*

21

SISTER'S LAST

*T*here she finally was in Dr. Ousterhout's waiting room in San Francisco the day before the cheek and jaw operation, having been photographed and relieved of gigantic checks, $10,000 here, $15,000 there. All her treatment from now to the end of her transition, she reflected as she sat there happily, was going to be paid out of her own pocket and was not tax deductible. Blue Cross and the IRS take a dim view of gender reassignment surgery, which the same people or their colleagues then declare as the very meaning of "female." They take an equally dim view of cosmetic surgery to make one passable and therefore less likely to be murdered; also of voice surgery for the same; also of fixing the glitches from all of these. Donald had complained to Blue Cross before he realized he was a gender crosser: "The DSM-IV you rely on calls transsexuality a 'disorder,' and unusually among such 'disorders' this one has a cure—surgical, including facial surgery. But then you won't pay for it. You can't have it both ways. Either it's a personal choice, in which case the psychiatrists should butt out, or it's a disorder, in which case medical insurance should pay for the cure." Donald was always engaging in little campaigns for justice. Dee was more realistic: ***Blue Cross will never pay for this, not in America—except in Minnesota, if you turn yourself over to an ignorant and self-important psychiatrist for two years of "cer-***

tification" as "genuine." We Americans like telling people what to do, as in Prohibition or the War on Drugs. It's not even Blue Cross's money: Over the years I've paid ten, twenty times more in medical insurance than has been paid back to me in expenses. From an actuarial point of view there's no moral hazard. It's not as if millions of men will step forward to take advantage if gender reassignment and jaw pointing are paid for. The policy is sheer, stupid crossphobia. Sweet land of liberty, and of stubborn, self-justifying hatreds.

Dr. Ousterhout's office manager Mira came into the waiting room and interrupted Dee's reflections on American character.

"Dee, I have some bad news."

Uh, oh.

"Your sister has been calling and writing the hospital and threatens to sue if we go ahead."

"Oh, no, no, *NO!*" Dee wailed and raged through the waiting room. "A *third* time. She's tried *four* times and succeeded three. When, *when* is she going to leave me alone?" Ousterhout came out to comfort her.

"It's a setback. But I'm going to do everything I can."

"She claims I'll go crazy when I wake up and realize what I've done."

Ousterhout laughed. "That's silly. I've done thousands of plastic surgeries. People *like* what we do. I've never heard of anyone waking up and being anything but thankful. What's her evidence?"

"She doesn't have any. But the psychiatrists will believe anything about this, they are so frightened."

"That's their normal state."

Dr. Ousterhout called the psychiatrist in charge at Chicago. His letter about Dee had been ambiguous in its last paragraph. It sounded to Dee like more of the self-protection that seemed to be the main object of psychiatric practice. Ousterhout later told Dee roughly what he had said to the doctor on the phone to Chicago:

"Do you think Dee is competent to sign the consent form and be operated on?"

"Yes." He had said the same to Dee a couple of weeks earlier.

"That's wonderful! Could you write that down, in the same words? You can send it to California by fax."

"Uh . . . My typist isn't here."

"You can write it on a sheet of paper and fax it. You know how to write, don't you?"

"Umm. I don't know how to operate the fax."

"I'll tell you how over the phone."

Nothing worked. The psychiatrist wouldn't do it, wouldn't put in writing what he had said twice and what he believed. *He's afraid,* thought Dee. *He half believes my sister's theories about my waking up and regretting it all and going crazy. He doesn't want to be responsible. Psychiatrists don't. Cowards. Unlike surgeons, who must decide now, they can always wait. "Let's see how she looks after a month in a madhouse. A year."*

But Ousterhout kept working and told Dee to check into the Davies Medical Center as though the operation was going to happen at dawn the next day as scheduled. The nurses that afternoon were Irish and Australian and had no trouble spelling "Deirdre," a new experience. Ousterhout then arranged for still another psychiatrist to examine her that very evening in the hospital. Dee moaned to Esther, who had canceled her appointments as pastor in Berkeley and driven across the Bay to the Davies to comfort her during the evening of terror, "Another psychiatrist! I am so *sick* of being treated as crazy because I dislike my gender. Would I be thought crazy if I disliked a cleft palate, or a congenital heart defect?" The psychiatrist came in late, brought away in the dark from a dinner party, but he seemed sympathetic. Esther stayed outside in the hall, speaking soothingly to Dee before and after: "It will be all right. He seems sensible."

"Unlike most of them," said Dee. "I am so frightened."

About 11:00 at night the psychiatrist passed her. "You are competent to sign the consent forms to have the operations." Dee slept.

But next morning the operation was still held up. Ousterhout still needed the examining psychiatrist in Chicago to yield. That would make two psychiatrists, enough to calm the hospital's lawyers, frightened by his sister's letters on Harvard stationery. Again it was up to this man who seemed so ignorant and frightened about gender crossing. All morning Ousterhout worked on him. It was an expensive employment for a surgeon, negotiating on the phone for a plain statement. Eventually he did yield, as he had yielded to the lawyer's expensive pressure in Chicago, and the fax came to California. This time Ousterhout did not tell Dee what he had said.

The operation started six hours late—another, separate surgery would have to be scheduled because of the lost time that day, making it three days of operations—face, breasts, and tummy tuck—instead of two, with three distinct setups, the first morning wasted. *Oh well, another $10,000. Thanks, sister dear.* The additional bill mounted toward $25,000: legal costs, extra travel, extra days of surgery. *Where* *am I going to get THAT?* Later Deirdre's mother paid $10,000 of it, by way of apology for her other daughter, but then she financed the other daughter too. When Deirdre's sister announced proudly that she was buying a new house, Deirdre was irked: *On the ruins of my bank account.* Her sister never paid for such adventures in control and would present the bill to Mommy or Granny or Donald. *That's something about secular stoicism she didn't get, the tragedy of opportunity cost. Do X and you can't afford to do Y. Unless someone is bankrolling you.*

But *Let it go,* said Dee to herself, as secular stoic. The surgery was going to happen.

She was told to make herself ready: rings off, bracelet. She came to her ear studs, which since her electrologist had inserted them six weeks before in Cedar Rapids she had taken out only once, in the paddy wagon in Chicago. *How hard do you pull to get them out?* She didn't know. *I know so little of this.* One of the Australian nurses helped her. "There: that wasn't difficult, was it?" Later she would get bold about pushing and pulling tiny posts through her earlobes. *Amazing what you can do to ear tissue.* One earring, a homosexual or a pirate. Two, a woman. **Well, in the old days.**

She was wheeled into the operating room. The sister's crazy hypothesis kept coming back: *What if I wake up and go crazy? Crazy, crazy, crazy,* as the anesthesia took.

■

When she woke up: *Am I crazy? No, just covered in bandages.* Richard and Susan visited, Richard reporting that "she looks like roadkill." Ken and Alan, editors on a book project that Dee was supposed to be working on, visited, and Alan's wife Gail, who brought a meal with dishes and all. The following day Esther came and took her home to El Cerrito across the Bay, and Dee waited in the empty house for the craziness to come.

The next operation was all right. And the next, the third. The order of operations was unclear to Dee afterward, since some were combined: nose job, bones under the eyebrows ground down, hairline moved forward, jaw pointed, lip scar fixed, eyebrows lifted, breasts augmented, tummy tucked. Her recovery was quick, though she looked puffed and bruised for a while each time. You can't have your face taken off and put back on three times without looking odd for a while. More than the wounds, she was worried about the repeated general anesthetic, because some people have reactions to it months afterward. But it didn't happen. None of the surgery then or later hurt;

the pain in recovery was masked by drugs. The recovery was inconvenient and embarrassing, because you needed to nurse yourself and you looked a mess. But not painful.

Between surgeries she stayed home at Marty and Esther's and went to church a lot. The First Baptist Church of Berkeley, American, not Southern, Baptist, said on its coffee mugs, "FBCB—*Not your typical Baptists!*" Theologically, Baptist churches of any sort are libertarian, though your typical Baptist doesn't act as though he believed it. Every Sunday for the six weeks she stayed with Marty and Esther she would go to the music-filled service and listen to Esther's elegant sermons and for the first time experience a church-centered life. The congregation was "welcoming and affirming," which meant it had a varied membership. A gender crosser with a face horribly bruised seemed not to give them pause. At the coffee hour after the service Dee would move among the ladies of the church watching her manners and observing theirs, welcomed and affirmed.

Marty came to California from her last term at the University of Massachusetts after grading her final exams, and the three women prepared for Christmas. Marty brought Dee into her birth family, scattered around the east shore of the Bay, suburbanites who talked daily by e-mail. They were accepting of Dee: she's Marty's friend; she's all right. Dee made sure to help with the dishes, talk to the women, dote on the children. It wasn't hard. Joyous.

Marty's father had died some months before. Marty had given up tenure at Massachusetts and came back to live permanently in El Cerrito. Esther's church was being "disfellowshipped" by fundamentalists who didn't like its open character. A few months later one of Marty's brothers died. And more and more blows piled into that year, including sheltering Dee for a month and a half and being a daily friend for months. Brave womanhood.

The back room of Marty and Esther's house had stacks of the mysteries Esther favored, but among them was a copy of Elinore Pruitt Stewart's *Letters of a Woman Homesteader,* published in 1914, by a "housekeeper for a well-to-do Scotch cattleman. . . . She took up a quarter-section in Wyoming." Dee read it in a night, entranced by Stewart's womanly strength in making a women's world of love among ranches twenty miles apart, bringing Thanksgiving dinner to sheepmen, working her own claim. Strong world of women.

■

Women would say to Deirdre, "You've got us wrong. We're not that brave or strong or good. We're capable of greed and cruelty and pettiness and cowardice too." To the women Deirdre would reply, "Yes, I understand and of course agree. Your virtues and vices—ours—are merely shaded differently from men's, and commonly the same. We're human or American or middle class as much as male and female. I know this from the inside, carrying over most of Donald's vices and acquiring a whole new set. But allow me to celebrate virtues that my former tribe too often undervalues. Believe me, women's virtues are undervalued by men, when they're noticed at all."

The very word "virtue" contains in Latin the word for "man." "Virago," too—a manly powerful and therefore frightening woman. What women do is viewed from the male tribe as good (or from a misogynistic perspective, threatening) to the extent that it approximates a man's virtues—struggling bravely through the snow, say, or being stoic about honorable injuries in battle. But most men can't see women's virtues from a woman's point of view. In Wallace Stegner's *Crossing to Safety* Deirdre was startled to read the declaration: "What I am sure of is that friendship—not love, friendship—is as possible between women as between men." Well, thank *you*, Wallace Stegner! He adds some guarded remarks that it doesn't have to have anything *sexual* about it, you understand, not "love"—as though love and sex were the same thing. The passage struck Deirdre as so male, this pomposity by Stegner's alter ego, so lacking in understanding of the female ability to make real friendships, which between men arouse anxieties, some of them sexual, especially among Americans of Stegner's generation. The narrator speaks of his best male friend (whom he never levels with, a woman notes): "I was the person he was most likely to confide in, and I feared his confidence and had on tap no word of consolation or comfort." No quick cure on tap, so don't trouble to listen. Be afraid to listen, as Donald had been afraid to listen to his wife's accounts of horrors in the hospital. "Inside our wives would already be deep in confidences, but Sid and I would pretend that . . . we were getting organized for a picnic." There's male strength in that, the strength to ignore pain and go on alone. But it's a failing, too, Stegner half realizes. And then he pointedly fails to celebrate what he has observed, the ability of two women friends to get quickly to the emotional point, to be real friends to each other.

It's irritating, this male inability to get it. To the women Deirdre would reply, "Let me exaggerate." Her friends were dubious, wanting her not to be disappointed when she learned the truth. Deirdre thought, ***They forget that I have seen evil in women too. My own. Others'. There is sin in the world.***

And good too, she thought, with balanced theological backing. A secretary in an economics department sent Dee an e-mail supporting her when she came out in a column she wrote regularly for an economics journal. The secretary was terrified that her boss, who was a conventional homophobe, would find out. But she did it. Dee got support from an e-mail group called Luti, gay and lesbian Christians. Deirdre ate once in London with a Deirdre supporter from the group. It was surprising that strangers from across the world would care what happened to her. Marty had told them. The secular stoic thought, ***What love is this?***

■

At home at Marty and Esther's, Dee shopped a little, wrote a little, but mainly used her AT&T calling card. She called Dick, who had been an assistant professor with Donald back in 1968 at the University of Chicago. He was now a high-level portfolio manager, moving billions in his own firm in New York. He said, "If a year ago God had told me that one of us—you or me—would become a woman in the next year, I would have been amazed. But given that God had promised it, I would have bet the farm on me: never Donald." He was accepting. ***Some of the men aren't so bad.***

Dee went on a "date" in Berkeley with Gary, a friend in economic history, a business school dean. Dee kissed him on the cheek when she got into the car.

Gary said, "This is the safest date I've ever been on."

Dee laughed and said, "I want you to thank Linda for lending you to me."

Gary took her to an agreeable restaurant in Berkeley, but it had bright lights in a small space, and the two of them were placed right in the middle. Everyone in the room read Dee, and the waiter was startled when she spoke.

■

The damned voice. Dee called the office of the speech surgeon in San Francisco to check on the voice operation she had scheduled there for early December.

"Oh," said the secretary, "That's been canceled."

"*Canceled?* What do you mean?"

"The doctor decided not to do it."

"Why didn't you tell me? Did he say why?"

"I'm not at liberty to say."

"Oh. So my sister got to him." ***The coward,*** thought Dee. "Why didn't you call?"

"I'm not at liberty to say."

"So you canceled a surgery because the patient's sister threatened you and then didn't tell the patient? May I speak to the doctor?"

"I'm sorry, but the doctor's not in. I have to go."

"Good-bye. Have a nice day."

Great. I've found a surgeon who's a coward. All psychiatrists and at least one surgeon.

Dee felt that the surgery on the voice had to be rescheduled with someone else. *Can't go to Holland to teach with this male voice.* The other name that the speech therapist in Iowa had given Dee was Robert Sataloff. Like the cowardly surgeon in San Francisco, Sataloff was internationally famous, but he worked in Philadelphia, three thousand miles away from Dee's refuge. *Thanks again, sister dear: some thousands of dollars of airfares.* While Dee was having one of her San Francisco surgeries Marty Olney got through the busy-signal wall around Sataloff's office and made an appointment for a preliminary examination.

■

Dee spent some days calling her family on the telephone. She spoke to her mother, her brother, her grandmother. Granny was ninety-eight years old, in good health, with few gray hairs, but tired of life and worried about disability. When Dee got her on the phone she had resolved to end it. She had just given up her driver's license, that symbol of freedom since she was a girl in Indiana.

"Granny, it's such a brave thing you are doing."

"Oh, don't you worry about me, dear. I worry about *you*. Donald, do you really think you should do this?"

"Yes, Granny. I've never been happier."

"Your sister told me you were sick, and I believed her. That's how she got the money for the fancy lawyer in Chicago."

"I know. I'm not sick, Granny. I love you."

"I love you, dear. Good-bye."

"I love you, Granny." Dee did love her, this hard, bustling woman from another century, with her strengths and her prejudices and her history deep in the Midwest: her repeated story, for example, of the little girls who about 1900 tried to walk from Williamsport, Indiana, to Chicago "to see Papa," who sorted mail on the railway. She had baby-sat for her grandchildren, including Donald. "All my grandchildren are welcome in my house, but they *have* to behave. Even the dog Simone knew that." "Yes, Granny, I remember." And now she would die.

That morning she did, using the exhaust in her garage, a life framed by the automobile. At the end of December Dee flew to the house in Saint Joseph, in southwestern Michigan. She traveled and arrived in her usual clothes, of course, her lovely, matronly green dress from Truly Talls in Des Moines. She was through with closets and with Donald. *No more shame.* When she came into the familiar little kitchen her mother and the cousins were there. A female cousin talked easily with Dee the woman. A male cousin, a big man with a kindly, open wife, strode over right away and gave Dee a hug. Later someone said to him, "This will hurt Donny's career," and he replied, "No it won't." Maybe he was thinking that good professors, like good electricians, are not a dime a dozen and find work if there is any. It was like the *rector magnificus* at Erasmus: Can the horse teach? Why are you telling me this?

The next day her mother and brother and she went to the memorial service at the Congregational Church. Dee's sister was said to be traveling and not reachable. *I wish she could have been here, for her love of Granny. But how would it have gone, she still so confident of her psychiatric creed?* The big church was full, suitably for a member of the congregation since the 1920s. The family sat in front, and Dee spoke briefly. The audience must have been jarred by the male voice, but no one snickered or gave any hint that Saint Joe would be anything but welcoming to a gender crosser. *Don't count on it.* At the reception some high-school friends of her mother's chatted amiably with Dee, and they all half jokingly planned a trip to Greece together.

22

PROFESSIONAL GIRL ECONOMIST

*T*hat December in San Francisco Dee needed to buy some serious clothing. Marty said the idea was for Dee to present to the American Economic Association convention, meeting downtown in early January, as a "professional girl economist," with ironies about "girl" and "professional." Christmas came and went with elegant parties, and then Dee, Marty, Esther, and a couple of other women from the First Baptist Church went downtown for the clothing sales and wandered a big department store in a slow-moving herd to outfit the professional girl economist, the other women bringing likely items to the changing room. The clerks took her for a large woman. In the end she bought a blue blazer and two suit dresses that she wore a lot afterward, one red and the other blue.

That evening they went to the movie *Pride and Prejudice*. After the movie the other women had to go to the ladies' room. With her large bladder Dee didn't, and she was still hesitant about urinary segregation, so she waited outside, nervous before the large crowd in the foyer. No one gave her a second look. *It's OK. I pass.* She felt like crying again, as they all had done in the weepy movie.

The debut for the professional girl economist was on the day before the convention started, a meeting at the San Francisco Hilton of the twenty-person executive committee of the Association. Dee had been elected to it as Donald, and the staff of the Association had been broad-minded about her crossing. Yet she worried as she went into the meeting room: *Will my professor colleagues be broad-minded, too? Economics is not the most progressive discipline. Will they merely laugh and dismiss me? Better a committee of anthropologists. They know "strange."*

She was acquainted with most of the economists there, in the slight way of academics. Being a professor is not something you do in a team. The committee was mostly men, with only three other women. Before the start Dee went up to an older man who had been a colleague at the University of Chicago. He looked at her puzzled. Who is this woman? Do I know her? Dee said, "Haven't you heard? I'm the former Don McCloskey." He hadn't heard, but he was amused and courteous and instantly started calling her Deirdre. Another committee member, who had been an assistant professor with Dee at Chicago, was genial and had indeed heard, as most of the profession had by then. They chatted about their families. *My lost family. No. It will get better.*

The committee members used her name—"I disagree with Deirdre," "As Deirdre said"—because it was hard to substitute "she" for "he" on short notice, and Dee's voice was still Donald's. She didn't talk as much as Donald would have, not because Dee had less to say but because like most other women she did not view conversation as a hockey game. Who knows? Biology or core identity or social role or socially constructed performance of a lifetime? In any case Dee was less pointlessly assertive than Donald had been. The chair was a woman, the second woman president in the history of the Association. Economics is a macho discipline, like chemistry or engineering. In a while Dee found herself exchanging significant glances with the chair and the two other women about the little-boy behavior of the men, *io, io.* Dee later sent cards to the women. Pleased to meet you.

After the meeting there was a cocktail party. The secretarial staff, who lived in Nashville, were womanly and southern and courteous about the new woman. Ordinary people are theoretically repelled: How can you *stand* to be with him/her? Dis*gust*ing. Craaazy. But he/she walks up to you at a cocktail party and you have to decide whether to imitate Jesus.

At the party Dee was trying to persuade a dean to hire her at Berkeley, the way academics sell themselves, doing a little business, and said to him without choosing her words carefully, "If you want that, I'm you're man!" As soon as it was out of her mouth she felt the idiocy.

The dean looked at her and smiled, "Not my 'man'!" She laughed nervously. *A month and a half: I need practice.*

The next day her sessions seemed to have larger audiences than one might have expected. *I'd be curious too. Very.* She commented on papers or presented her own papers in a professional girl economist style, and Marty was pleased. The women economists were mostly welcoming, the men mostly tolerant though sometimes uncomfortable. Economists tend to be libertarian: "If he . . . she . . . wants to do it and does not by the action hurt anyone else, *laissez faire.*" The definition of "hurt" is crucial: mere annoyance is not to be counted, or else no individual freedom in a society could be justified. Until 1997 you could be committed in Iowa as a danger to others if you merely annoyed them, a tyrannical clause that a law school friend of Dee's caused to be modified.

Dee went up to a bar table where a professor from Notre Dame and his students were gathered. The professor had long struggled with Donald as though Donald was some sort of older brother he was unhappy about.

"Hi!" Dee said with a bright smile.

He looked puzzled. She waited, smiling demurely. It took him a full ten seconds to recognize her, so slow that she rewarded him with a kiss, older-sister style.

She ran into Judith, a British economist she knew slightly and who later became a girlfriend, and she and a male economist and Dee went out to eat in San Francisco. Judith took her shopping at the department store across the street from the Hilton, and Dee bought a handbag to reward the store for not reading her. Judith bought a striking outfit, though later Dee couldn't recall its details. Deirdre later got better at fashion recall.

A columnist for the Boston *Globe* whom Dee knew a little did a favorable story about her work at the conference, which was reprinted in the Chicago *Tribune* and some other places. He emphasized Dee's sober participation as speaker or chair in four sessions, a professional success for the new woman. But he also wrote that she had on a "brilliant red dress, a major wig and lots of gold jewelry." It made her sound like one of the less restrained participants in the Mardi Gras parade and helped distance the straight author from his queer subject. The phrase kept coming up in stories derivative from the *Globe,* such as a squib in *Fortune.* It made the guys feel better.

23

FAREWELL SPEECH

The last job before Holland was to get the voice operation in Philadelphia. She had to go there in December for tests, and then again for the operation. She had it at the Graduate Hospital in a six-hour outpatient procedure (an hour in the operating room) and went back to California scribbling notes, silent for a week. It was interesting to have a note conversation with the woman beside her on the plane, who therefore did not read her. Write but do not read. "How many children do you have?" the woman asked. "Two," she wrote.

The voice didn't seem to work, but Dee hoped. She would have to go back to Philadelphia for a third time to have the operation assessed. Three transcontinental fares. *Thanks, Sis.* January was complicated by a big snowstorm in the East, so she went first to Iowa City and cleared out. She needed to rent the house, settle the new mortgage, say good-bye to people. She would stop off in Philadelphia again on the way out to Holland.

■

She came back to the deserted house in Iowa City, hers now by purchase with a new mortgage, opening closets to see what Donald's wife had left. The division of the property had been fair, on a day in November walking through the rooms. His wife bargained, and wept the tears of things: the sideboard from Chicago in 1980, the antique clock carried back from England in 1976, the cherry table liberated from the Nurses' Residence in 1965. So now about half the furnishings were gone. Dee opened the hall closet, expecting nothing, since nothing had been bargained for. But the good wife had left three pairs of winter boots that no longer fit her and a scarf and matching winter cap, one of her favorites.

■

Dee glided around Iowa City in the cold not being read, though wary. Her friends needed to adjust, the men especially. She noticed an older colleague spotting her downtown, a pained look spreading over his face. *I suppose he regards it as madness.* Some thought it was an anthropological experiment in moving the gender boundaries. The thought appealed especially to progressives. They talked of the tradition of the berdache, the crossdressing medicine man/woman among Native Americans, as did one academic woman at a seminar later in Holland, before they had met. The woman was proving her own progressiveness without having to think too much. A third sex. Ah, I see. Later Deirdre became clear about her distaste for the third-sex talk. It was the usual way of talking about homosexuality in progressive circles about 1910. Such talk was better than hatred, but it robbed homosexuals of their familiar humanity. It was a condescending toleration, and ignorant. After all, gay men are men, lesbians women. "I am a woman," Deirdre would say, "not a third thing of neuter gender."

Some regarded Dee's identity as fashionable drag, RuPaul and all that. A simple version was something like, "He's doing it out of boredom with being a man, or to show his fashionable edginess. Careerist PR, you see." Deirdre could only sigh. As Sara Buechner, a concert pianist who gave her first performance as a woman in September 1998, put it wearily, "Why would I ruin friendships and devastate my family for some dubious gain?" To the literary people who might think the RuPaul way, Deirdre would explain, "No. One doesn't do such a thing to get attention or to deconstruct the male imaginary. And neither Donald nor Deirdre could be called fashionably edgy."

A sophisticated version still supposed that it was the act of a man, not of a woman misplaced. In the downtown shopping mall in Iowa City she ran into a literary colleague, an intelligent, sensitive woman who proved to be a good friend. Dee was dressed in women's clothes, had been legally named Deirdre for two months, and had just spent tens of thousands of dollars remaking her face. Her friend said, "I'm so glad we talked. I've been thinking, 'If Don can't talk to me, who can he talk to?'" Another English professor, a friend even from college thirty years before, saw Dee in a restaurant in town. His e-mail that evening was cheekily embarrassed: "Good to see you this noon, if only in passing. You almost passed, in fact." *Very funny,* thought Dee with oversensitive indignation. *Don isn't serious about passing, of course. He's just a man in a dress. Man-to-man jokes deprecating such an ambition are what's needed, showing incidentally that we are sophisticates together about the vocabulary of "passing."* (He later apologized, a friend.) It was the premise that Dee was still a man that irked her.

■

She gathered what she could for the trip to Holland, packing books and clothing in two enormous bags, stuffing a big crinoline into one of them. In the last five years of his marriage Donald and his wife had learned square dancing, frozen in the styles of 1960. Dee wanted to take up square dancing as a woman, but the Ocean Waves Square Dancing Club of Iowa City did not welcome her now. *Maybe if I move to a new place,* she thought. *The steps are almost the same. Change sides.* Her last purchase on leaving for Holland was her very own crinoline, from the square dancing store in Cedar Rapids twenty miles up the interstate. But she never wore it, even among the tall Dutch. Her voice was no good for going to the square dancing clubs in Holland. The Dutch are tolerant but not permissive.

Her graduate students threw a good-bye party at Steve Ziliak's house. They gave her an elegant gold-and-silver colored ring, which she wore ever after. The students had no problem. A generational difference.

Set to go. The day she was to leave Iowa for Philadelphia and then Holland a bill arrived from the Graduate Hospital, where the voice operation had taken place. They had required $6,000 up front checking into the hospital back in December. For those six hours of outpatient care, an hour of which was in the operating room, they now wanted over $18,000. *This is some sort of silly mistake,* she thought, stuffing the bill into her purse.

■

And so to Philadelphia after the blizzard. Gayle and Herb housed her cozily in the city of snow while she got inspected for her voice (a failure, but Dr. Sataloff wouldn't say it just then, and Dee therefore hoped for months) and made final preparations to leave. Her passport had been caught in the federal government closedown that December, and now three days before she was to fly she was still pleading with the National Passport Office in New Hampshire. She wanted an "F," female, passport. An antique regulation in the State Department said that only if you were traveling to get the operation could you have it. The operation again was the criterion. People focus on sex and reduce it to surgery. Why the State Department should have an opinion about the gender choices of American citizens was not clear, as Dee's congressman's office argued. You can change your occupation and even your nationality on your passport. If fraud is not involved—and the name-change procedures took care of that—why hassle gender crossers?

Oh, because we like to, and because we haven't considered the issue since 1965, and because we have primitive anxieties about gender. And because you're weird. Probably lower class. Shut up.

Dee called and called and finally got a sympathetic bureaucrat in the New Hampshire office to issue the F-labeled passport and send it off by fast mail to Philadelphia. The woman couldn't endure Dee's crying to her on the phone and saying, "Are you comfortable enforcing such a vicious, pointless policy?" That and the pressure from the congressman.

On her frequent trips back to the States over the next couple of years she was stopped and her bags were searched unusually often. Twice in a row it happened. During thirty years of earlier travel, fifty or so reentries to the United States, Donald's bags had been searched two or three times, and never twice in a row. Dee wondered if Customs had been told by the passport people at the State Department about how weird this citizen was. Weird people do weird things: search her. She thought, *Even paranoids have real enemies. I'll fight.* In her confident, middle-class way she resolved to make a scene if it happened *three* times in a row, to hire a lawyer and force Customs to reveal whether her computer records had a notation. Next time, with Dee primed for legal action, nothing happened. Then they did it again. Then the searches stopped.

Dee noticed that her gender-crossing acquaintances who did not have the arrogance of class power were abused by bureaucracies. They expected abuse and had never had the rank or money to get practice in effective complaint about it. Working-class gender crossers in Iowa were routinely abused, for example, by the Department of Transportation when they went to get a driver's license with an appropriate photo and the right gender, F instead of M. The right license entails no financial fraud and helps the Iowa crossers to avoid murder at the hands of crossphobes. "Imagine an Iowan stopped with her M license and women's clothes by some sheriff on a dark stretch of highway," said Deirdre, pleading on the telephone to the director of licensing in Des Moines. The director denied heatedly that she wanted to put Iowans at risk but could offer no defense of a standard far above that of neighboring Illinois. The richer, more clever, better-educated gender crossers would realize that their petition to the judge for name change in Iowa should include a phrase, "now female," in which case the Department of Transportation would give the person a safe identification card—as it did for Dee. The less intelligent or less well educated would not, and the Department of Transportation would give them a document that could get them murdered.

Poor people who are gender crossers get damaged. Blue Cross, which extracts money from gender-crossing workers for its plans, will not pay for the operations that would keep them from being abused or beaten or killed. The hospitals, the psychiatrists, Blue Cross, the State Department, the Iowa Department of Transportation have a free hand to abuse the powerless among gender crossers. Deirdre felt as Donald had felt thirty years before, when working-class men in his Massachusetts mill town were sent off to Vietnam while he, the college student, the graduate student, the son of the upper middle class, was deferred: ashamed. The injustice stirred again in the conservative economist a long-dormant feeling. *Class matters,* she noted, *even in America. One does class like doing gender.*

■

She went to the Graduate Hospital in Philadelphia to complain about the $18,000 bill for less than a day as an outpatient and was directed to the accounting office upstairs. The woman who was to reply had family photos on her desk, and Dee half-sincerely gushed over them. The insincere half was prudence. Make womanly connection to save yourself from aggression.

"The bill seems excessive. I was in the hospital for about six hours."

The accountant worked for a while on her calculator, then replied brightly, "It comes out to $18,461." Dee thought as an economist: *People like precision in numbers, especially crazy ones. The extra digits vouch for accuracy.*

"You mean for this service lite the Graduate Hospital proposes to charge me about $18,000?"

"Uh, yes."

"This can't be correct. I don't believe I paid that much for five or six overnights in the Davies Center in San Francisco."

"Do you have insurance?"

"What does that have to do with it? Now that you ask, no, I don't. Gender crossing is a 'disorder' according to DSM-IV, but Blue Cross won't pay for it. I've paid for everything myself. I paid you $6,000 on admission to the hospital and assumed that for such a short procedure I'd get money back."

The accountant ran her calculator some more.

"Well in that case we will charge you $9,230."

Dee realized that the accountant was simply halving the bill. "You mean you're going to charge me 'only' $9,000 for six hours of outpatient care, about $1,500 an hour, instead of your regular price of $3,000 an hour, *because I don't have insurance?*"

"Yes. It's our policy."

"Isn't your policy insurance fraud?"

Pause. "Uh, no."

"I think so. You were going to charge twice as much to Blue Cross. So the policyholders pay for your extortion."

"It's not extortion. It's our policy."

Dee didn't pay. The hospital threatened each month and would not respond to the central point she made in letters she sent from Holland: the sum is nuts. The bills from the thuggish hospitals piled up monthly in her mailbox downstairs—the University of Iowa, the University of Chicago, the Graduate—demanding gigantic sums. *Hospitals are the robber barons of modern life,* she thought, *extorting from victims called patients.*

Exhausted, she boarded the plane for Holland. Good-bye for now, oh my sweet country, cruel and violent, loving and generous.

24

DUTCH WELCOME

Arjo Klamer met Dee at the airport in Amsterdam. He told her later that when he spotted her in the customs and baggage area at Schiphol he thought, Is that her? The motions handling the bags are like Donald's. But those legs?

Until she found a flat she stayed with Arjo and Marijke. When Arjo came home from work the first day Dee kissed him. She was growing accustomed to kissing men, in the nonpassionate way of friendship, and to the funny feel of their beard stubble. Marijke looked on placidly. It was not about sex. It was about identity: women kiss men they are close to when greeting them or leaving them. Three times, Dutch-style, right cheek, left, right. ***Don't leave lipstick, dear.***

A few weeks into the term Arjo and Dee and a colleague were eating lunch in the university cafeteria, Arjo still adjusting to Dee's not being Donald. He had known Donald a long time as a colleague in teaching and writing, and by the standards of men they had been close. Dee used her pocket mirror to check for bits of food and found that her lipstick needed work. She started doing it. Arjo was embarrassed and said so, but the other man defended her: Women do it, Arjo. And Dee said airily, "Arjo, you don't want to see how awful I look without lipstick!"

She found a flat a mile or so from Erasmus University and her office. The flat was furnished and expensive, and her house in Iowa was still not rented. Donald's wife had suddenly decided not to live in it, so during the frantic week home in January Dee had made arrangements with a realtor. Still no tenants. She was anxious about money. She had exhausted the financial assets she had started with from the divorce and was paying a higher mortgage. She had to get ready to pay for the operation that summer. The university in Holland fouled up her salary payment, and month after month embroiled her with Holland's Napoleonic bureaucracy.

But the light was good in the Rotterdam flat, important for the darkness of a Dutch winter, and she snuggled into the bed. The worst climate in the world, she would say, like living on the deck of an oil tanker in a force nine gale; and then she would delight in traipsing to the office in the cold rain.

■

A few weeks after Dee arrived, a full-page article with a flattering photo of her appeared in the leading Dutch newspaper, *NRC Handelsblad,* the *New York Times* of Holland. It focused on her views about economics and love, treating her gender crossing as an interesting sidelight. That's how the Dutch press reported on her. A Dutch-language business magazine did a long article on the revival of Adam Smith, noting that "Deirdre McCloskey is een Chicago girl," a free-market feminist, and quoting her at length on an economics that might make sense to women. A sidebar noted that "Donald is Deirdre," and reported her opinion that "tolerant Nederland is de goede plaats om te transiteren van het mannelijke naar het vrouwelijke bestaan": that tolerant Holland is a good place for the transition from a masculine to a feminine way of life. Yes. So Dee was not shocked when a magazine aimed at the embattled Dutch businesswoman (Dutch women believe in staying home with the children, and so the labor force participation of mothers is the smallest in the developed world) ran a long story on gender crossers in government and industry, titled "Vroeger man, nu vrouw": formerly a man, now a woman. Later in the year Deirdre herself was part of a panel discussion in the magazine about women's work. It was a discussion with three women and one man, which ended up being dominated by the man, pushing, pushing, *io, io.*

■

Part of the Dutch tolerance came from mere familiarity. The hostess of a Dutch daytime talk show is crossgendered. Any television show that treats gender crossers as human beings is enough to take them out of the shadows. Dee had been getting an electrocardiogram in a clinic in Philadelphia and warned the male technician, who had shown no signs of reading her, that when he went to put the tapes on her chest he'd find a male body. He replied cheerfully, "Heh, I know that! I've seen Donahue!" In Holland the show that everyone had seen a couple of years before was a lengthy, dignified treatment of three crossers, two male-to-females and one female-to-male. Four years later, in October 1998, A&E ran a sympathetic story on American gender crossers, Bill Kurtis resonating with tolerance in prime time. Oh: They are people, with lives, who could be our children or siblings or parents. "I know that," Deirdre would be told in Holland. "I saw it on TV."

One of the stars of the Dutch TV show was a director for Dutch radio. When she saw the newspaper article in the *NRC* she introduced herself by postcard and invited Deirdre over to Utrecht: "I was worried you might be isolated," she said with womanly care as they ate at a candlelit café. She was divorced but saw her two young children frequently and got on well with her ex. She was good at her job and good at friendship, a combination that Deirdre found to be Dutch: *handel en vriendschap,* business and friendship, could be the Dutch national motto. ***Thank God for Holland,*** she thought daily.

■

The world's largest program on gender crossing is at the hospital of the Free University of Amsterdam. The program is well known among gender crossers. The radio director was a graduate. Dutch people are amazed at where the program is, because the hospital is part of a university founded in the late nineteenth century by religious conservatives (thus "Free": free to be reactionary), and the university still tends a little that way. It would be like Oral Roberts University developing in its second century a program for the support of gay marriage. The Free University program has helped many thousands of gender crossers on the model of "illness," with diagnosis and treatment. Dee needed to visit it to get hormones, since American prescriptions are not honored outside America.

They wanted a psychiatrist to interview her, though to Dee it seemed pointless. She was not officially in the Free University program, which for political reasons has to extend the transition to two years of agony between the genders, following the Benjamin Standards. But the program would prescribe hormones, so she couldn't offend its personnel by standing up for patient rights. Anyway, she liked the Free University program. ***It's good,*** she said to herself, ***a lot better than the hospital programs in the United States domi-***

nated by the example of Johns Hopkins. The big university hospitals at home, run by psychiatrists, try to cure gender crossing, and fail. The Free University Hospital, run by an endocrinologist, tries to help, and succeeds. Though on the silly model of illness.

The young woman psychiatrist asked Dee the usual questions, mentally running down a checklist of the gender-crossing illness. "When did you first want to be female?" "Were you effeminate as a child?" Dee could see the psychiatrist's eyebrows rise when she got an answer that did not fit the conventional "diagnostic" list thrown together for the *Diagnostic and Statistical Manual of Mental Disorders* out of junk science. Dee thought, *She does not realize how silly the list is.*

So what? Does it matter? Can she hurt me? Can she stop my prescription for estrogen or tell my potential surgeon in Australia that I'm not "really" a gender crosser?

Damned right she can.

Time for action.

Dee started lying. They all do it. A psychiatrist proposes to withhold a desired and harmless life from a free, sane adult based on no scientific evidence and no intelligent empathy for the patient and no understanding that the DSM's list of symptoms rewrites the society's myths about gender. We need to examine you. For two years. Wait, wait. We might not ever approve you. Chances are we won't. Dee knew a gender crosser from Galesburg, Illinois, an otherwise normal if working-class person, who after two years and $2,500 of "therapy" from a local psychologist was still being delayed: You have more issues to work on. You will *always* have "more issues to work on," dear. *It's therapy for the therapist,* Dee thought indignantly. Daphne Scholinski described the psychiatrists sicced on her in 1981: "They're not interested in what you think. They want you to give them the right answer so they can walk away smiling, pleased at the progress they have instigated."

Of course the gender crossers lie. They can read the DSM just as well as the psychiatrists can. Pat Califia, who wrote the book on it, notes, "None of the gender scientists seem to realize that they, themselves, are responsible for creating a situation where transsexual people must describe a fixed set of symptoms and recite a history that has been edited in clearly prescribed ways in order to get a doctor's approval for what should be their inalienable right."

"Oh, yes," Dee said to the Free University psychiatrist, "I've always had these desires. Oh, yes, Doctor, ever since I can remember. Oh, yes, it's *just* like being a woman in a man's body. Oh, yes, I *hate* my penis." ***Oh, yes, Doctor, whatever your dopey list says.*** The psychiatrist's eyebrows returned to normal.

It was Dee's last encounter with psychiatrists—except a year after she returned to Iowa, when she tried to get the Department of Psychiatry to take the thirty pages of medically misleading notes out of her file. Every doctor who saw her at the University of Iowa Hospital would see the wodge of "psychiatric information," and she could be misdiagnosed as a result. ***Maybe I already have been,*** Deirdre thought suddenly. ***It might account for the casual way my physician brushed off my attempts to get Blue Cross to pay for the second operation on my vocal cords. Maybe he thought, "Look: it says here she's nuts anyway." Probably not. But more nonsense to worry about.*** Deirdre made an appointment with the chair of psychiatry, the same who had asked, "If you're not homosexual, then why are you doing this?" Now he was resentful and uncooperative, like a bad boy caught in a lie. He didn't want to fix the damage that he and his department had been tricked by Deirdre's sister into doing. The lawyers at the hospital had to be whined at for months to do the little they said they would do. They would "sequester" the psychiatric parts of the file. But when Deirdre went to look at her file, to check that they had done what they promised, there was a large notice ONE OF TWO FILES and no assurance she could trust that doctors could not get access to the "sequestered" set. Back to the lawyers. Anyway, the curiosity of even one judge would make all the sequestering irrelevant. Deirdre finally gave it up and resigned herself to being misdiagnosed in future at the University of Iowa Hospital as having "mental" disorders when she in fact had physical ones. Welcome to womanhood, dear.

■

There's no case, Deirdre would argue, for letting psychiatrists get at a gender crosser. People say, "Wait a minute. It's an irreversible step. Better check it out." But the psychiatrists don't know how to it check out. They know nothing about it and are not interested in learning. To make them assess gender crossers is like making a brain surgeon do open heart surgery. It's not in their competence. The excitement these days in psychiatry is about drug treatment of psychoses. It's wonderful that some clinical depression and even schizophrenia can be helped with drugs. But gender crossing is not a psychosis, and there is no medical evidence that it is associated with psychosis in any form. We might as well have psychiatrists check out people with brown hair or people with cheerful dispositions or people who like to visit Venice as often as they can. Just to make sure.

And The Step is not irreversible. When Deirdre made this point people would get indignant. They at least know *that* much. "What are you talking about? Someone cuts off his penis and you say it's *reversible?*" Please, listen. Operations—not that the operation is the essence of it all—can be reversed, sometimes. For example you can take out cheek or breast implants. True, with current techniques reconstructing a penis is very expensive. That's the only advantage that males-to-females have over females-to-males in cost and effectiveness: because it's easier to remove than to make, their male-to-female operation is a fifth the cost of the female-to-male one, a compact, low-end car instead of a Mercedes. But so what? Forget about reconstructing the penis. Many men do not have penises, on account of war or accident or disease. This does not for most purposes make them less men. A man is a man because of his look and behavior, not because of what is secretly in his pants. And beyond the contents of pants, one's behavior and dress can be changed back. The hormones, too, have partly reversible effects. Deirdre would smile and say, "If I stopped female hormones and started testosterone, in five or six months I'd be acting like a jerk again!" The joke worked best if there were lots of other women present.

Anyway, Deirdre continued, we need to ask whether we want to invite psychiatrists to have power over all the comparably important business of life. Having a baby is well and truly irreversible, more so than gender reassignment. A new human being is brought into the world. Well, shouldn't everyone have many years of psychological-psychiatric counseling before having a child? And getting married, though reversible at some cost, like cheek implants, is pretty serious too. So likewise is choosing a career, or buying a house, or taking up golf. If these were treated the way gender crossing is treated we would need for each a certification from psychiatrists achieved through hours and hours of expensive conversation; maybe some drugs; or if nothing else works hook 'em up to the house current. Such certification and treatment would be absurd for the reasons it is absurd for gender crossing. The psychiatrists don't know anything worthwhile about having a child or buying a house or being a gender crosser, as most psychiatrists admit. And even if they did know, in matters not affecting other people's rights we regard ourselves as free individuals. The freedom question is, Why not? There's no case for a special enslavement of gender crossers to the psychiatrist except that there are so few crossers that no one troubles to care.

Gender crossing is also called "gender dysphoria," Greek for being uncomfortable with your birth gender. Being uncomfortable with, say, poverty or brown hair or lack of fluency in French is not labeled a disorder. Drunk and disorderly. A threat to order, the order that gender is irrevocable. A gender crosser Deirdre knew in Iowa City lived under threat by a psychiatrist at the University of Iowa that if she appeared there for treatment of her easily controlled depression (having nothing to do with her gender crossing) she would be sent to the state madhouse for three months. She has posted on her door a sign: "If you are coming to take me to a hospital, take me to Mercy," the local Catholic hospital—anything but the University of Iowa and its crossphobic psychiatrists. Deirdre was surprised that psychiatrists allowed themselves to be cast as gender police. Nowhere in the literature has a cure been reported for the "disorder," except the cure of letting people be who they wish to be, which has done its work for tens of thousands. But when the psychiatrists get the chance they lock people up; and if they don't have locks they deny permission. The patients wait, and go slowly mad, which then confirms the prior judgment of unsuitability. Doctor sickness.

The world's anxieties about gender authorize the psychiatrists' presumption. For God's sake don't let him do *that.* The residual crossphobia in the DSM justifies parents on the religious right in sending their children to jail camps to butch up the boys and femme down the girls, scaring them straight. "After all," the parents say, "whatever the allies of Satan claim, homosexuality is not an identity or a biological fact. It's a choice of lifestyle, a sin and sickness you can cure. Why, not long ago even the liberal psychiatrists thought of homosexuality as a 'disorder,' not a trait of character. And gender crossing, right there in the book, this 'gender identity disorder,' it's the same thing as homosexuality, isn't it? The liberals still think *that's* a disorder. Darn right. No son of mine."

Unfairly, Deirdre developed a low opinion of psychiatry. She was acquainted with the places of unconscious fraud within her own field of economics and wrote books as she imagined exposing them: statistical significance, blackboard proof, inability to face facts. So she knew about pseudoscience from the inside and knew that within economics as within psychiatry the real and good science is often hard to distinguish from the junk. It uses almost the same rhetoric, even from the same scientists. In her experience—the experience, admittedly, of a nonpsychotic who was being stuffed into a psychotic box—psychiatry felt like the junk parts of economics. Of course it's bad news that psychiatrists on the whole have a limited understanding of what's going on in their patients' heads. We wish they had the unlimited knowledge that their professional rhetoric and the threat of lawsuit require them to claim. In this they are no different from other doctors: look at the misdiagnosis and mistreatment of chronic fatigue syndrome, or for that matter tonsillitis. Organic weariness in women has been treated as psychiatric, tonsils have been pointlessly ripped out, breasts unnecessarily lopped off, all with cheerful confidence. Doctoring has gotten better since 1925 (the year Lewis Thomas reckoned it stopped killing more people than it cured), but psychiatry has not been one of the fastest-moving fields. Certainly the psychiatrists know little about gender crossing. Even the experts. The conclusion to be drawn from the fact of ignorance reminded Deirdre of her economic views about government policies: Since we know so little about the economy, or about gender crossing, better *laissez faire.*

A resolution was passed in August 1997 at the annual meeting of the American Psychological Association in Chicago, a quarter of a century after homosexuality was removed from the *Diagnostic and Statistical Manual.* Homosexuality "is not a mental disorder and the American Psychological Association opposes all portrayals of lesbian, gay and bisexual people as mentally ill and in need of treatment due to their sexual orientation." A year later the American *Psychiatric* Association said the same. Most American gender crossers want the same liberation from psychological/psychiatric torture. They want gender identity "disorder" removed from the list of madnesses and another sentence added to the resolution of 1997: "The same is true for gender crossing and crossgendered identification." The Canadian gender crossers object, because under their national health service they get money for the operation as long as the "disorder" is in the *Manual.* Consistent Canada. *Merci bien.*

■

Dee would sometimes wake up at night and be unable to sleep, though it was rare. *The sleep of the just,* she said to herself. But she watched for signs of doubt. At 3:00 A.M., stripped of the day's masks, doubt would surface. It never did, and she slept better as Deirdre than as Donald.

She could recognize doubt. Donald couldn't sleep for doubt when he was chair of economics at Iowa. He knew from the experience that he should not go into administration. Just or unjust, you have to be able to sleep. The new president of Harvard in the 1990s had a similar problem and took a year's leave. When Donald left a permanent job at the University of Chicago in 1980 he knew doubt at 3:00 A.M. His wife would become angry if he talked of his Chicago doubt, for it was tedious after a while to listen to the whining. *My ex-wife would like Deirdre better if she knew her,* she reflected. *No angst.*

■

One late afternoon in Rotterdam she negotiated in her office with a producer for Dutch TV, a woman with United States experience. The show was to run in prime time after a popular sports program. The university director of public relations came along to advise Dee on whether the show was zoolike or serious, Jerry Springer or Brian Lamb. It was somewhere in between. The presenter was a sportscaster, very macho.

A week later the producer called up apologetically.

"I'm sorry, Mevrouw McCloskey, but we're not going to do the show."

"Oh?"

"The presenter can't handle your gender crossing."

"I understand." Dutch people are tolerant in official theory, but not every one of them is therefore enthusiastic about social deviation or comfortable with a threat to masculinity. *The poor man. Maybe he should see a psychiatrist.*

25

D U T C H   W I N T E R

Sunday, February 25: Tomorrow, Monday, two frights. I go again to the Frijeuniversiteit, for blood work and to talk to a speech therapist. My fear is that they will not do enough to speed the transition—for example, prescribing effective doses of the hormones. I'm afraid that intrinsic conservatism or fear of criticism from reactionaries will make them go slow. I fear this of all my medical practitioners. They have a terrifying power to grant. Usually you go to a doctor because you are seeking treatment for a disease, not to get a service that should be yours to purchase.

■

Tuesday, February 27: Things were not good yesterday at the *ziekenhuis* ("sick people house": the expressive Dutch word for hospital). Idiotically, it turns out that all they had scheduled was a blood test, no consultation with the speech people. I had come on an all-day trip from Rotterdam to Amsterdam to get a blood test I could have got five hundred yards from my office at Erasmus University.

It must be easy to stop taking care when the patients are so eager to avoid making a fuss. It's bitchy to complain about people who are helping, but they terrify me. If you are a naughty girl they have the power to stop your hormones. The imbalance of power makes abuse inevitable.

■

Friday, March 1: The procedures canceled without notice on Monday had been rescheduled for yesterday. I was so frightened that Eugenia, the young American woman who lives in the flat downstairs, volunteered to come with me, and she suggested in her generous feminine way that we drive to Amsterdam for a day of sightseeing too. So we set off for Amsterdam early, and from the hospital parking lot we took the subway to the center of town to the Rembrandt House and the inexpensive market that surrounds it. Eugenia and I talked and talked. She is a graduate student in psychology at Oklahoma, where her husband, a specialist on Dutch politics, teaches political science.

We arrived back at the hospital in time for the 1:30 appointment with the speech people. I was ushered into a room with a chair some distance from three women seated together at a table, doctors and therapists it seemed. They didn't introduce themselves—no one did in my visit unless I initiated it—but I think this is Dutch. The chair I was told to sit in was far from where the three sat because it was close to a big machine to be used on me later, so the interview took place at a hostile distance.

They talked to each other about me in Dutch. I can hardly come to a country and demand that people speak my language, but more frequent summaries would have been easy, since they all spoke excellent English. When I made a joke about it they translated a little more, but then they slipped back into Dutch secrets.

The young woman doctor started filling in a form, asking idiotic, pro forma questions like "What is your complaint about your voice?" or "Do you have a profession?" She later apologized for her clumsiness and explained that she had never done this for a gender crosser. I was at the biggest gender-crossing program in the world and it was still amateur night—I was still having to explain myself over and over again to people with no knowledge of my life or my "illness," people who had not bothered to prepare for the interview.

The junior doctor looked in my throat with a sort of periscope, taking a video of my vocal chords opening and closing.

Then a senior doctor named Greven came in, also a woman. I had told them before that I had had a voice operation, yet they were surprised to find an orange fixture in my vocal chords. I told them as well as I could understand it myself that it was part of Dr. Sataloff's procedure back in Philadelphia a couple of months earlier. The senior doctor said emphatically in English, after a lot of Dutch talk, "We will have to examine this ourselves under general anesthesia." Huh? We, if we have listened to what the patient has just said, already know what it is. Sataloff put it in. Talk to Sataloff. She brushed aside the suggestion. Though I was by this time close to tears, I felt enough alarm at her medically dangerous attitude to resist. After some back and forth we politely agreed that she needed to have a closer look but that it was only prudent for her also to talk to Sataloff. She did not actually do so, I imagine out of professional pride: I look, I decide, the doctor, *la dottoressa, moi*, me, *io, io*. It seems strange for a woman doctor to act in this characteristically male way. It's like resisting asking for directions when you're lost.

The speech therapist, who was more courteous than the doctor in accord with the law of status in medicine, took me for voice tests, after which she gave me the unsurprising news that I had a male voice, worse than before my operation. I wish they would not feel it is their duty to give bad but obvious news in as brutal a form as they can think of: Ms. McCloskey [presenting with an obviously broken leg], your problem is that you have a broken leg.

I showed my distress at the offhand treatment I'd been given. The therapist seemed to sympathize. She was to give me the name of a speech therapist in Rotterdam, so she took out a sort of phone book and was about to offer some possibilities randomly, or by how close the therapist was to my postal zip code. When I saw what she was doing I broke down and said through my tears that I was tired of being an education for people who know nothing of gender crossing and that it would be much better if the person was experienced, or at least mildly interested in it. She understood and said she would ask around.

It was a hard day, even with Eugenia's support: the doctors and therapists treating me like a case, the speech therapist telling me I had a worse voice than before the operation, the big doctor holding out the prospect of a better voice operation but being coy, expecting me to beg.

It was worktime back in the United States, so when I got home I called MidAmerican Energy, the gas and electric company in Iowa that has been taking big checks from me to heat an empty house but won't change my name despite repeated written requests, with copies of my court document. It reminds me of American Express, which has never responded to requests to issue a card in my new name, or the TWA frequent flyer program. I opened again the complicated proposal from my travel agent for my next United States trip and started crying. I thought weepily, *My life is so complicated. I am so alone: my son and probably my daughter have abandoned me; my wife, who could have been a true friend, and my sister, who could at least have been a sister, have turned against me. I feel so alone.* I cried and cried.

It was daytime in America, so I called Marty, but the line at work was busy and then she wasn't there, probably in class. I couldn't call my mother in this state. *I must present to her as strong—she has enough doubts.*

■

Saturday, March 2: Today I feel better and not so vexed at the Free University Hospital and its program, which after all is very good by the medieval standards at home. And the brusqueness was merely Dutch. The Dutch view it as candor, directness, plain speaking. The word is *openhartig,* which does not mean only "openhearted" in the English sense, but candid, direct. These are the Dutch who have been so accepting and generous toward me in the month I've been here, the Dutch whom I celebrate in my writings on bourgeois virtue.

Deirdre went weekly to speech therapy on the other side of Rotterdam. The therapist was a tall, vivacious Dutch woman a little younger than Dee, a singer with perfect pitch. Sataloff's operation had left Dee with little in the way of range, and just as low a voice as before. The weekly visits were a repeat of years of speech therapy as a child. Deirdre didn't practice, and in part couldn't with the voice she had after the operation. The vocal cords gradually stretched to half their preoperative flexibility, and the therapist was professionally optimistic and supportive. They became friends, Deirdre coming over to her house to eat. In the end the therapist said, "You better have the second operation." Dr. Sataloff had by then conceded that the first one hadn't worked. He offered to try again for free. Except for the robber hospitals of Philadelphia. *Another thing to save your Dutch guilders for.*

26

PASSING

When she first got to Holland she worried about passing. When she left Holland she worried about passing. When she had been back in Iowa for a year and half she was still worrying. *Do I pass?*

She worried, and monitored her success, not from pride in trickery but from anxiety about being scorned. She wanted not to worry. She wanted merely to walk down the street or climb onto the bus because she was owed the right to be taken for a woman. But wanting is not the same as getting, not for a six-foot, big-boned, low-voiced former man. "Don't worry, dear" is useless except to say I love you and wish you peace.

One Sunday, a month in Holland, she went for a stroll in the big park with a windmill a mile or so from her flat, practicing her walk. She forgot to go to the bathroom before setting out, but in the park there was what looked like an English pub, with pub casualness about who arrives and leaves. *I'll just march in and do my duty.* Standing in its hallway she realized: *No, this is a restaurant, not a pub. Someone is going to try to seat me.* She noticed a woman customer staring intently. The woman smiled in that way women do, the apology for the aggression of eye contact and the assurance of goodwill around the fire in the cave, and Dee managed a grimace back but quickly turned and fled. *What I have to learn,* she said to herself, *is to act as a woman would in the situation. That means smiling back, and not fleeing.* A year later she was skilled at the womanly smile. Men know nothing of it. It's like a secret handshake.

The next Saturday Dee worked at the office until in the Dutch way they closed the building at 1:00 in the afternoon, turning off the electricity, and she went downtown on the subway to shop. Her goal was a store with large sizes of shoes that a Dutch friend had shown her, but she got distracted by other possibilities. She bought three rings at the fancy department store on the Coolsingel in the middle of Rotterdam and got them sized for her big hands. She was nuts about rings, her theory being that big ones made her hands look smaller.

She thought the woman who served her in the department store had read her, because she seemed annoyed. It was always a worry, this frightening or annoying of women. She didn't want to do that. She just wanted to join. But the clerk had not read her: she was merely frustrated at her poor command of English by Dutch standards. Dee told her woman-kindly that her English was amazingly good, and they parted with smiles.

She needed some hooks to repair the closure on a skirt, so she stopped at a big fabric store on the Coolsingel, the only one she had spotted riding the number 3 and 7 trams. It was a first time as Dee in a fabric store. She came up the stairs after buying the hooks and some thread in hard-to-get colors she might need for her sewing box and said to herself, *This is a women's domain.* No one looked at her. She was in her place. It made her want more to learn to sew when she got back to Iowa and her sewing machine. She wanted nothing in the women's domain to be foreign, at any rate when it could be learned or experienced at her age. She couldn't give birth to a child — though she was much more interested in the matter than she had been six months ago and found herself thrilled about pregnancies in the camp the way most women are. But she could sew and cook. Her attitudes were old-fashioned, yet most women her age knew these skills, taught in a girlhood of the 1940s and 1950s that Dee could never have.

Each new first time as Dee had subcategories. For instance, the shoe store she finally got to that Saturday was not an unqualified first time, since she'd bought shoes at crossdressing shops and conventions, and later in a North Bay mall with Marty and Esther. But it was the first time in a regular shoe store alone, without a genetic woman friend. Like an obscure category in the Academy Awards. Yes: for acting. She kept her eyes to herself in such circumstances, since she did not want to know if she had been read. *I would do better,* she told herself as she scanned the shoes on sale, *to have as much eye contact in shops as other women have.* In serious shopping women do not have much. Dee thought of it in terms of cocktail party paleoanthropology: The ancient alertness is turned on, she said, and women are working not on making common cause with each other but on finding the right herb for the roast of woolly mammoth tonight. She got a pair of boots on sale for 19 guilders, about $12, then bought two pairs of shoes on sale for more. She was just able to resist a beautiful pair of Italian flats full priced at $100. *That's why they have such sales,* Dee the economist reminded herself. *Price discrimination for the rational and temptation for the irrational. We have both in us, always,* the free-market feminist said to herself.

Walking along in the neighborhood thronged with Saturday shoppers, pleased with how well she was passing, she noticed a thirty-something man in a camel hair coat staring. She looked away, as women must respond to the male gaze, and so didn't notice that he turned and followed for a few seconds. Then he said to her in Dutch,

"Do you speak Dutch?"

"Nay," she answered, startled by his approach. It later occurred to her that he was checking her voice to be sure.

"Well," he continued in English, "I just wanted to say how much I liked the article about you in the newspaper." He meant the favorable article in the *NRC* that week. The man seemed embarrassed, but not enough to stop. *This could never happen in England,* she thought, *or for that matter in America east of the Sierras. The Dutch are different:* openhartig.

"Thank you. I'm glad you liked it."

She was unhappy afterward. *I am so easy to read that walking down the street in a city of a million a man says to himself, "Hmm. Odd-looking woman. Wait a minute: I wonder if she's that American professor at Erasmus. Is his voice female? I'll try."*

A few days later on a train she noticed that a woman across the way was eyeing her. *Admiring my outfit? Yes: it* **is** *good looking.*

"Excuse me," said the woman in perfect English a few minute before The Hague.

"Uh, yes?"

"I'm sorry, but I couldn't help noticing that you are the American professor."

Dee was resigned. "Yes."

"I just want to say how much I liked the article." *As though I had written it,* she thought. *The journalist* wrote *it, dear*. "And how much I admire your courage."

"Thank you."

The train pulled in. "Well, I have to go," said the Dutch woman. "Nice to meet you!"

"Yes. Nice to meet you, too. Good-bye." *Nice to meet you and get read. She "couldn't help noticing." Wonderful.*

She got advice from genetic women about passing. Wear this; do this to your hair; change this about your makeup. She loved the advice, because it was lovingly intended and showed the woman friend as understanding the situation from Dee's point of view. The friend was working on her problem, as Dee herself did when a girlfriend complained about her lover, Dee listening and sometimes offering advice. But a genetic woman's advice about passing was usually mistaken, for the same reason that Dee's advice about handling lovers was usually mistaken. Passing as a woman is not a problem that natural-born women have. They get no practice thinking about it. (There's a comedienne in the United States who is six feet two and tells about coming into the women's locker room and having to shout, "I'm not a guy! I'm not a guy!") It therefore takes an actress to see what makes a born man into an acceptable woman.

Anne Hollander points out in *Sex and Suits* that women's fashion makes use of crossdressing gestures, appropriating items of male clothing to be cute or stylish. The little girl's sailor suit is an old example, or the grown woman's adoption of jeans and workboots and tough-guy T-shirts for the 1990s. Dee had an overcoat that she and Marty bought in San Francisco, a quotation from a Russian soldier's coat of 1810, though by now thought of as feminine. But styles recently male don't work on a big woman with a male-type body and a not perfectly feminine face. In the summer of the Dutch year Dee went out in Rotterdam with her British girlfriend Judith, who approved of a malelike choice of garb, matching her own outfit. Judith was short and cute with cascades of black curls, and when she adopted male clothing it just looked fun. But the butch garb that looked fun on Judith got Dee read all day long. Everyone looked at her a second time. A young male cashier in the Boymann's Museum souvenir shop was startled by her and then laughed out loud, the first time anybody in Holland had done such a thing. Dee wept about it in the restaurant of the museum, and Judith comforted her. It will get better, dear. It will.

It's harder for a natural-born man to pass as a woman than the other way around. A figure is assumed male until enough gender clues contradict the hypothesis. A big woman born male is giving off the message "man" by her sheer size—Dee's tall Dutch friends, genetic women, were amused that on holiday visiting the Castro district of San Francisco they were read as gender crossers. So Dee had to counter the size. Lose weight. Dress femme, but not campy. Learn to walk right. A Dutch girlfriend in Rotterdam would tell Dee when she saw "male" in her behavior, as when she walked over a little traffic barrier in one step. "A woman would do it this way," she said, and stepped from sidewalk to barrier to sidewalk, instead of over in one gulp.

27

YES, MA'AM

It's hard to pass. You just try it, Dee would say. I mean really try to pass as the opposite gender, not just put on a joke dress and a lampshade hat for the Lions picnic. You'll be surprised at how many gender clues there are and how easy it is to get them wrong. Scores of them, natural and unnatural, genetic and socially constructed.

No, hundreds. Women stand and sit at angles. Men offer their hands to shake. Women put their hands to their chests when speaking of themselves. Men barge through. Women look frequently at nonspeaking participants in a conversation. Men don't look at each other when talking. Women carry papers and books clutched to their midriffs, men balanced things on their hips. Women smile at other women when entering their space. Men never smile at male strangers. Women put their hands on their hips with fingers pointing backward. Men use wide gestures. Women frequently fold their hands together in their laps. Men walk from their shoulders, women from their hips. And on and on.

Dee watched other women in her culture for characteristic gestures and practiced them on the spot. *The way the hands gesture together, as though in a little dance. The way the fingers lie up the arm when the arms are crossed. Standing with feet in a ballet pose. Pulling your hair from under a coat just put on.* (It was some time before her hair was long enough to make that feminine gesture useful.) Years into her transition she could amuse herself in a dull moment in a mall or airport by breaking down other women's gestures and trying them out. Like square dancing: hundreds of calls.

Rest one elbow on the back of the other hand, laid horizontally across your middle, the free hand stretching vertically to frame your face from the bottom, palm out. In touching your face, which you should do frequently, hold the hand in a graceful pose. For situations such as display at the dinner table, learn the hand pose used in ballet—fingers arched and separated, middle finger almost touching the thumb. Pinky up, but not too much, since it's an obvious parody of the ladylike. Overacting evokes the theatrical tradition of drag. Try to create a somewhat splayed effect with the fingers, angled up, instead of masculine cupping. When shaking hands—don't be the first to offer—use no strong grip, and place your hand sideward into the other person's. Check your hair frequently. Play idly with your jewelry. Check your clothing (a set of gestures that women's clothes require more often than men's, or else you stride out of the ladies' room with the back of your skirt up around your behind). Always stand more on one foot than the other. Stand with your legs crossed (a youngish gesture, this). Never stand manlike with feet parallel and legs spread wide. Angle your feet when you stop at the corner before crossing. Rest with hands together, not sprawled all over like a man's. When sitting cross your legs, either knee over knee angled to one side (never lower leg crossed horizontally over the knee, like the Greek boy in the statute removing a splinter) or to one side beneath the chair ankle over ankle. Never slouch when you sit. Stick your rear end solidly into the back of the chair, and never stretch your legs out, crossed at the ankles. Keep your knees together when you sit—"close the gates of hell" used to be the misogynist joke about it—which is easier if your knees are naturally angled inward, as girls' and especially women's are. If your feet are not crossed when sitting, keep your legs together from feet to knees. "Take up less space" is one formula; another is "keep your wrists loose," and still another "keep your elbows close to your body," this one imitating the effect of a female angle in the elbow, a piece of biology. But the formulas are hard to apply, like formal grammatical rules. Imitate, imitate, the way girls learn it. Deirdre was congratulated three years into full time: "Last year your motions were a little abrupt; now they are convincingly feminine." The gesture language is probably imitated with the same ease and at the same age as the spoken language, and like the spoken language it is hard to learn as an adult. Little girls act different from little boys, independent of the slight structural differences in their bodies. By age ten many girls even know the secret smile.

Much of behavior is gendered. A lot of it is culturally specific and variable from person to person. European men cross their legs in a way that in America is coded as feminine. American soldiers in Vietnam would sneer at what they read as femininity in their Vietnamese allies and enemies: "They're all queer, you know." Mediterranean and Middle Eastern women make broader gestures, not the little dance of hands that upper-middle-class women in America use. The gender clues figure in any culture in an abundance that only a gender crosser or Dustin Hoffman preparing for *Tootsie* can grasp.

Of course if you are *aiming* to be funny then you want to be read, even if you are skillful at giving appropriate gender clues. Passing is not at issue. The Australian comedian who has developed the character "Dame Edna" is good at it. Without a leer or a nudge, he simply *is* the absurd Dame and sometimes spends hours in character, yet of course his audience knows. Miss Piggy of the Muppets is similar. She is gloriously who she is, yet everyone knows it's cross-speaking—her voice is always that of a man using falsetto. Getting read is part of the joke.

If you are not trying to be funny, you do not want to get read. Really, you don't. A sincere but detected attempt to jump the gender border from male to female—and no joking about it—creates anxiety in men, to be released by laughter if they can handle it or by a length of steel pipe if they can't. A 1997 survey claimed that 60 percent of cross-gendered people had been assaulted. Deirdre knew a gender crosser who had been beaten by four young men outside a bar even in peaceful Iowa City. The director of Gender PAC noted that "RuPaul is funny so long as she stays in a television studio. But try walking to the subway and she'll be a grease spot on the sidewalk before she makes it home." (If a female-to-male crosser was read by men maybe he would be regarded as cute, or rational: after all, it's rational to prefer to be a man, isn't it? Like the daily prayer by Orthodox Jewish men thanking God for not making them women. On the other hand, Brandon Teena, a pre-op female-to-male thief outed by the Falls City, Nebraska, police department was raped, complained about it to the police, who did nothing, and the next week in 1993 was murdered. Not by women.)

The anxiety is weirdly strong. A standard routine in the movies is that two men are forced to sleep with each other by circumstances (oh, sure), and then one of them dreams that he's sleeping with a woman. The other man, horrified by the amorous advances, rejects them violently, and the awakened dreamer is ashamed. The routine enacts over and over again the male anxiety about being homosexual, much less being a woman, and the violent reaction the anxiety arouses. With this threat of violence in mind, Donald's sister had given him her own pepper spray. The pepper spray, though, wouldn't be much good against a steel pipe.

Women who read a crossdresser are not violent, but frightened and indignant. Who is this guy? What's he up to? Deirdre knew from being a woman on trains late at night in Holland or walking by Dutch cafés in the summertime or living later in the less demonstrative but more dangerous environment of America that women have daily experiences of men in fact being up to something, often something sexual, often enough something dangerous. At first it was flattering, the knocking on windows of the *eetcafé* as she went by, the propositions to come into the jazz club and have a drink. Then it was tedious or frightening. Women experience dangerous men all day long and are on the alert. The alertness is not male bashing, merely prudence in the company of people with greater upper-body strength and the inclination to use it, intoxicated by lethal fantasies about What She Really Wants. Women who read a gender crosser are putting her in this category of dangerous men. To be read by women is utterly demoralizing. After all, the gender crosser is trying to join the women, to pass as one, and instead they are treating her like a man, maybe nuts, probably dangerous, definitely another one of those bloody *men.*

On all counts it is better for a gender crosser to pass rapidly to the other side, and making the crossing rapid ought to be the purpose of medical intervention, such as facial surgery, and social intervention, such as counseling on gender clues. Women acquainted with a gender crosser sometimes think of her interest in facial surgery as vanity. Natural-born women have no problem passing as women. "You're silly to want operations," says a woman out of a face with pointed chin, no browridges, high cheekbones. Deirdre's mother declared that getting electrolysis, which she regarded as merely temporary, was "vain." But a nose job or a facelift or electrolysis that will make a gender crosser passable will also make her less likely to be scorned or raped or killed—at any rate at no more than the shocking rates for genetic women. Deirdre knew a not very passable gender crosser in tolerant Holland who had been raped three times. It is merely prudent to pass.

■

Some radical feminists object to gender crossing. They complain of the gender crosser that she (when they have the ruth to call her "she") is adopting oppressive stereotypes about women and therefore contributing to society's discrimination. The gender crosser, they claim, is pulling women back to the 1950s, white gloves and pillbox hats, lovely garden parties, and a *Leave It to Beaver* vision of a woman's life.

There is little truth in the stereotype argument. The crossphobe who uses it ordinarily doesn't know any gender crossers. A gender crosser with a job or career outside the home tries to keep it and does not in practice dissolve into a 1950s heaven of full-time cookie baking and teatime gossip. Far from becoming passive and stereotypically feminine, the gender crossers Deirdre knew often retained much of their masculine sides. The crossphobes mix up gender crossers with drag queens or female impersonators, whose shtick is indeed a parody of women—sometimes demeaning and stereotypical, though often enough loving and amusing. In 1958 the sociologist Harold Garfinkel described a gender crosser named Agnes. Latter-day crossphobes attack Agnes as "displaying rigidly traditional ideas of what a woman is" or having "stereotypical views of femininity" or "constructing an extremely narrow and constricted view of womanhood." Agnes was nineteen, a typist, at the height of the feminine mystique. But no allowances: "I don't support you in your effort to have an operation, because you have stereotypical views of what it means to be a woman." Unlike all the other nineteen-year-old typists in 1958. (Agnes had the operation, and was fine, because Garfinkel and a psychiatrist named Stoller did support her.)

A gender crosser trying to be a woman must reproduce enough of the characteristic gestures to escape being read, and often—especially in voice—this is difficult. It becomes second nature, and a comfort to oneself even when alone. But if you fail you are classed with people stereotyping women. Or murdered. The crossphobe radical feminists are allies in hatred with the gay-bashing murderers of Matthew Shephard.

The complaint about stereotyping will be delivered by a genetic woman whose every gesture and syllable is stereotypically feminine. At seminars in which Deirdre was attacked for stereotyping she would reply with the same stereotypically feminine gestures or turns of phrase just used by the crossphobe—who had been practicing them since she was a little girl. This was Garfinkel's point, that gender is something "done," a performance, not an essence springing from genitals or chromosomes. Deirdre would say, "Of course I [putting her hand to her chest in the feminine way of referring to oneself, just used by the crossphobe] would never [doing a deprecating double flap with her hands in the style of American middle-class women] want to damage women by *stereotyping* [raising her voice in the falsetto of emphasis stereotypical of women, for instance the crossphobe attacking the genuineness of gender crossers]."

■

The passing worked better, slowly, each month, if she dressed carefully and worked at it. Each little acceptance delighted her. The signal was being called "mevrouw" in Holland, "ma'am" in America, "madame" in France, "madam" in England. ***Yes: call me madam.***

She is getting up to leave a Dutch tram at Oostzeedijk, intent on how to make the transfer to the subway. ***Let's see: across there and down. Remember to watch for the bicycles.*** The tram has almost stopped and she is pressing the exit button when she hears finally through her English thoughts and the haze of a foreign tongue, ***"Mevrouw! Mevrouw!" It's me they're calling,*** she thinks. ***Oh. I've left a package.*** She smiles in thanks and snatches up the package, slipping out the door as it closes, still smiling. They see her as "ma'am."

At the grocery store she is accosted by a woman giving out samples of a Dutch delicacy. It doesn't look very good. The woman babbles at Dee in Dutch, and Dee catches only the blessed "mevrouw." She smiles and shakes her head no thank you and pushes the cart toward the canned goods.

In May in Paris with an economist friend, Nancy, who is visiting there for a year, she walks out of a hat store, wearing the lovely lace floppy number just purchased. An elegant Frenchman goes by and says with a smile, "Un beau chapeau, madame!" Deirdre's French is poor, and she is still wondering if he could have said what she thought he had said when he politely repeats it in English over his shoulder as he walks on, "A beautiful hat, madame!" She would say when telling the story, "I could have kissed him. If he had proposed, I would have married him on the spot. Even though he was shorter."

A month later she wears the hat (which can be worn only in Paris or at special events) to a daylong concert of classical music in the park in Rotterdam. Sitting at luncheon on the grass with some members of her women's group, she feels particularly lovely. A Dutchman passes by and makes in Dutch the same remark the Frenchman had made, "A beautiful hat, mevrouw!"

The women's group meets at a restaurant in Rotterdam. It is a year since she abandoned the male role. The waiter asks the *"dames"* (DAH-mez) what they want, including Deirdre without notice or comment. ***One of the dames. Yes.***

■

The bad stories, not being accepted in the tribe of women, come down to "sir." Standing in a line at an airport in Philadelphia, before Holland and before much practice, though dressed modestly and appropriately, Dee is ordered into the correct line by a woman member of staff with a pointed "sir." Dee is weepy with vexation: ***Do I look like someone who wants to be called "sir"? What a crummy thing to do.*** As she is shopping for gloves at Harrods in London, after a triumph as Dee the professor, speaking to journalists and members of Parliament about bourgeois virtue, the clerk calls her "sir." Many months later it happens again in Harrods, although this time — and maybe the first time too — she thinks the clerk is reacting unconsciously to her voice, which is still male. The clerk probably doesn't know what she said and says it hundreds of times a day.

In the cold spring of 1996 a trip to The Hague with Joel Mokyr, one of the Chicago rescuers, is mixed. Joel is princely, buying her a flower at dinner, her first flowers from a man. She cries. They visit Joel's brother, named Mok, a high court judge, who is genial and is interested to hear that this is the daughter of the authority on the American Supreme Court whose book sits on the coffee table. But the day is mixed because Dee is read as a man all day long, perhaps because Joel is shorter or Dee's makeup is an experiment. She arrives late at Rotterdam Central Station and decides in her unhappiness to take an expensive cab instead of waiting in the cold for the tram. When he sets her down the cab driver calls her "sir." She cries and rages and throws his fare in his face, then goes in and weeps and weeps. ***Will I ever just be?***

And then many months later, in the late fall of her Dutch year, she is chased by little boys in the dark at a tram stop close to Erasmus. Terror, even in law-abiding Holland. They want her money. She is afraid to hurt them but afraid they will hurt her. Later she learns that such boys are routinely armed with knives. She speaks in English to one: "Go away." The boy shouts, astonished, to his confederates, "Zij is een man!" "She's a man!" Real trouble, but they give up as she crosses the highway and gestures threateningly toward the one boy who follows. Perhaps they say to themselves, Uh-oh, this isn't a defenseless woman. "The streets belong to men," a Dutch girlfriend said. It had not occurred to Deirdre that at some age even little boys start to own them.

But the exceptions, "sir" or "meneer," become rarer and rarer. She has almost crossed to the other side

PART THREE

DEIRDRE

TREES KETTING AND MARIANNE KETTING OF ROTTERDAM

NANCY, IN PARIS

DAVID AND HÉLÈNE, IN IOWA CITY

KATE CUMMINGS OF SYDNEY

DR. HAERTSCH, GENDER REASSIGNMENT

GAIL, ALAN, AND NOE OF SAN FRANCISCO

FRANK AND LIEKE OF ROTTERDAM

STEVE OF NEW ZEALAND AND DUNDEE

SUZANNE AND FIONA OF DUNDEE

PATTY

CAROL

SUSAN OF OXFORD

JUDITH

```
┌─────────┐
│   28    │
└─────────┘
```

V R I E N D I N N E T J E S

"Girlfriends." The Dutch word *vriendinnetjes,* pronounced "frreen-DINN-et-yuhs," says it. It means a friend (*vriend-*), female (*-inn-*), affectionately diminutive (*-etje-*), a plural few (*-s*). You can't have more than a few. Deirdre would ask every woman she came to know how many girlfriends she had, and each would pause and count mentally: one, three, five at most. You can have a dozen or more inactive girlfriends in the background, such as Janice in Colorado from junior high school whom you call twice a year, Janice with whom at fourteen you tried on tight jeans by lying down in the department store dressing room and hauling with all your might. But five is a high limit for *vriendinnetjes* on active duty.

"Friend" doesn't mean the same thing to a straight American man. An American *vriendinnetje* of Deirdre's asked a man she knew well how many friends he had. He said, "I've lived in this town for decades. I have hundreds of friends." No, she said, I mean, how many people can you really talk to about your deepest feelings? Who you can call at 3:00 in the morning to come to you at once?" He paused. "Uh . . . No one. . . . I don't have any friends like that." It is the tragedy of being a straight American man, like Donald, who had had no *vriendjes,* though he knew hundreds of men who would not actually draw a gun on him in the street. Mass "friendship," pub and gang, team and regiment, club and clan, the nation-state and the brotherhood of man, is for men, because they don't grasp *vriendinnetjeschap.*

Most women need a few women friends. In Whitney Otto's *How to Make an American Quilt* the character Constance does not, but she is unusual in this. She rejects an imagined female roommate: "Things were being made 'nice' [that American word] and there was supper together and emotional confessions and tales of personal histories—no, she simply was not patient enough for such close contact," and she gets along without *vriendinnetjes.*

Real friendship is costly, as economists would put it. It's not painful—that's not what economic "cost" means. It's expensive in the things you have to do without if you're going to have a real friend. You haven't got time for more than a few. You must call her or write frequently, and the calls or letters must not be businesslike. You must level with her. Not about everything, but always a little more than you intended to reveal, always a little embarrassing afterward. Secrets. The linguist Jennifer Coates speaks of "reciprocal self-disclosure," which "plays a key role in structuring the talk of women friends." In Carol Shields's *The Box Garden* the narrator, Charlotte, talks with her sister Judith in the dark before they go to sleep in their mother's guest room: "'Poor Char,' Judith says softly. Her sympathy is all I need. Now I can't stop myself." In Deirdre's weekly phone conversations with Marianne Ketting in Holland she told the details of her troubles, and Marianne told back. Being a girlfriend requires you to open yourself. You can't keep up a manly front.

It doesn't work to say that husbands have *vriendinnetjes* in their wives. Many women think when they get married that they are about to embark on a girlfriendlike relationship with a man. It's not likely. You can't be a one-way girlfriend. That he can level with her is no help unless he's good at listening too. Listening does not mean "coming up with a quick solution to the problem raised by the woman and then closing the subject." As Deborah Tannen points out in *You Just Don't Understand,* men think that when women engage in troubles talk they are asking for the big, brave men to solve their problems. (They are asking for sympathy, real sympathy. Poor Char. Poor Deirdre. Get it?) A few husbands and wives have a *vriendinnetjelijk* relationship, but it's rare.

Donald's relationship with his wife developed more and more as one-way. In the last decade or so Donald was the listener, playing the wifely role of sympathy without manly attempts to "solve" the problem, his wife acting toward Donald's personal talk like a man impatient with listening. Can't talk now. Would sometime next week work for you? Have your girl call my girl.

Deirdre's first *vriendinnetje* in her transition, and the first she had had since Donald's wife stopped listening ten or fifteen years before, was Marty Olney in California. At its height their relationship was real 3:00 in the morning stuff. It's hard to make or keep such a relationship by mail, or even by e-mail, but Marty and Deirdre were both articulate and sometimes would be exchanging e-mails in real time, one typing while the other sent. They had two e-mail periods framing the month and a half that Marty and Esther protected Deirdre in California.

Trees Ketting was her first *vriendinnetje* in Holland. Her first name, which is a nickname for her official one, Theresia, is pronounced "trace," not like the plural of "tree." She knew English even better than most Dutch people and would perform little English jokes like wearing a T-shirt reading "Save the Trees." Trees ("trace," remember) was the department secretary for Art and Cultural Studies. Deirdre knew she liked Trees before she met her, because when Arjo showed Deirdre her new office the first day on the job it already had the title on the card as "Mw. [*Mevrouw,* My woman, or Mrs.] prof. [Professor] McCloskey." It's not compulsory in Dutch academic naming to announce your gender with the "Mw.," and a person less sensitive than Trees would have missed the importance of this for a new woman.

She is an *echte Rotterdamse,* a real Rotterdam woman, born just south of the Nieuwe Maas, in which she and her sister learned to swim by being dunked with a rope tied around their waists. Trees and Deirdre ate once at the Hotel New York, the hotel-restaurant made out of the old head offices of the Holland-Amerika Line (Donald had embarked twice in the 1960s from the pier they now ate on), and Trees pointed out her old house and the very swimming spot. The Maas, which is the Meuse in the French areas of its source and is joined by the Rhine, draining all of northwestern Europe, is dirty now; it was corrosive then.

Trees took Deirdre on. They liked each other's sense of humor, though they joked about the cultural difference, and especially about the saccharine conventions of American womanhood, greeting and thanking and praising people all the time: "Oooooh, *honey,* it's so *wonderful* to see you! Thank you *sooooo* much for the birthday card. And, my, what a *lovely* outfit. Where *did* you get it?" It's southern especially, "a certain amount of obligatory social hypocrisy stemming from the southern tradition of manners, which does rather tend to emphasize pleasantness more than honesty in social situations," as the Texas columnist Molly Ivins observes. Deirdre explained that American women don't *really* believe it and make jokes about it among themselves. When Ivins met a Texas woman with a garish pink blouse and asked politely where *did* she get it, the woman replied, "Honey, it came from mah cou-tour-i-ay, Jay Cee Penn-ay." Dutch conventions among women are what in Scotland are called "dour." No gushing. Barely say hello. It can sometimes mean "No emotion, please, we're Dutch." Secular stoicism gone mad. Another Dutch *vriendinnetje* noted that her mother had never once praised any of her children. It might spoil them. Pre-Spock.

Trees called up her sister Marianne, a businesswoman in Rotterdam who does consulting on public relations, and then they both took Deirdre on. Deirdre embarrassed Trees and Marianne a few months later by calling them in the acknowledgments to her inaugural address "the Ketting sisters," like some sort of vaudeville act. *But they* are *a vaudeville act,* thought Deirdre, *Marianne the perpetual big sister to me and Trees. We could go on the stage. A situation comedy for Dutch television.*

Marianne arranged to have Deirdre invited to join a women's club she had founded, a *damesnetwerk* of professional women in Rotterdam. (The word is pronounced DAH-mez-net-vairrk.) The first time was terrifying, a dinner on Monday night in Rotterdam's yacht club. Deirdre rushed home from work, rushed to Marianne's house, rushed with her to the restaurant, rushed to put on her earrings in the ladies' room, rushed to powder her nose. *What will they think?* They proved gracious, women welcoming a new member of the tribe. Women are practiced at social games, games that for practical purposes become the realities of who you are: doing gender. "It's so *wonderful* to see you! Thank you *so* much!" The twenty or thirty women arranged themselves around a long table, which was good because it meant that Deirdre imposed English only on her immediate neighbors. An art-historian member of the *netwerk* presented a discussion on mosaics, switching to English from time to time when the slides did not speak for themselves. *These are people I can be friends with.*

They met once a month, next in a Chinese restaurant, and Deirdre talked to an architect of Indonesian Chinese descent named Timmi. Deirdre thought there was an opening to discuss recent immigration, something Americans know about. "How long have your people been in Indonesia, Timmi?" Deirdre expected an American-scale span of decades. "Four hundred years." The Damesnetwerk met once downstairs from Deirdre's apartment in a kitchen-design store owned by a woman named Pien, and Deirdre glowed with happiness in the snapshots taken among the Italian sinks and refrigerators. They met out at the lake house of one of the members, a music director, and Deirdre sat on the dock with the other women sipping white wine and laughing into a landscape-perfect afternoon. Deirdre herself once gave a presentation about her transition. She arrived early at the Rotterdam high-rise apartment, and the conversation turned to the important Dutch word *gezellig*. It means "cozy, comfortable, snug, socially happy" and is sought by Dutch people in all their gatherings. Candles are part of it, the feeling of friends fast at home while the wind and rain beat outside. A late arrival saw the group gathered in a corner of the apartment around candles and drinks and exclaimed in Dutch, "*Ach so, gezellig,*" and they laughed at the way she had accidentally supplied a punchline for the conversation. At the end of Deirdre's presentation ("When I was fourteen years old I prayed for two things . . .") she turned away briefly, stripped off her blouse and turned back to reveal the T-shirt Trees had given her: "Wonder Woman." A wonder indeed, *gezellig* with the other women.

The Damesnetwerk supported Deirdre in the Dutch women's way. No gushing, but nothing of the imprecision in friendship that is acceptable in America even among women. When Deirdre was in the hospital in Sydney that June for her operation, twelve thousand miles from Rotterdam, a bouquet of flowers arrived. "Congratulations from the Damesnetwerk." It had taken trouble to find the right place to send them, but the Dutch are expert at flowers and at international transactions—the arts of friendship and the skills of trade: "De Bloem is noodeloos in 'tKoren, en nochtans, / Daer's geen weerseggen aen, sij geeft de Tarw ee' glans." The flower's profitless in the grain, but nonetheless / There's no denying it gives the wheat some splendor.

Her best *vriendinnetje* back in America came to be Patty, the wife of a student Donald had taught long before at the University of Chicago. Patty and her husband lived in New Jersey. They first heard of Deirdre's transition in her Christmas letter from Holland, and Patty sent an e-mail when Deirdre was back in Iowa City. How are you? How does it feel? Patty is a quickly loving person, open and intelligent, and Deirdre liked chatting with her by e-mail. They became friends in the way women do, by exchanging confidences, leaning on each other in crises, helping and being helped. It was an advantage Deirdre had in making women friends, since she had bizarre things to tell (and no compunction about telling them) and plenty of crises to be helped through. Other women felt they had to reciprocate, if they had the inclination and the gift of friendship. Patty had them, and soon Deirdre was visiting the family in New Jersey when she came east on business. Patty and Deirdre would sit on the two white couches in the living room, near the point of the L the couches made, with a bowl of hard candy between them, and talk for hours. Patty's husband was astonished, amused, tolerant, a little disturbed: here was his tough-guy professor crying with Patty about little miseries and joys. Big ones, too.

Patty's daughters became honorary nieces, and Deirdre would bring presents. She and the younger daughter read *Little Women* together, and the honorary niece came out to Iowa to visit for a few days. Deirdre took her to the local version of Take Your Daughter to Work Day at the university. Deirdre's New Jersey family and her Dutch family stood in for the lost McCloskey children. *No **whining, now,** said the stoic to herself. **Remember, you disassociated from your birth family when you went to college. It's what kids do even in normal times. And what you have done is not normal.***

■

Downtown in Iowa City one day that Dutch spring, on a flying visit back to the United States, she kept running into an elderly couple she had square-danced with as Donald, and she finally stopped the husband and reintroduced herself. He was startled but courteous. God seemed to be nudging her (four encounters in a few hours), and anyway she had been disappointed by the reaction of her square dancing club. No one had written, these people she had thought of as friends. "Friends" is not a word taken too seriously in America, the country of caravans, as Arjo Klamer puts it. One of the couples in the club did write, some months after Deirdre sent them a card, and they invited her over for dinner when she came back for good.

■

Women ask Deirdre what she found most surprising about her crossing. What's most dissimilar on the other side? She answers: Women's friendship. Men, such as Wallace Stegner, do not understand it. It varies by era and culture. Margaret Mead's circle of friends at Barnard in the early 1920s were the "Ash Can Cats." The Ash Can Cats, Mead wrote, "firmly established a style of relationships to other women. 'Never break a date with a girl [thus 1923] for a man' was one of our mottoes in a period when women's loyalty to women usually was . . . subordinate to their possible relationships to men. We learned loyalty to women, pleasure in conversation with women, and enjoyment of the way in which we complemented one another." As did Deirdre, seventy years on.

29

WOMEN'S WORLD

You become a woman by being treated as one of the tribe. Nothing else is essential. Being Dutch is being treated as Dutch. Deirdre had many Dutch clothes, and so in Holland people came up to her in the street and asked directions in Dutch. You can be a masculine woman, as by some stereotypes many women are, yet still be treated as one of the tribe. No piece of conventionally feminine behavior is essential if the overall effect makes you accepted in the tribe. Biology is not decisive. Big hips, small frame, high voice, hairless face, sexual interest in men, more-than-male amounts of sympathy and readiness to cry: we all know women who vary on these dimensions, in this direction or that, but who are still part of the tribe.

And you treat yourself as one of the tribe too. Being Dutch is being homesick for Holland, inside your head. The dialogue with other members of society about whether Deirdre was part of the women's tribe has a personal side. Does Deirdre treat *herself* as a member of the women's tribe? ***Am I a woman? Yes.*** For months after going full time she still dreamed as Donald. It reflected a lifetime of practice in telling stories to herself, not some secret doubt. The stories a man tells are dreams of courage. Save the maiden in distress. She had to practice telling dreams of love. *Be* the maiden in distress. A Dutch woman friend told Deirdre of her tomboy childhood and of how disgusted she

Donald at age seven

Harvard fencing team, 1963 (Donald is third from the left, back row)

Chicago professor with son and dogs, 1973

Cricketer, age thirty-five   *With daughter, 1977*

Iowa house, 1980

Teaching economics,
University of Iowa, 1985

Square dancer, 1994

In drag, 1995

Iowa Artistry picnic, July 1995

Dee with women at the Social Science History Association, November 1995

*Dee with Nancy at the
Johnson County Courthouse,
November 1995, for name change*

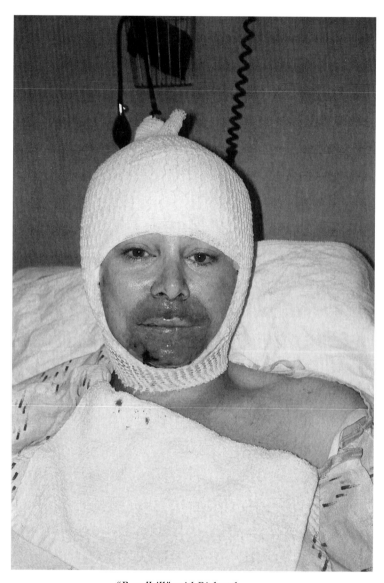

"Roadkill," said Richard

Arjo Klamer on a tram in Rotterdam

Trees Ketting, Deirdre, and Marianne Ketting, 1996

Deirdre in Paris, Nancy behind the camera, May 1996

Deirdre feeling lovely in her Parisian hat, with Marianne, Rotterdam, May 1996

A good hair day

*Dick and Deirdre in
New York, 1997*

*At a performance of <u>La Cage aux Folles</u>,
Iowa City, 1997*

Patty and Deirdre on the couches in New Jersey, 1997

Deirdre shows Patty and her daughter how to get
beautiful skin, 1997

In Mexico with Nancy and Norwegian women, summer 1997

Susan of Oxford and Fiona and Suzanne of Dundee, 1997

Judith in the Amsterdam flat, August 1997

Two presidents of the Economic History Association, September 1997

A Dutch conference, 1998

Dutch fame: the corner display at the Atheneum Bookstore in Amsterdam

The television camera crew at Scheveningen, 1998

Frank and Lieke and Janie at the park in Rotterdam, 1998

Makeover at Georgette Klinger salon in Manhattan, 1998

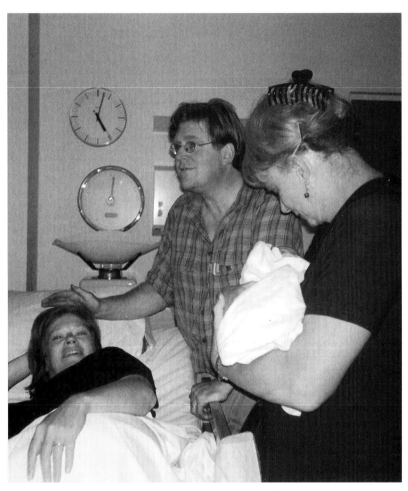

Marijke, Arjo, and Deirdre with Rosa Deirdre Klamer, August 1998

was when in adolescence she started dreaming about being saved by men and living happily ever after. Another woman told of growing up in Baltimore, an Orioles fan, especially admiring the pitcher Tom Palmer. She was chagrined when she realized in adolescence that she had started thinking of Palmer as a love object, not as a model for behavior.

Deirdre dreams one night of her wife, and for the first time she tells the story as a woman, not as a wife's protector and sparring partner in the way of marriage. Deirdre and the ex-wife talk to each other as women with a long and deep friendship. When Deirdre wakes she thinks: *She will not come to it. Sad,* one of the three things that can make tears rise, beyond sad stories on TV: her former wife, her children, her dim prospects for someone to share her dreams of love. *Am I not lovable? I am a nice woman. People say they like me. I don't try to hurt people. I am responsible, loving, intelligent, fun, aren't I? I am even a little pretty, aren't I? Why doesn't anyone love me? Why am I alone?*

Welcome, dear, to the women's world of unrequited love.

Deirdre made up an imaginary lover, as girls do. Hers was a big Dutch fellow, a handsbreadth taller even than Deirdre, named Joop, pronounced "Yope." There's a popular perfume by that name, and Deirdre was disappointed when she didn't like it. She made up Joop to help her with her posture. When she imagines Big Joop looking at her she stands tall and proud and womanly. She amuses a friend at the Damesnetwerk one night by telling about him, describing him as strong yet sensitive, manly yet insightful, passionate yet inclined to stay home evenings with her. The friend says, "If you find one like that, ask him if he has a brother."

■

Why then did Deirdre join the women's tribe? The question does not make sense, because it asks for a prudential answer when the matter is identity. Choice of a holiday in Indonesia rather than Australia can be explained with "I like Indonesian food better" or some other appeal to prudence, taking care, getting what you want. You are prudent, though, within an identity fixed on some other grounds. If you are Dutch you just like the sandwiches called *broodjes.* Asking why a person changes gender is like asking why a person is a midwesterner or thoughtful or great souled: she just is.

An identity is both made and not made. It is a romantic idea, which is strangely paired in the modern world with the antiromantic ideas of positivism in social science, that we all have an internal identity, fixed and ready made, and the only task is to express it. Will the real Deirdre please stand up? The "realness" is not right. We make ourselves, which is our freedom as human beings. One evening after supper Deirdre is explaining to a Dutch *vriendinnetje* how women stand and walk by contrast with men. The friend has not noticed the details, since she has no reason to. To show her, Deirdre stands up and tries to walk like a man. She can't. She can only do the woman's parody of a man's walk, with lots of loud clomping and macho swaying like Popeye the Sailor Man. After a year of making herself walk like a woman, she has forgotten how to walk like a natural man. She says to herself, *Good.*

Late in her Dutch year she is scorned by an elderly academic she thought was friendly. He is stiff with age and maleness. Deirdre cannot feel what it is like to perform as a boyish if old man in emotions, an old bear making attacks on people who trust you, brushing off blows as part of the game, valuing pride before consideration, unable to apologize, not caring about love. Deirdre is forgetting manhood the way one forgets a place you once lived in or a former job. *Good.*

She has made herself a woman. But everyone does that. She had made herself a man, too, learning to suppress her femininity, becoming an athlete and lover and tough-guy debater. A male version and a female version are available for everyone, one's own sister or brother, mother or father. No one thought Donald the slightest bit feminine, and repeatedly people would express astonishment: "You're the last person I would have thought." A good performance.

For all the performing, though, the romantic view has something in it. You make yourself Dutch or American, a nurse or an accountant, a recluse or a social butterfly, piece by piece. But you have tendencies, which can be traced back to childhood. Anyone who has watched a child grow is impressed by the thrust of character. The dismal, fretful infant in arms will in eighty years be a dismal, fretful old lady. The cheerful infant will always be an optimist. No wonder people devised a word for it, the soul.

■

Male editors found it hard to grasp why Deirdre wanted her new name to appear on her publications, even republications and new editions from Donald's day, even in reference to his work. Years afterward the more polite men would send puzzled inquiries. Almost no woman found this difficult. Perhaps the men felt, without bringing the feeling to consciousness: It is a shameful thing to be a woman; why would he—"she"—want the honorable male name changed? A woman economist told her that no male economist she knew could bring himself to call this new female economist of old acquaintance "she." Her male colleagues sometimes misspoke her gender, "he" instead of "she," "Don" instead of "Deirdre," with no malice. It's hard.

■

She goes to lunch in Rotterdam with a British woman professor and acquaintance who had given the economics seminar. Two male Dutch economists are there, so she keeps an eye on her own style of talk: masculine or feminine? She gets into a friendly dispute with one of them, a superb economist who doesn't read much beyond economics, about whether philosophy is worth anything to the practical man. Trying in a big sisterly way to set him straight, she says, "Come now, dear: are you a fact man? Yes? Well, then, read the facts about philosophy." The turn is a little masculine, and she worries afterward about finding an academic style that suits her. That night she cooks for the woman professor her dish from the Amsterdam High School of Domestic Science, her one Dutch specialty of broccoli with brie and tagliatelli, and they talk woman to woman. That's how to find a woman's academic style, among women.

■

Deirdre was glad to publish with her student Stephen Ziliak a technical paper that appeared in the largest-circulation journal in economics in March 1996, shortly after she arrived in Holland. *Just so you realize I can still do it.* The paper attacked "statistical significance" (not statistics or numbers or measurement, about which Deirdre was ever enthusiastic, but a silly and very particular technique that has taken over modern economics), and she gave a talk on it to a crowded seminar in economics at Erasmus. The men did not know how to treat this new lady who claimed to have found a dreadful mistake in their intellectual lives. Deirdre was amused to get a little stack of letters about the published paper from male economists, saying, "Yes, I agree, and in fact here is a copy of *my* paper on the subject." All of the men missed the point in their eagerness to draw attention to their own point. *They aren't listening,* she thought, *as boys often don't in the excitement of the sandbox. I have come upon a criticism of modern economics that makes the field seem boyishly silly, but the boys can't see the silliness and draw proud attention to their new sand castles. Look, Aunt Deirdre, look at what I have done.* Io, io.

■

An Iowa City woman came to Amsterdam on holiday with a friend, and Deirdre traveled from Rotterdam to meet them one evening for a meal. It was funny to talk to the two other women about men and women and crossing. The three of them giggled when the people at the next table caught the drift of their peculiar conversation. The Iowa City woman said, "Just you wait until you get home. I'm going to introduce you to some other women in town." She meant the businesswomen outside the circle of the University of Iowa. Deirdre was pleased by the prospect: *It would be like the Damesnetwerk,* she thought. *Yes. Just another* **DAH-meh.**

30

TO MAKE UP FOR GOD'S NEGLECT

One afternoon in the spring she felt ill, so she turned off the lights in her office and stretched out to nap uneasily on the extra desk. Since her daughter had stopped bringing home cold viruses from school sixteen months before Deirdre had not been sick, not at all, except the self-imposed sickness from operations. This was the first time sick as Deirdre. *Isn't that lovely: first time as a woman.* She canceled her class—she did not have to put on a brave front and appear in front of the class groggy and close to vomiting, as Donald would have. Trees asked one of the secretaries to drive her home. The secretary was a policeman's wife, and she and Deirdre talked about how hard that was. She was shy about her English, but they got on. The next day Deirdre brought flowers in thanks, as one does in Holland. Trees called after she got home, concerned that Deirdre had support. Eugenia was there downstairs, helpful and loving.

Women help each other, Deirdre found. In the dedication to Deirdre's book about her transition she wrote the first names and last initials of women who had gone some distance to welcome her—a luncheon here, a gift there, a comforting letter sent, introductions made, defenses drawn up, all the things that few men would think to do (Arjo, Gary, Joel, David, Richard, Stephen: a short list, and Donald would not have been on it). She was stunned when she counted out the names gathered from her memory and from old appointment books (ever the empirical and quantifying lady): 258 acts of grace. The list would have been impossible for a man. Female-to-male gender crossers must face the unhappy fact that American men don't help each other. The theory of American maleness is that your special woman takes care of you when you're sick, but aside from that you are supposed to do everything alone. Help among men is shameful, because it shows incompetence. Among women help is the point, because it shows love, "love" in its full sense: care, sympathy, providing for need.

Gifts, it seemed to Deirdre, are similar. A theologian friend wrote of a sequence from exchange through "gift exchange" to grace. Women are always giving graceful gifts. In Margaret Atwood's *The Robber Bride* the heroine Roz is moved to give even to the dangerous Zenia: "She would like to give Zenia something, just a little something, to make up to her for God's neglect." It is never the purpose of a woman's gift, as it is ordinarily with men, to establish how big and powerful you are. Thus men give diamonds. The diamond monopoly De Beers insinuates in ads that a man should spend two months' salary on the engagement ring—or else his penis will fall off. Waiters in the United States prefer male customers because the men give bigger tips, for the same reason. The woman would actually have to care. When Deirdre gave an expensive scarf and a few extra trinkets to her economist friend Janet in Toronto, Janet sent a card of thanks, and thanks especially for the funny little keychain with tiny wooden shoes. She liked the scarf, but women are on the watch for tokens of love. When Deirdre gave her secretary Deb a vase from Iowa Artisans Gallery, Deb loved it, but she loved especially the big-key calculator from *Reason* magazine that she had jokingly coveted when it came into the office the week before. A token.

Deirdre had to learn the women's culture of gifts. Marty Olney taught her how to remember birthdays. Surprise, dearie: write them down, and care. Henceforth she was on the alert for birthdays, noting them down when they arose in conversation, and was delighted when she could surprise Carol Fethke with a birthday card. She got a long Dutch birthday calendar and hung it on the wall facing the downstairs toilet, the traditional location. The joke among women in Holland is that men forget birthdays because they don't face the calendar when they relieve themselves. Though they *could* turn around once in a while.

The Ketting sisters taught her how to give and receive favors without the thank-you-thank-you that American women use. "Oh, *thank* you: how *wonderful! Thank* you. It's *just* what I wanted! *Thank* you! *Thank* you!" Thank-you-thank-you is read in Europe as establishing indebtedness, or perhaps as canceling the debt. In the eyes of European women it is vulgar to draw attention in this way to the debt aspect of a gift. It is grace, not the guys' gift exchange. Deirdre would explain that American women were not actually doing such a thing—like European women they viewed gifts as unrequited acts of love—but Trees and Marianne did not believe her, and thereafter they would joke about the thank-you-thank-you.

All this started to affect Deirdre's view of economics. People have two ways, exchange and identity. Men can grasp only exchange. In his one letter Deirdre's son declared that love is an exchange and that he wasn't getting enough value in exchange from her to continue. Male anthropologists and economists have found gift giving mysterious and have interpreted it as a kind of exchange, as among men it is. Failing to pay back a gift is shameful.

Among women the gift makes connections, expressing love and solidarity: a meal, a keychain, a life. It feels like a conversational move that says, Yes, I love you. Trees gave Deirdre her lipstick holder right out of her purse, Trees's sister Marianne gave Deirdre the dress for Deirdre's inaugural address right out of her closet. Gail gave her a scarf right out of her drawer in San Francisco. Barbara gave her a hat right off her hat rack in Gothenburg, just a little something to make up for God's neglect. Virginia sent Deirdre her own copy of a book on style for the professional woman. Saskia gave Deirdre earnest advice on hair curlers and showed her where to buy them, and in a square in Leiden she demonstrated how to put them in, as the manuscript they were doing business about began to scatter in the Dutch wind. Such giving was partly tuition in being a woman, and in a man it would have served to establish who was the expert and who the mere student, creating a debt of equal value that would have to be paid off. Among women, it seemed to Deirdre, it's nothing of the sort. Just before she left from a brief, intense visit to her college roommate in Stockton, California, his wife Judy, whom until that time Donald/Deirdre had known only slightly, gave Deirdre, literally, her hair—two hairpieces Judy had had made from her cropped tresses long before when she and Derek were in the Peace Corps in Korea. "I don't use them at all. You have them," she said at the door, thrusting them into Deirdre's hands. Deirdre felt like crying, and thinking of it later, she did.

Women's lives, Deirdre noticed, are collections of gifts; men's, of trophies. When she stayed with David and Hélène on a trip back to Iowa

City she admired Hélène's collection of pigs, two hundred or so little cloth and clay and wooden pigs of all sorts in displays around the house.

"You know who gave you each one, don't you?" said Deirdre.

David looked disbelieving. "Oh, I don't think she does."

Hélène cocked her head at him. "Of course I do," and ran along a row of varied pigs on the mantle, naming each giver and the occasion. David was impressed.

"All two hundred?"

"Of course." Hélène was surrounded not by model pigs but by tokens of love. Deirdre wore the ring given by her graduate students when she left for Holland. It was beautiful and expensive and attracted compliments, but that was not the point. Every time she saw it she saw their love, and she was likely to get weepy.

Some women find it incredible that men do not grasp what gifts are about in women's lives. But Deirdre knew, because Donald hadn't. She remembered the last time Donald gave his wife flowers. He had to be out of town for a few days and felt guilty, so he arranged, bright boy, to have a florist deliver enormous bunches of flowers to her office for three days running. His wife was annoyed by it, this industrial and commercial approach to gift giving, which showed Donald as rich and powerful, diamond-style, but said nothing about his feelings toward her. Donald was stupidly puzzled at her annoyance.

Deirdre later could only sigh, "Men!"

> April 1996: I still, in the fifth month of full time, do not quite have the gift culture down. It's coming. I see absurd joke gifts for Trees on my travels. She has a wall of funny schlock in her office to which she steadily adds, so I help and show her my affection. I was full of thought for Trees's funny project in a souvenir shop in Oxford or an airport stall in San Francisco. I tried and tried to get flowers to my Australian friend Kate Cummings on her sixty-first birthday, but I'm not Dutch and businesslike with flowers and therefore failed and had to send them late, covering up in a male way by claiming it was an after-birthday gift. But I succeeded better for her when in the Philadelphia airport I spotted the card about men turning into women and instantly thought of her and bought it with a smile of affection. There's nothing like it, this blessedness of giving.

Deirdre learned the blessedness. Home in her Iowa year she gave Louise a shooting stick for Louise's brother right out of her closet, to make up for God's neglect.

31

MERRY MAY

*I*n May Deirdre was to give an oration, an *oratie* (oh-RRAT-zee), to the assembled professors of Erasmus in the great hall. In British English the occasion would be called an "inaugural address," but because America does not have the powerful professorships characteristic of European academic life, at home there is nothing to inaugurate. Her Dutch occasion was a trifle artificial, since her chair was then only a visiting one, a folding chair, but Deirdre agreed with Arjo's and the rector's suggestion for an *oratie,* and she wrote her speech on the crisis she discerned in modern economics.

Her mother decided to come over for the week. Deirdre knew she was expressing the family's support, and also checking to see if her new daughter was safe and respected. On that score and others the *oratie* was a success. The speech as delivered was terrible. Deirdre had forgotten her Harvard Ph.D. gown at her flat. and in her borrowed gown she was flustered by the poor lighting and inadequate microphones of the great hall. She tried to read from the prepared text, a bad idea because she always stuttered more that way. But she was hardened to performances' sometimes working and sometimes not. Nothing could spoil the warmth of the celebration, with Arjo and Marijke and their children in attendance, and Deirdre's students and colleagues clapping as the berobed body of the professoriate, Deirdre at its head, marched out of the hall as at a wedding. Her mother was pleased to talk to the other professors at the reception afterward and to hear their words of praise. One of them said to her, "You know, your daughter is an unusual woman." That says it. A reporter from the *New Yorker* was there, and had been for some days, doing a story about Deirdre that was not published. Deirdre arranged an expensively catered party at her apartment, at which Arjo made a loving speech about the new professor and everyone gave gifts. Deirdre was thrilled at the outpouring of little tokens of love: scarves and books and jewelry.

The next day she and her mother went to Paris, Deirdre to see her friend Nancy, her mother to see an old friend from opera-student days. On the train down from Rotterdam they shared a European-style compartment with six other people, including a Russian physicist and a rich Indian couple. Deirdre's mother has always found it easy to talk to strangers, and soon the compartment was buzzing with geniality. But by accident of fifty-three years' acquaintance she sometimes called Deirdre "Donald," and sometimes "he." The other travelers were puzzled.

They arrived at Gare du Nord to be insulted by a languid youth smoking in an information booth. He was asked a thousand times a day, "Do you have a map of Paris?" and each time he pretended not to understand either an English or a bad French version of it. This trick was for his own amusement, wholly Parisian, but Deirdre found it endearing as Donald would not have. Deirdre loved Paris this time. She stayed with Nancy and her husband Bob in the garret flat near the Odéon on the Left Bank that they had rented for the year of Nancy's fellowship. Deirdre and Nancy wandered about when Nancy was not working, into an upscale clothing store to handle the exquisite suits starting at $1,500, through the Luxembourg Garden, to Nancy's hat store. Nancy cooked out of a French bistro cookbook that Deirdre then bought for herself, burning a bistro stew back in Rotterdam and thereafter leaving the book on the shelf. *Take it down,* she advised herself, *when you're more advanced.* Nancy's aunt and uncle came through, Texans like Nancy who did not fit the prejudices of Yankees. Deirdre and her mother and her mother's friend Joe, also from Texas a long time before, roamed the museums and tried to have a drink at the Ritz, but it was closed and a less famous hotel nearby had to do. Deirdre arranged one night to meet a younger woman colleague from Iowa, and they dined on such a crème brûlée that Deirdre wished she could spend the rest of her life eating it. The next night she met Barbara from Sweden and her German academic husband at the café where Sartre and Beauvoir had hung out half a century before, then they went to an actual bistro and had a long, long talk about life and gender.

■

Later Deirdre took care of Arjo and Marijke's children for a week while the adults were on holiday in America. The two older children spoke English well from living three years in Washington. Arjo's sister took the little one, mostly. Deirdre acted as Tante Deirdre, the maiden aunt, a role she found comfortable. Love them, but make sure they get to school on time. When they ate their meals Tante Deirdre used the Dutch customs of the house, such as candles at dinner and holding hands in a ring for grace. The eleven-year-old girl made hot chocolate one night for the three of them (when the little one was still with her real aunt), and Deirdre and the girl and her younger brother played the board game Snakes and Ladders endlessly. The day before mother Marijke was coming home they all cleaned the house, even little Anna doing a job of straightening her room. It reminded Deirdre of raising her own children, or before that of baby-sitting her sister and brother. Taking care, a womanly task. Marijke spoke of taking care of her horse as a girl. Girlish enthusiasm for the great beasts thus foreshadows the big-time caring for children and husbands and parents.

Two years later Marijke had her fourth child, a girl. Deirdre was in Holland at the time and briefly took care of the house during the delivery. Forty minutes after it Deirdre came to the hospital in Hilversum, and Arjo handed her the bundled babe. "I'd like you to meet Rosa *Deirdre* Klamer," he said, making up for God's neglect. Deirdre was stunned and wept for joy and for her own lost children.

32

STARTING

In June 1996 Deirdre had the operation in Australia. She could make people laugh by saying, "I was on a business trip there, and thought, 'What the heck.'" Yet it was a truth. She had been invited a year before as Donald to come that June to a conference at Australian National University, a little second trip to Australia long after a three-month visit Donald and his wife and children had made in 1983. The director of the National Humanities Institute was not alarmed when Donald declared in the fall of 1995 that she was now Deirdre. No problem. Why are you telling me this? At the "Southern Comfort" convention in Atlanta she had met Kate Cummings, an academic librarian from Australia. Kate's doctor had been Haertsch in Sydney. *Outside the circle of the Benjamin Standards,* Deirdre thought. *He can do it when I'm ready. Six, seven months into full time.*

Donald had never loved his penis the way some men do. So much seems obvious. Dee didn't care when he lost the use of his penis for sexual purposes a few months after starting on hormones; Deirdre didn't care when at last in Australia she said good-bye to it, and she didn't care any time afterward. She hadn't known Donald was different from most men in this way. Arjo mentioned later that he had sensed the difference long before he knew Donald was a gender crosser. It was an absence of push. Donald was annoyed when people thought of him as competitive the way men are, disregarding opportunities for cooperation. He thought of himself as cooperating on the common thing, the res publica. Other men were always putting forward Their Things. Or so it felt to him. (Others found him as pushy as the pushiest of men.)

Deirdre's nonchalance on the matter struck many men as strange. Gary, her first date in Berkeley, wrote to her, "I would hide anywhere on earth, anywhere, in order to avoid such an operation." Deirdre on the contrary yearned for it and worried it might not happen. The anxiety that many men feel about gender crossing, which Donald and Deirdre found it impossible to feel, seems rooted in their male identities. "I am a boy. Look at my weenie." It was why some said, "I can't handle it," and why some friends stood silent. They feared for themselves, for their pleasures and their pride. *I suppose,* she said to herself, puzzled.

As soon as Deirdre made the arrangements with the surgeon in Australia she started counting the weeks and days until. In the months before the operation she came to view her male parts with increasing distaste. Some gender crossers feel like this all their lives. Every time Deirdre went to the bathroom she was reminded of the deformity. And yet she never had the intense feelings that some gender crossers express and that justify the operation in the minds of gatekeepers. The operation was important but not defining. It was living as a woman that was defining, not an operation on parts usually secret and that one can in any case hardly feel one way or the other, except in urinating.

She told lots of people about the event, to get support, to give them time to adjust. In view of the aggression by her sister and Galenson during the fall and winter before, it was not prudent to blab, but she couldn't be prudent about such a thing. She was apprehensive all the time about the operation's being called off, blocked by her sister or a typhoon or the beginning of World War III. She had occasional moments of doubt, which seemed normal. "It's a big step," her friends kept saying, wiping their brows. She concluded that she was feeling her friends' anxiety, not her own. She viewed the operation as one would view the removal of a malignant tumor, not the removal of a functioning leg. The operation is major surgery, but not particularly dangerous. It's not "experimental," as crossphobic congressmen got the Veterans Administration to declare it in order to stop the few the VA did. (Donald's endocrinologist resigned his appointment at the Iowa City VA Hospital over that policy.) In a sympathetic article about gender crossing in its issue of July 20, 1998, *Time* reckoned that more than twenty-five thousand Americans have had such operations. Only a few surgeons in the country do it regularly since the Johns Hopkins psychiatrists took over the field and imposed prohibition, but not because the operation is difficult. It is similar to a hysterectomy or a bowel resection. Gallbladder.

People are haunted by the worry that "he'll change his mind." It doesn't happen any more than changes of mind over gallbladder operations, but people worry nonetheless. It's something they would darn right change their minds about—they can't conceive of anyone's wanting such a bizarre thing in the first place. It's craaazy. *Weird.* The gender crosser must be nuts, they reason. Make him wait: he'll snap out of it.

It's funny, she thought. ***Once you've decided to be a woman (that's wrong; not "decide," once you must), there's a premium on getting swiftly to the operation***—not that for most practical purposes it matters a lot, she would say. They would balk at "not that it matters a lot," and she would ask, How many times a day do people check your genitals? Your face, yes, your gestures, voice: hundreds of times a day. But what's between your legs is seldom tested. Yet being able to say you are finished, complete, really a woman by the no-penis criterion is the most powerful rhetoric for acceptance of behavior that otherwise does not inspire acceptance. Jamison Green, a female-to-male writer Deirdre met once, said that in some cultures people will simply enter an agreement that Washtano is henceforth to be regarded for all social purposes as a woman. In our medicalized culture the ceremony that seals the agreement is the operation. People think they understand the operation, at least in the primitive way that most people are able to reflect on gender, because they merge genital sex with gender roles, as though people were salmon being checked for sex before being either clubbed to death or returned to the stream. Cruel or ignorant women might object to a pre-op gender crosser in the ladies' room but are less inclined post-op. Where else do you propose I go to the bathroom, dear?

■

Her route to Australia, and to a social agreement that she was a woman, was Amsterdam to Chicago to Iowa City to Los Angeles to Sydney. While the plane was boarding in the Amsterdam airport a man her age took the next seat. He was a talker. He found that Deirdre was an economic historian, and over the next ten minutes he outlined his theory of economic and political history. She smiled and agreed with him, for in truth it was not a stupid theory, though mistaken. She reflected that as a man her impulse would have been to put him down, to show Donald as the prime male. After all, she was the expert on such matters, the president-elect of the Economic History Association, writer of books on the subject, not he. But as a woman her impulse was to take care, to avoid bruising him. *I mean, why hurt him?*

The stewardess came over with a list and asked for "Mr." McCloskey. Deirdre smiled and acknowledged that she must be it, and the stewardess corrected herself, "Oh, *Miss* McCloskey!" and told Deirdre that as a frequent flyer she had an upgrade because they had overbooked tourist class. Deirdre moved away from her loquacious seatmate, who joked that he always had brief relationships with women. She was re-seated next to a young man who didn't show interest in forming any relationship, short or long. *The talkative man was a fling,* she thought, *I like being a woman to a man.*

Late that evening her history graduate student Jon picked her up at the Cedar Rapids–Iowa City airport. She embarrassed him by kissing him, but she was inclined to do that now with all men she knew well and hadn't seen for a while. She worried: *Perhaps kissing isn't appropriate between student and thesis supervisor, even if done chastely on the cheek.* But she wanted no piece of feminine behavior to be uncomfortable to her. During a seminar at Erasmus she had announced that she was going to give a Dutch economist named Albert a kiss for some good intellectual deed, and he expressed at first mock horror, the sort that straight men are supposed to express at homosexual encounters. Deirdre thought ruefully, *A real woman would not have been treated so.* The same thought must have occurred to Albert, because afterward he came up and presented his cheek. "Well, are you going to kiss me or not?" *Good, sensitive man,* she thought, and gave him the kiss.

Deirdre had come to Iowa City to give a Ph.D. examination for her economics graduate student Stephen. She stayed in Iowa City with David and Hélène. When Donald came out as Deirdre they had invited her over to dinner at once when others who knew her better were embarrassed. A few men in her acquaintance stood up quickly, but most kept mum, and Deirdre remembered the feeling of Donald in similar situations, divorces and deaths and the like: *I'm not expected to be good at love; maybe it will pass. What do I say?* Hélène had written a loving letter that came at Deirdre's worst time in Holland. Deirdre had not replied and felt guilty, worrying that she had failed as a woman. Hélène was gracious. They shared womanly intensities about ideas and clothes, and later they exchanged e-mail when Hélène was in China and Deirdre still in Holland.

A little group of faculty and graduate students went to lunch at Givanni's after Stephen's successful exam. The students seemed to be making good progress in her absence, as though the emotional test they and Deirdre had gone through together had made them more focused than average graduate students. She daydreamed about this pleasant notion but doubted it.

■

She had worried that her height would be a problem in America, away from the giantesses of northern Holland, but that was not so. There's enough genetic variation in the United States that people are ready for a big woman. She passed without comment in the Osco drugstore, at J. C. Penney's, on Clinton Street, and got no second looks. The average resident of Iowa City is no hick but is no gender sophisticate either. *Good. Gender sophisticates are pains in the neck.*

■

There she was again at the little Iowa City–Cedar Rapids airport, finally on the way to Los Angeles and Australia, to the operation, to genuineness and the end of fear. *Thanks be to the Lord, blessed be her holy name!*

The agent looked at her passport and handed it back to her.

"Ma'am, you might as well go home."

Huh? What! No, no.

"You need a *visa* to go to Australia," a stamp in the passport made by the Australians allowing her to come into the country.

Oh, my God. I forgot. Of course. The Australians and their bloody visas. Guy-type retaliation for the Americans and their *bloody visas.*

All the terrors of the last November and December rose again. *The operation isn't going to happen. Oh, my God, my God.*

33

FINISHING

She was tearful, frantic. She had the agent give her a ticket as far as Los Angeles, at least. In Los Angeles she might possibly get a visa quickly and still make the operation. There was no chance in little Iowa City. *Oh, my God,* the prereligious Deirdre chanted to herself. *Please, please, dear God.*

Deirdre sat in the airplane as it took off, nearly crying. *My God, my God.* She took out her cross-stitching project, an antique pattern from Holland. In Cedar Rapids, Denver, Los Angeles she called Kate Cummings in Australia and left messages on her answering machine, less and less hysterical. Dr. Haertsch's office and he himself were Australian laid back. "G'day. Oh, yeah. Kate told me. Sure, love, it would be fine to come for the preoperative checkup on Saturday morning instead of Friday afternoon."

When she got to the Australian consulate in Los Angeles early the next day the clerk admitted that the Australians impose visas because the American government imposes them on Australians. *That's intelligent.* The French also did it for a while in retaliation for the American policy, and Donald once spent an afternoon in the white persons' line (the shorter one) at the French embassy in London. But even the French gave it up. *Feminine good sense. Dopey Australian ma-*

choness. (A year or so later the Australians changed their policy.) ***Dopey American xenophobia in the big nation of immigrants.***

She ended up enjoying the extra day in Los Angeles. After the consulate she sat in the sun at an outdoor café and wrote postcards, a womanly duty she now understood and loved as Donald had not, then went over to UCLA to see if she could find people she knew there. A colleague in economic history was in his office, and friendly. He organized a luncheon with a couple of other economists. They discussed whether economics would change with more women in it. She joked: "I've taken a somewhat radical approach to changing the ratio!" which became one of her lines among other academics. Afterward she spent a couple of hours with a retired economist at UCLA who was one of Donald's and then Deirdre's heroes. He was in his early eighties, flexible of mind, friendly and understanding. At the business school coffee room they talked about economics and life. He wanted Deirdre to meet a woman economist friend of his, the wife of an economist who had been a classmate of Donald's in an economic history course in graduate school. "You and she would get along great," he said. ***Probably.***

Later Deirdre went over to the English Department to see a friend from Iowa by that time at UCLA. Kate was not in her office, but the light was on and the door ajar, so Deirdre went in and waited. Kate returned.

"May I help you?"

"Uh, yes. Do you recognize me?" The voice had a manly timbre, but Kate did not understand. *Who is this woman?* "I was once Don McCloskey."

"Good Lord! Don! I mean . . . "

"Deirdre. Pleased to meet you!"

Kate told how a few weeks earlier a student in her graduate seminar had shown her Deirdre's coming-out piece reprinted in a magazine for literary academics called *Lingua Franca*. Kate was certain it was a spoof. Things are that way in the Department of English, irony upon irony. "I'm sure it's a joke," she declared to her graduate student, and to show her certitude about this obvious truth she added, "If Don McCloskey has changed into a woman, I'll turn back my Ph.D.!" A student piped up: "Can I have it?"

Kate invited Deirdre to her house, which was close to the Los Angeles airport and the evening flight to Australia. The two women took her husband and her husband's father out to a Thai restaurant for Father's Day, a feminine duty, Deirdre observed, with Kate wrapping presents and organizing ceremonies for her men. Deirdre couldn't tell if the men read her, which merely showed that they were courteous, because they must have. Kate's father-in-law asked Deirdre how it felt to be such a tall woman.

At the airport that evening she picked up her stored luggage from the Mutual of Omaha booth. It was late, and her makeup was slipping. The clerk laughed at her and called her sir. She flared up and got weepy angry, scolding him for enjoying hurting people—Did his mother raise him that way?—and the clerk retreated in confusion. *People around airports are the pits—savvy, and impolite about their savvyness. The worst ones are in the worst jobs, like the dopey clerk at Mutual of Omaha.*

The flight was fourteen hours, but for some reason easier than going to Europe. She could not figure out how to think about the international date line, but she arrived in Sydney at a time that left no jet lag. Maybe it was her sheer desire to fit in. She got a window seat for leaning and sleeping and was engrossed for hours in a woman's novel off the rack. The young Australian woman in her row was pleasant and didn't seem to read her, despite Deirdre's croaks and stuttering from tiredness. Stuttering is five times more common in men than in women, which made stuttering another gender clue in the wrong direction.

A second caring Kate in two days, Kate Cummings, met her at the airport in Sydney, on a Saturday in winter like a New York autumn, and drove her home. and then across town to Dr. Haertsch's office. Kate the gender saint. Deirdre was the seventh post-op to recover at Kate's house. They dined a couple of nights later at Kate's mother's house, and Deirdre learned why Kate was so generous: she is a loving daughter of a loving family. Kate's former wife was still furious and managed to get their long marriage annulled, the Church lawyers refusing to acknowledge the evidence that a marriage had happened there. One daughter, whom Deirdre met, was supportive and treated her father like a human being. The others were suspended in their mother's hatred and shame like insects in amber. Deirdre worried.

Dr. Haertsch himself is a big, masculine man who tells it like it is. The old operation used the penile tissue supplemented by a skin graft to make the neovagina. Haertsch, who had done nearly four hundred gender reassignment surgeries in a large practice of surgery of the hand and various cosmetic procedures, was adopting a newer technique that used some of the large intestine (the "ascending colon"), which has its own blood supply and is internal tissue, as should be.

The operation was developed in Sweden, he explained, for girls born without vaginas. "Are you sure you're ready?" he asked. Yes, yes. Kate claimed to be envious of the new procedure: she had had her operation the old way ten years earlier. Deirdre left the office ecstatic.

I've made it. I've made it. The day after tomorrow!

Deirdre, Kate, and Kate's friend went out shopping for an hour in a Sydney neighborhood. Deirdre was the tallest, and if they were going to get read it would be her fault. Kate and her friend were beyond caring about whether people were reading them, and anyway they looked like Australian women out for a Saturday stroll. But the little group didn't seem to cause heads to turn, and Deirdre was happy.

> June 17, 7:00 A.M. Sydney time. It's the day of the surgery. I sit in a small room in Westside Private Hospital after a good night's sleep. The staff are pleasant. They are accustomed to Dr. Haertsch's patients and treat me like another woman. I am calm enough to pull out my computer and beaver away.
>
> Yesterday afternoon when Kate brought me to the hospital I was weepy happy about making it, and then weepy sad about having no special lover. These past months I've begun to look on men as consumption items rather than as competitive suppliers. I certainly have not had sexual desires directed toward women since the epiphany, and even some months before. One thinks of sexual desire as unalterable. In this case perhaps not.
>
> This morning I feel cheerful and confident—less apprehensive than I was before the first facial surgery back in November. I feel like an experienced patient, and I was foolishly pleased when the nurse praised me for refusing milk in my morning coffee: no milk before operations involving the colon.
>
> At 8:00 on the morning of the operation (it will be at 12:00 noon) I showered, to shave my pubic area. I say good-bye to my penis, hanging there unprotected by hair. Poor thing. I wonder if I'll grow to enjoy them in a sexual way in men. At fifty-three maybe not, even if men are consumption items. For my own I have no regrets.

"Regrets?" she replied to a woman who asked. That's always the first thing people want to know. Even sympathetic observers believe the mythology of regretted gender change. "No. Good Lord, would anyone do it if she was going to have regrets?"

Regrets: none, zero, nada. She still had Donald's memories and embarrassed herself a couple of weeks after the operation by reflexively introducing herself to an Australian journalist as "Don." Almost a year after the operation she signed "Donald" in a book inscription. But the habits faded and got reworked. In Australia she started dropping her married life from accounts, especially when it signaled maleness. Yes, she answered to inquiries at the academic conference on eighteenth-century culture at Australian National University, "I" was here in Canberra before, in 1983. Not "we." *Sad.*

It was taking longer to recover than she had imagined it would, and she hobbled around the conference at Australian National unable to stand for a long time or to sit. Lying down worked. So she missed a debate going on over drinks after one of the sessions, a few yards from a couch she was laid out on, though she heard snatches of it. The academic men were of two types, pushy or gentle. The pushy ones were self-important and careerist, "forceful" in the way Donald had thought of himself. One of the pushy men had given a paper that consisted of forty-five minutes of slides of droopy breasts in the art and anthropology of the eighteenth and nineteenth centuries, and all the women, including Deirdre, took exception. The women said: Suppose one of us gave a talk consisting of forty-five minutes of slides of droopy penises? No one could figure out what the droopy-breast man thought he was doing, showing drawings of women with pendulous breasts thrown over their shoulders. At the party the fellow stood there satisfied with himself, with the unreasonable self-confidence certain men have, *io, io,* surrounded by women trying to reason with him. In reply he addressed one woman as "baby," which for some reason she found offensive. He was puzzled. Hey, if I called a black man "boy," would that be a problem? Deirdre noted that not all men, even academic men, treat women as equals. No surprise. She had known it as Donald, but there's nothing like being one.

34

A WOMAN ON HORMONE
REPLACEMENT THERAPY

It's not a career move. One doesn't become a woman to better one's career, not in economics or in most jobs. Arjo told Deirdre that when he was attending a convention in Washington on feminist economics while Deirdre was off in Australia having the operation he was asked repeatedly, "Why is he doing it?" Arjo was startled by the question. In ten months of talking about it with Donald and then Deirdre, he had come to understand that she was doing it because of who she was. You can understand by answering the question, What would you, a fifty-year-old woman, do if you woke up tomorrow and found you had grown a penis? Or if you, a thirty-year-old man, woke up and found you had grown entirely female-looking breasts? You'd get them cut off just as quickly as you could, yes? Damn the expense—which isn't that much, actually.

But economists, whether conservative or radical, think the answer to a "why" question is always "some material advantage." Economists don't seem too smart about identity. Arjo finally realized that the people asking the question thought Deirdre was doing it for some sort of political advantage. He explained gently that she was not, pointing out that it's hard in any case to think what the political advantage might be.

July 6: Starting home from Australia, three weeks after the operation. The main event was a success, though I'm still sore. No great pain. But my digestive system took a week to start up again, so I had some sick, sick days in the hospital, retching violently. I'm still a little feeble. When I left the hospital a week after the surgery I used colored pens that Kate got me to make an International Certificate of Excellence to hang in the nurses' station at Westgate Hospital, thanking them.

The doctor had to use part of my small intestine instead of the ascending colon, because the part of the colon he had in mind turned out to have been damaged decades earlier by a botched appendicitis operation. My tummy tuck made it hard to get up to the small intestines, and the operation was longer and more difficult than usual.

After two and a half weeks of what I took to labeling to women friends as "the mother of all periods," during which the neovagina excreted like mad, it calmed down some. I'll need to wear at least a small pad indefinitely, no hardship, because the intestine, of course, still thinks it's an intestine and secretes a little colorless and odorless fluid. I have to dilate daily for a few months. This is not something you look forward to, although it's not agonizing, either. The idea is to stretch the vagina and keep it open, especially at the juncture between penile tissue and the piece of intestine, until it is thoroughly healed. (The doctors in Holland neglected to tell this to a friend, and her neovagina closed up and had to be reopened surgically.) Then sexual intercourse or dilation two or three times a week will do it. The chore takes about half an hour. Though it's now the most advanced use of my new equipment, it hurts too much now to be pleasurable.

Two months later she was still trying to get the big dilator in. When she forced it the wound would bleed fresh, red blood, so she stopped, terrified. Ten months later, back in Iowa, her gynecologist got her an intermediate-sized dilator (a test tube, actually), and Deirdre went back to it, when she could bring herself to do it. *Will it never end?* Finally her doctor said, "You have enough depth," and she stopped even her infrequent and cautious dilating.

Dr. Haertch's procedure is supposed to give a sensitive clitoris, but with the swelling and then the trouble with the dilation Deirdre was not eager to try it out. People told her of having multiple orgasms even while sleeping. She didn't. She thought perhaps that the unexpected length of the operation had left the neoclitoris damaged in some way. But anyway her libido was low and stayed that way. ***Better.*** Then she would think, ***Unless,*** and turn gloomy.

She went back home to Holland in July by way of another literary conference, in New Zealand, dragging a little less. Her presentation went fine, as had the presentation in Australia. The gender crossing acted as an *exordium*—in the classical theory of rhetoric, the beginning of an oration that fixes attention and claims authority to speak. A woman came up after the New Zealand talk and told what she was going to say to her colleagues back in the Department of English: "I've met an economist, and she's a sweetie." Kind womanhood.

The conference had contrasting films, one by a French filmmaker on his own death from AIDS, another by a woman nurse on the life of a woman with rheumatoid arthritis. Deirdre noted the difference between the two films. It reminded her of the droopy-breast man in Australia. The French AIDS film was emotionless, substituting shock for feeling in the way of male sexuality. The man filmed, for example, an experiment in suicide in which he drank from one of two glasses, one filled with real, deadly poison, the other harmless, after switching and shifting them like a con man doing the three-penny scam. There was a fifty-fifty chance that he would die on camera. It was an event, the macho gesture that high modernism takes for art. If art doesn't shock and revolt you, it isn't worth much. The woman's film, by contrast, was a story, not an event, not *io, io.* Rather, *noi, noi,* we, we. It showed the courage to live a life with arthritis. The wife of a friend in Holland was diagnosed with the disease when Deirdre was there; back in Iowa her roomer, Sister Marilyn, had it and showed the iron courage. The man's film had showed courage of a male sort, bravado, the officers at Waterloo sitting placidly on their horses in plain sight of sharpshooters. The woman's film showed courage of a female sort, endurance, a courage to live and love under a daily weight. Mommy, I need you. Yes, dear, I'm coming.

Deirdre stayed in a remote suburb of Auckland with Steve and Lynn and their grown son, a little younger than her own lost son. Steve had been a research student with Donald in the late 1960s in London. All three were now cheerful and accepting, and Deirdre talked long with Lynn. Said Steve gently, "It's quite something you're doing. I worry about you."

■

Deirdre's brother sent her a wise and beautiful letter. Her brother is the best writer of the scribbling McCloskeys because he is in many things the best thinker, using a sentence as a digging tool, as Annie Dillard says, for picking out the thoughts like coal, an archaeology of self-knowledge. On the operation: "I hope you feel yourself affirmed and know yourself better—*know yourself easier*," which was right. Jamison Green said that people did not see him clearly until they saw him as a man, and Deirdre felt that way: what you see now is me.

■

She was in the hospital in Rotterdam to fix a terrifying stoppage of her urine flow. It was the sixth procedure under general anesthesia since November 1995. Clip, clip, snip, / Woman problem fixed. A middle-aged nurse came in and started removing the catheter.

"Good job!" she said, looking at Haertsch's Australian handiwork. She meant the cosmetic appearance of the labia.

"Thanks."

"I'm like you: I had the operation." Deirdre looked sharply at her. "I mean, I've had a hysterectomy."

So just like me, thought Deirdre, *she has a vagina but no ovaries.* Deirdre was like her, like a woman on hormone replacement therapy after a hysterectomy or menopause. *Goodness,* she thought, *I* am *a woman on hormone replacement therapy*.

FACELIFT

That September, three months after the operation, she went from
Holland back to San Francisco for a conference of the Economic
History Association and a facelift. ***Getting to be a habit,*** she thought,
amused, ***this combining academic work with general anesthesia.*** The conference was held at a resort hotel in the Berkeley Hills, a
swank tennis club officially in Oakland. (One afternoon she went
down with another large-footed woman to the African American part
of Oakland to buy shoes at a favorite shop and to admire the hats they
sold. White men can't jump, and white women can't wear hats.) The
main reason for going to the conference, trekking across the ocean
and the country and back, was to show the flag. For a long time she
believed she needed to prove that her operation had not involved
scooping out her brains; that she was just a woman professor, not a
frightening object.

She was to be inaugurated as president of the Association. It was
glorious, affirming. The previous president was one of Deirdre's
teachers, and at the end of the conference she received the necklace
of office from him.

She talked with old male friends to reassure them and with new
female friends to make contact. Not "contacts," plural, the utilitarian
male idea of friendship, but "contact," singular, affirming an identity.

The women's luncheon out on this pool veranda is charming, Deirdre thought as she sat placidly in the sun, trading minor confidences, laughing at herself, allowing for the needs of other women, dissolving into we. *Noi, noi.*

After the conference she was to have her facelift with Ousterhout in downtown San Francisco. By this time she had settled on the argument for it with other women. It was about security, she explained to one woman after another looking dubiously at her, not about vanity. The facelift would help her pass. Passing is the thing, not beauty. ("Though if beauty comes," she would joke, "I will accept it graciously!") Gail and Alan took care of her the night before she went for the fourth time in a year to the Davies Medical Center in the gay heart of San Francisco. The hospital felt homey. ***It's a good hospital,*** she thought, ***at least compared with the robber barons of the Graduate Hospital in Philadelphia and the*** openhartig ***carelessness of the Frije Universiteit Ziekenhuis in Holland, not to speak of the psychiatric thugs at Iowa and Chicago.*** She slept as at home, now before operation number seven.

The facelift was a bigger operation than she had imagined. It took six hours on the operating table, with a brow lift and lip augmentation, neither of which worked. The next day she shuffled out of the hospital into the care of Gary of the Berkeley "date," who drove her to his home out in the Central Valley. Each time she stayed with friends she made deeper contact with the wives than with the husbands: Linda; Lin; Judy and her mother (Judy's husband Derek was a college roommate; Donald had been best man at their wedding out on Long Island, dancing the hora; now Judy gave Deirdre the hairpieces, for God's neglect); Laura, who had videotaped Deirdre in Berkeley in the spring for a class project; and back to Gail in San Francisco and an afternoon of shopping with daughter Noe in the fancy consignment shops of the North Bay. At the shops the other women took her for one of them despite her apparent encounter with a surgeon's knife, forming tiny relationships the way women do over what looks good on whom, waving good-bye from their cars, inconceivable in the world of men. The pleasantries didn't mean anything, really, Deirdre knew. You couldn't depend on such an acquaintance, of course. But it's nicer to go through life with pleasantries than with the scowls compulsory among men.

Alan drove her at dawn to the airport in San Francisco, her lip still puffed like the monkey people in *Planet of the Apes,* eyes and neck bruised. The battered version of Deirdre got read less. People seemed to think, "Oh, look at that poor woman: she must have been in an auto accident . . . or been beaten up by her husband," then they would look elsewhere. By the time she got back to Rotterdam she was hideous, which was the best disguise. *Three weeks of this,* she thought. *Oh, well. Just look straight ahead, dear, and go about your business.* She made a little sign one day that she wore on her blouse to the cafeteria downstairs in the L Building at Erasmus: "It does *not* hurt!" She learned later that hers was an unwomanly attitude. Most women will not leave the house after a facelift until healing. She had that male self-confidence, her unfair advantage. Looking pretty had not been drilled into her by praise and blame since infancy: "Oh, aren't you *pretty* today!" "Don't you want to be *pretty?*" "Look at that *hideous* dress on that woman!" So she was not ashamed to be strange looking—as long as they saw a strange-looking woman, not a man.

> October: After a week of an unusual amount of being read, which I cannot understand, I had one of my rare middle-of-the-night anxiety attacks. Nothing pathological, just waking up too early and being unable to go back to sleep while thoughts tumbled. Is the genital surgery healing right? Am I just too tall? Will the facelift work? Can I ever get the voice right?

One cold morning she went on the subway to the hospital for her urinary problems and learned that she would have to dilate her urethra for the next year. A urethra she could not find. (She didn't have to at last. After some thousands of dollars her flow was all right, though misdirected as it is for many women. Another little glitch for her money. *No matter. Medicine is not like car repair. Or is.*)

She went back to the office at the university, and after lunch and some work took the subway to the hospital again to get her stitches from the facelift removed. The hospital's architecture, like much of sweet Rotterdam, was brutalist. The doctors found a blood blister and lanced it, but it was going to take two weeks of self-care to heal. *More screwups.* Her hair looked a mess, and she was read a lot on the way home. She felt a drip-drip of anxiety, no one to care, hurrying through the ugly city. At any moment the doctors can tell you news of disaster, thousands of dollars, months of self-nursing, your own dissolution. They are terrifying to speak to, though of course you put up a rational front, as though threats to a normal life were daily and cheerful occurrences. She missed Eugenia, now back in Oklahoma, who would have been there for a cup of tea and a long, feminine plaint.

She got to her flat and looked at the new facelift, the staples and stitches removed, and started sobbing. It was not what she had hoped for. There were still heavy, masculine wrinkles around her mouth. *It's a little better than before, but I'll still get read on a bad hair day.* The lip job had not worked and merely made her face between her mouth and nose thicker without emphasizing her lips. The eyebrow raise had not worked either, and Ousterhout had worried for a while that it had paralyzed a nerve. *For about $15,000 I have got a slightly tighter neck. It was worth maybe a third, a sixth of what I paid.*

After she stopped crying she reflected bitterly: *I am weary of being grotesquely overcharged for medical procedures that don't work. American medicine. They've got to pay for their bloody yachts. A "surplus" of doctors, says the American Medical Association.* The economist sneered. *Funny if there's a "surplus" that the doctors are paid three times what comparable professionals are paid, and have been ever since the AMA started in the 1930s getting medical schools to close.*

The check paying for the procedure with Ousterhout had bounced, in the confusion of bank accounts in two countries, and it went through Deirdre's mind to stop payment on the second try. But she had no animosity toward Dr. Ousterhout, who had so gallantly defended her against her sister, and after all had given her face a woman's bone structure. He had tried. She could not understand why he had failed. *Maybe he's a bone man.* She could push her skin a little with her finger to achieve the result she wanted. *Why couldn't six hours of surgery do the same? Jesus, when will it end?*

In time, in time. The facial operations and the slow effects of hormones, and morning and evening applications of Estée Lauder products by the half gallon, finally left her unread. Two years later she had stopped testing for passing. Almost.

36

THIS IS HOW WE LIVE

Back in Holland that fall she opened a letter from her sister, which to her surprise contained an apology. Sort of. Her sister still believed that what she had done a year before was defensible, even if its outcome was bad. *Not very good, dear: check your manuals on secular stoicism.* But the letter was a start. She called her mother and read it to her. Her mother so wanted her offspring to forgive. Deirdre was cheered enough to vacuum the apartment.

∎

After work on a Friday she had stopped at her colleague Frank's office and he and his wife Lieke ("LEE-keh") and she went to a café for dinner. They bicycled, and Deirdre sat Dutchwoman style on the back of Frank's bike, sidesaddle in her tight skirt. Deirdre had been astonished at the casual way a Dutch woman has of plopping her rump onto the rack of a moving bicycle and then sitting there upright, not even holding on. Her first ride had been on a dark February morning at Arjo's house in Hilversum. They needed to catch an early train, and when Arjo said it was time to go she thought he meant for a fast walk. But he pulled out an old bike and had Deirdre hop onto the rear rack. The bike wobbled through the dawn to the station, Deirdre holding the sides of Arjo's coat, not at all in the stylish Dutchwoman's way.

This time she had seen examples and knew it was possible. Soon she was perched and pretty, not even holding on. Frank's job, besides hauling her weight, Lieke explained, was to warn her of bumps, at which she was to tighten her rump for the shock. The skills of womanhood. Lieke and Deirdre joked with Frank on the one little hill, "If you're a *real* man you'll be able to do this without stopping," and on and up he labored manfully. Lieke said, "That's how you get them to give you diamonds, too." They had a joke about diamonds. The bicycles zipped to the restaurant and then back to Deirdre's flat for decaffeinated coffee and Belgian cookies.

■

The daughter of Gail and Alan from San Francisco, Noe, had been touring Europe student-style, sleeping on the trains with her railpass, and Deirdre promised Gail, woman to woman, that when Noe visited she'd take care of her, seeing that she ate well. Gifted in music and other things, Noe was the same age as Deirdre's daughter. When they were in the tiny kitchen of the flat making spaghetti Noe taught Deirdre how to make garlic toast, and Deirdre taught Noe the trick Mom had taught her last spring about rubbing the oregano between your palms as you drop it into the sauce, a trick Mom in turn had learned from a neighbor. The skills, hints of Heloise or Helen, are passed woman to woman. Men don't do this, because unless you are officially a student you are supposed to know already. It's insulting to be taught. When Deirdre started paying close attention she noticed that being taught was a problem for some young men in college.

■

Deirdre was to come across from the L building at Erasmus to the H building for a couple of months to have an office in Economics. Three departments shared her: Economics, Philosophy, and Art and Cultural Studies. Economics needed some actual presence to ensure that it got its share of the expensive professor. Deirdre's temporary appointment as Tinbergen Visiting Professor was a big deal, and the Dutch newspapers took an interest in who filled the post. Jan Tinbergen, an economist recently dead whom Deirdre had admired since doing engineering economics at age twenty-one, had been the founding father of Erasmus University, merging his Netherlands School of Economics with the same medical school downtown to which Deirdre traveled that autumn. In 1969 Tinbergen had got the first Nobel Prize awarded in economics (four years later his brother got one in medicine), and even before that he had been a national hero, a figure in Dutch socialism. Deirdre was proud to later become a permanent Tinbergen Distinguished Professor at Erasmus, though she criticized Tinbergen and the other giants of economics in the 1940s for leading economics toward the sandbox.

So this morning from her new office in the H building the Very Distinguished Visiting Senior Figure in Economics went to get a cup of coffee from the drip coffeemaker near the sink. *Empty. Some man has poured out the last cup at 9:30 A.M. and walked away. The truth about men: they believe in the coffee-making fairy. Brewed coffee, like ironed shirts or birthday parties for the kids, is a natural phenomenon, social rain.* Oh, well, she sighed, and made the coffee. *In 1996 we do not leave that to secretaries.* From then on the Tinbergen Professor made the coffee, as the senior woman on the floor.

■

She cried. Not "more," because she had hardly ever cried as a man; a few times in the final months of her marriage. The popular notion is that because they don't cry the men are brave or repressed, and in some cultures men do cry more than in the macho West. Ulysses did. Mostly, she thought, it's not moral or cultural but biological. Deirdre's crying started soon after hormones. She usually did not cry for any length of time, but tears were ready in a way they had not been since childhood. She cried of course when she was sad, but also when as a man she would have been angry, blustering, shouting, aggressive. Her medical glitches such as her nonfunctioning vocal surgery or her nonfunctioning urethra or her nonfunctioning facelift often made her cry, as did the chasm between her and her marriage family. But small things, too. Her Dutch landlord's delay would make her want to cry. She would hold back tears at the keyboard over e-mails, at the TV over stories of lost love or sick children. On the plane flying back to Holland after the facelift she cried over the movie *Jane Eyre* between bouts of crying over the novel *How to Make an American Quilt.* Her seatmate, a male biochemist from California, was delicate about it. Along with millions of other women in the world she was sad watching the funeral of Princess Diana, in the coffee room of a motel in Dallas before electrolysis. When the British prime minister read Deirdre's favorite passage from the Bible, 1 Corinthians 13, she wept at the peroration: "Faith, hope, and love, these three. But the greatest is love." She noticed in the coffee room that while their wives watched the TV transfixed the husbands went on reading the sports pages.

Since it was biological, as she thought, she was neither proud nor ashamed. In Holland she watched a film on the BBC about the Battle of the Somme in World War I, in which twenty-one thousand British soldiers were killed outright on the first day of five months of fighting, and she wept at the waste. ***Some mother's boy, some wife's husband.*** A colleague in Rotterdam took a small group to the battlefield itself, a long drive into France in the rain. The battlefield was unimpressive, for the grass had done its work:

> Pile the bodies high at Austerlitz and Waterloo.
> . . . .
> Shovel them under and let me work.
> Two years, ten years, and passengers ask the conductor:
> > What place is this?
> > Where are we now?

But she looked at the monuments and names, thousands and thousands and thousands of British men, whole villages of men named Maclean in the Hebrides, and tears welled. As Donald she had been appalled by the story of the Somme, but never moved to tears. When Donald had taught the big introductory history course at Iowa he had lectured on the battle, finishing with a reading of Wilfred Owen's poem about mustard gas, "Dulce et Decorum Est." "In all my dreams before my helpless sight / He plunges at me, guttering, choking, drowning." She wondered how Deirdre would change the lecture. Not, she hoped, by professorial tears.

∎

She had started to forget what it was like to be a man. She was still certain about some things to tell people—that men live in a world of violence pitted against violence, for example, even if they are middle class and never use it. But she started to forget the actual experience, how it felt. She forgot what it felt like to not understand relationships because you find them boring. Or to feel that you are by rights the local hero. Or to feel that people should serve you. Or most superficially and most fundamentally to think of men as "we" and women as "they." When in a group of men and women, she would listen intently to the other women, join their conversation, giggle self-deprecatingly with them, compliment their jewelry, make mental notes about their clothing, hear out their anxieties about their mothers, their guilt about child care, their fascination with what's sad, and listen with only half an ear to the men standing there boasting to each other and trading data.

So she gave up male privileges. They exist, as she had known theoretically as Donald and as she slowly found experientially as Deirdre, with her girlfriends bitterly emphasizing it. Simone de Beauvoir traces the divergence of privilege to adolescence, especially the emotional shock of menstruation—"I do not have control over my body"—and the increase in the physical strength of boys, and behind their strength the knowledge of manly dominance.

Men, for example, are authorized to stare at women and make any proposals that come into their heads. Men think of the male gaze as cool, tough, assessing. A gentleman doesn't do it, but like brawling and heavy drinking he secretly admires it as manly. Since no woman, however beautiful, is permanently confident of her looks, the male gaze is often painful, much less welcome than men imagine. Anyway it's presumptuous, denuding, taking possession.

A male privilege that men are less conscious of, but that grates on women, is the freedom to wander. The Dutch girlfriend had said, "The streets belong to men." One can see the privilege in their loud and confident behavior in taking possession of the public places. Women enter as guests of the men and walk hurriedly about their business. Women loitering, except to feed the pigeons or to window-shop, are read as sexually promiscuous. As a man Donald could walk directly across the empty park to where he was going; as a woman Deirdre carefully stayed on the proper paths. Violating the proprieties says to men that you are an unusual woman, which excites their interest in a dangerous way.

∎

Deirdre was being driven batty by her hair. She and Lieke agreed that hair talk is the female equivalent of sports talk. Put two women together who don't know each other and they will establish common ground about hair, mainly bad hair. If Deirdre's hair didn't look good she got read, especially before the facelift. She needed simple hair. So she went to a hairdresser in the wealthy neighborhood close by and had them try to curl the hairpiece tight, together with her own now longish hair (wispy on top). The fancy hairdresser below the Oost-zeedijk was her first regular one, a step in normality beyond the cheerful woman from Suriname who worked at the hairpiece salon in central Rotterdam. The owner of the fancy place had just lost his lover to AIDS, and as he worked on Deirdre he talked about his feelings. *Gay men are different.* The employees all read her, of course: a big woman with ugly hair and a manlike voice turns out in fact to be wearing a partial hairpiece. But they were courteous. As she left she reflected: *Fine—it would be better to have most strangers not know, but as long as they treat me like a woman I couldn't care less. It's not about fooling people.* Deirdre had no wish to make anyone a fool. It was about living as who she wished to be. She walked down the Oostzeedijk feeling glamorous for a speech on business economics that afternoon at Erasmus.

But the hairdresser was too conservative, worried about ruining the expensive hairpiece, and in a couple of days the curl was gone. She went back, and he promised to fix it after she returned from a long trip to the United States. In the meantime he showed her how to style the hair using hair spray: comb, tease, spray, tease, comb, shape. Months later she learned that dyed hair is hard to perm anyway. She tried a Tina Turner shag for a while. Then she discovered that it looked all right just pinned up, swept into the clip American women call a claw. For a month she thought the claw needed to be put in horizontally, but finally she got it right. Edith Wharton said, "Genius is of small use to a woman who does not know how to do her hair." Everything is of small use without done hair.

■

Women learn the importance of graceful living. A single woman will keep her apartment clean and will engage in little ceremonies, such as occasionally bringing out the best china. On a visit to Laura in Berkeley she and Laura tried out a few of the best plates. Pretty soon they had redone the table, playing house intently with all the best silver and glassware for a simple evening meal. Straight men view such gestures as all right, maybe, but a trifle silly, don't you think? The women reply, There's nothing silly about treating yourself with dignity. When she got back to Rotterdam from her facelift two women colleagues invited her for an elegant dinner overlooking the Maas from a high-rise, with talk and more talk and the same dignified stylishness. And a few days later she went for a girl-to-girl dinner at Marianne Ketting's house, sipping chablis and talking on the balcony while Rotterdam shimmered in the Indian summer, then a tablecloth and salmon steaks. The women were teaching Deirdre: This is how we live.

37

THOU WINTER WIND

*M*ore trips for Mw. dr. prof. in the cold wet of northwestern Europe, jolly parties and amiable seminars at Brussels, Gothenburg, Copenhagen, then London for a triumphant talk at the Institute for Historical Research, and back to four days in the north of Holland at Groningen for one talk after another organized by a young *vriendinnetje,* Deirdre with a stomachache caused by overindulging in peanut butter, propped up to talk. At Groningen they honored Deirdre with a painting from the school of artists that flourished there in the 1920s, and then with a magnificent party at a house deep in the countryside, among medieval dikes, where Deirdre talked and talked with the women by candlelight over white wine.

Steve had moved from New Zealand to take a job at Dundee in Scotland, and he invited her to come across and speak, to which she joined an invitation to Dublin. At both she gave her talk on statistical significance, which the economists could not understand—at Groningen it had been the last and most controversial talk, and she got into a heated, *openhartig* quarrel with an elderly statistician who didn't grasp what she was saying. "Don't you understand?" she pleaded with him, "You have to *care* about what the numbers say. That's something about your feelings, about you, not about the world. The numbers themselves, necessary though they are as data about which you feel, can't tell you how you feel." He didn't get it, nor did the economists and statisticians at Dundee or Dublin or anywhere else she said it. They would reply, angrily, you are against statistics; you don't like numbers; my scientific life is being insulted. Truly a Cassandra was this Deirdre the Wanderer, cursed like the daughter of Priam warning about the great wooden horse filled with Greeks, to know but not to be believed.

In Dundee Deirdre met a lecturer in psychology, Suzanne, a quick-witted and deep-hearted American, who organized a session with a group of women faculty: "I bring bad news from the other side," Deirdre told them. "The men won't ever get it." The triumph at bonnie Dundee was a colleague's coming up to Steve after Deirdre's scientific talk: "This Deirdre McCloskey, is she related to Donald McCloskey?" *Yes, yes!* High fives. *His smarter sister.*

Then to Dublin, which she found more prosperous than when she had seen it last, three decades before, priest-ridden then and filled with street urchins and bold beggars. Now she strolled an O'Connell Street busy with new money, and she bought a Celtic pin in silver and less advisedly a massive shawl in the earth colors of the North. She stayed with Frank, whose Ph.D. was from Iowa, and Frank's sister Consuela. Con and Deirdre and a friend of Con's talked about what women talk about while Frank played the fiddle and others the harp, tin whistle, and uilleann pipes until 4:00 in the morning. Cormac, a colleague in economic history, got on better with Deirdre than with Donald and took her to a public house for a pint—well, a lady's half in a "snug" shielded from public view. At dinner with five men from the Department of Economics she could sometimes view the scene from the outside, the men playing their cards in the guys' game, and she, bored, watching them. *Why can't they talk about how they feel? They don't get it, this matter of life and friendship.* Another of the cheeky cards that Deirdre and her girlfriends exchanged said on the front, "Women share a special bond, because there are certain things that men can never understand." Open the card: "Life, for example."

■

Suzanne and Fiona from Dundee came across to stay in Rotterdam for a few cold days in December. The three of them traipsed around Rotterdam and Delft in wraps and blankets, Deirdre's purchases in Harrods and Dublin, as three sizes of women: little Fiona, midsized Suzanne, and giant Deirdre. Fiona is a lecturer in law, so they went to The Hague to see the International Court of Justice, closed, and then to a museum and dinner. Mainly they talked the deep women's talk about their lives and loves, and giggled and froze.

∎

She went to back England to give a talk at the London School of Economics, where she had been a student thirty years before. An old friend from the School, who had been awkwardly silent, like many of her male colleagues, was now gallant, walking her back to her little hotel close to Covent Garden. She noticed that when male friends met her and saw that she was after all a woman they knew how to act: pretend Don's a woman. The following morning she bought two jokey teapots in Covent Garden for Trees and Marianne, for the Dutch gift-giving day of December 5, then went up to Knightsbridge to meet a graduate school *doktorbruder* and his wife. Deirdre stood at the Christmas-drenched Harrods corner for some minutes before a woman came over.

Tentatively: "Deirdre?"

"Oh, I didn't see you!" They hugged.

"Deirdre, I wouldn't have recognized you!"

"That's good!"

They had lunch in a pub nearby, then the husband went off on business. The two women wandered down to Sloane Square and went into a department store. Deirdre got no further than the jewelry counter, looking for herself and especially for her daughter, whose birthday was near Thanksgiving. *A little piece of jewelry,* she said to herself. *Just the thing, to make up for God's neglect.* The other woman went off to look at British clothes. Deirdre found a selection of Glasgow-style pins and bracelets, art nouveau in the North. *Perfect for her age,* she said to herself. In as soft a voice as she could manage and still be audible she discussed the matter with a clerk and another woman customer. They did not give her second looks. *It feels so good,* she thought, *gathering with other women, looking for pieces of love.* A month later Suzanne and Fiona gave her a pin of the same style and she was reminded. *At the bottom of my daughter's jewelry box,* she thought, *sits the piece of love.*

∎

It was Christmas morning with Arjo and Marijke. Deirdre would keep an American Christmas among the Dutch. Sinterklas two weeks earlier had been the real present time, Christmas being just Christ's mass, a first day and then a second to accommodate both grandmothers. *But we do things differently,* she thought, imagining her Iowa family. Six hours later, as the sun swept from Holland to Iowa, they would be in their nightclothes around the tree, with cups of coffee, the schnauzers expectant for a present of food. There would be a fireplace burning with wrapping paper, if Donald's wife's new man was there and like most men a pyromaniac. The firestick of the aborigine.

In Holland the night before Deirdre had put her mother's CARE package of presents underneath the Klamers' tree, and now Arjo was acting the American Santa Claus.

"And another for Dee," he said, passing a funny package of one-size nylons, wrapped in the ironically hurried McCloskey style. ***Mom is so nice.***

"Oh, how lovely!" said Deirdre, self-mocking of her American woman's sugar. More little ironies. Then from the biggest package, which she unwrapped slowly, emerged a stylish light brown bag, of soft leather, capacious for the office or the plane. Without irony she gushed: "Oh! How lovely," a tightness in her chest. "How lovely. . . . And a card." She read unfluently: "To my . . . m-m-my . . . my new d-d-daughter." Alone she would have wept at the acceptance.

Later when she called her mother she clumsily did not mention the elegant bag. ***Stupid Deirdre,*** she thought afterward. During her weekly phone call the following Sunday she made sure to praise the bag.

"It's wonderful."

"Yes, such soft leather," her mother noted, and then added, proud of skillful gathering, "It cost $160, but I got it marked down to $90."

"It's wonderful."

Later on that Christmas day, at dawn in Iowa, Arjo proposed that he put in a call to Donald's wife, to see if the family would speak to Deirdre. She grabbed at the notion like bread to a starving woman. She left the room when he called, but she could hear the tone of Arjo's cheer and sympathy through the door.

"They want to wait for three hours," he reported. "They are in the middle of opening presents."

Fine. Good. That's sensible. They are willing to talk. Ob, please, please. But fifteen minutes later a call came from her son. He was being the man.

"Hello, Dad," said her son, distantly, with a hardness poorly done.

"Hello, Son. How are you?"

"Fine, just fine. Everyone's fine." ***He is learning the hardness.***

"That's good. How's your sister? Is she there?"

"Yes, she's here. She's fine, just fine. Everyone's fine."

"Wonderful. And, uh, how's your work?" She could not bring to mind the name of her son's significant other, so she skipped down the conventional list of health and welfare inquiries suited to failing conversations. It was not yet time to mention her son's mother, Donald's wife.

"Fine, just fine." *All right: Herself.*

"And how's Mom?"

Pause. *He's going to do his business.* "Look, Dad, everyone's fine. We don't want to talk. We're just fine."

"Oh."

"We're just moving on."

"Moving on," my ex's phrase, Deirdre thought bitterly. *How brave of you all. We shall erect a monument. Nothing has happened to you, except that someone you said you loved has had the crisis of her life and you are embarrassed and have walked away, leaving a bag of clothes in the madhouse.*

"I understand, Son." And to herself: *Oh, God, I am so sad.*

"We're just moving on. So let's leave it at that."

"Of course. I understand." She tried to pretend this was a real Christmas call. Sad. *But so is he, so is he.* "Thank you so much for calling."

"Yes. Well, good-bye."

"Good-bye, Son. I'm glad everyone's fine."

"Yes. Good-bye." She sat staring out the frozen windows,

When she came out of the room Marijke and Arjo looked hopeful.

"At least he called," said Marijke. "It's a start." *A start. Yes, yes, please, please. A start.*

But she knew it was an ending. "Yes, I hope so," she said for appearance. "A start."

■

And a happy New Year. On New Year's Eve she was invited to a party at the flat of a Dutch woman philosopher up the street. The Dutch shifted to English, and the women were friendly. At midnight all the boys and men, no females, all the male firestick holders, were out on the balcony shooting off rockets, dropping matches that had burned their fingers, letting firecrackers drop just before they exploded. The porch furniture of one flat in a building across the canal blazed, some man playing, and the fire brigade came and put it out. Inside one of the Dutch women said to the other females in perfect English, "Now we know who has the brains around here!" Agreed.

■

One of the few calendar things that Donald had done annually was
to write a Christmas letter, lately as poetry, one year in Dante's terza
rima, another in collected folk lyrics—entries for "Letters We Never
Finished Reading" in the *New Yorker.* At Christmas 1995, in California
hiding, Deirdre hadn't done it. Now for Christmas 1996 from Holland,
sent in January late, she wrote in couplets:

> My Christmas poem takes a measured tone,
> Iambic feet for Christmas spent alone:
> "Alone" in house, at least, though each Dutch friend
> Has joined to cheer me, at beginning's end.
>
> . . . .
>
> A cheerful flat she had near college gate—
> If late she rose, was not to writing late.
> She learned to stroll the city, ride the tram,
> Take trains to Utrecht, and to Amsterdam,
> Participating as a Dutch "Mevrouw":
> Remembrance Day, she curtseyed at the bow.
>
> . . . .
>
> Downstairs until they left in dreary June,
> The Coxes brought their love in cheery tune,
> Eugenia, girlfriends' gossip daily traded,
> And Robert's humor, and the dogs elated.
>
> . . . .
>
> She went with Frank and Lieke to the south,
> Exploring River Schelde, town and mouth.
> She shopped at Lulu's Resale for her clothes,
> Though driven wild by hair (of course) and hose.
>
> . . . .
>
> She wishes you and yours a cheerful season,
> And asks you wonder little of "the reason."
> It's not about some gain or secret pleasure,
> But who we are, from whom we take our measure.
> She's joined the tribe of women, without tear,
> And wishes happiness in *your* New Year.

38

H O M E W A R D

January in 1997 was the coldest for years, and the Dutch had their "Eleven Town Tour," the ice-skating race on the canals of the North. The nation stopped, Deirdre watching the race for eight hours on her TV, from the start before dawn until the first woman finished.

Two weeks to go before Iowa. The boxes of books and clothes made it feel true to her, no theory. Each box should be just under fifteen kilograms (to get the lowest rate per kilogram in the Dutch schedule of postal rates), checked on a bathroom scale she had borrowed from Arjo's house. She thought academically of the loss function and statistical significance. *If the schedule jumped from thirty* cents *per big box to forty cents, instead as it did from thirty* dollars *to forty dollars, the break in the schedule would not be "significant," no matter how accurately the weight was measured. You wouldn't care about it. It wouldn't have oomph. Amazing that my economist colleagues miss the point and have ruined their science missing it. Oh well, it gives me honest employment telling the deaf ears, Cassandra to the Econ.*

Let's see: Get it done, get it done. She moved the boxes artfully, a woman using her hips and the available tables and chairs. Donald would have manhandled them. Yet she injured her back, in the old way, lower left, sharply but not grievously. *It will heal in a couple of days of inconvenience,* she thought. *If someone could treat it now it would heal quicker.* At the twinges of pain she said to herself, *We used to call it the treatment,* bringing hot, wet towels to the back victim, relaxing the muscles. Right to the end Donald and his wife would do it for each other, among a dwindling repertoire of love.

■

The week before she was to go back to Iowa her Dutch friends held a party at Café Dudok in Rotterdam, a grand café in the Continental style where one could nurse a hot chocolate and study the magazines at a long reading table. The Dutch are good at ceremonies, blending plebeian geniality and *haut bourgeois* stylishness. There were joke gifts, such as an apron, a project of one of the woman students, who knew Deirdre struggled with cooking, inscribed with well wishing in indelible pen. Then they presented a pin they had commissioned in silver from a local artist. Three inches long, it was a familiar profile of Erasmus of Rotterdam (he spent more time in Gouda and Groningen, or for that matter Paris or Oxford, yet his place of birth gets the credit), but with a feminine leg in heels flailing out from his—her—robe, knocking down the sand castles. It was Deirdre, visiting professor at Erasmus University of Rotterdam, critic of the silly boys' games in the economic sandbox. She almost held her tears at the Café Dudok, and she wore the pin always when she went to Holland, and at other times with silver.

■

It was a terror to return to Iowa. Off the campus of the university she feared the fundamentalists and the gay bashers. On the campus she feared the radical feminists, with their notion that a "man is invading women's territory" and their ignorant disdain for cosmetic operations to avoid scorning and beating and death.

Her classes started as soon as she got back, an undergraduate class on American economic history, fifty students, and a graduate class on the philosophy of history, ten students. She dressed in a conservative but not frumpy suit to face the big class of undergraduates, explained her situation in the first fifteen minutes, and then dropped it. The students had almost all heard of the gender-crossing professor. She thought again: *The crossing works as an odd appeal to ethos, a character worthy to be heeded, which must be established in the opening lines of any speech.* The stuttering had long had the same effect: My God, people said to themselves, a severe stutterer is giving a speech! Now: A gender crosser!

It did not appear that any student dropped the course out of discomfort. ***Probably as many as drop because of the stutter,*** she thought. ***Admittedly, with too few undergraduate courses being offered the students are desperate.*** A few weeks later she talked to a group of a hundred or so undergraduates at a dormitory, and two of the students tried to raise fundamentalist issues.

"What if I am uncomfortable about what you have done?"

"Don't take my classes. And try to think of Jesus as a God of love, all right?" She said it as kindly as she could, without aggression. These children had one chance to be educated, and respecting their religious beliefs might break through. Probably not, in view of the hatred and ignorance that fundamentalism demands. Later she reread Saint Paul's letters and wondered at the influence of this hard man.

She ate at Givanni's, an Italian place for grownups among the sports bars. The maître d' saw her so many times that he gave her dinner one night without charge. Time to learn more cooking. Put on the Erasmus apron.

Women faculty in various fields expressed their support in the women's way—lunch or dinner, mainly at Givanni's, a full appointment book of Carol F. and Cathy C. and Kathleen F. and Mary T. and Helena D. and Nancy H. and Leola B. and Connie B. and Kim P. and Alice F. and Mary Beth C. But also Alan and Paul and David and Robert and Rich. There was a luncheon group of older women, faculty and wives in one of Deirdre's departments, who embarrassedly asked her over once when they saw her eating lunch alone in Givanni's.

She had an assistant, Deb, as part of a salary agreement years before: give me less money and hire me a half-time secretary of my own. Deb was a young mother pregnant with her second daughter. She had a loving husband and had no trouble with Deirdre's change. Deb grew fierce in defending Deirdre against insult and would toss out letters addressed to "Donald," at any rate the second-class mail unlikely to contain checks. Some of the secretaries wondered about the bathroom question, that American anxiety, but in Deirdre's second week back from Holland the dean's office held a bag lunch for all the female secretaries and faculty in the College of Business, at which Deirdre gave a talk and answered questions and laughed with the other women, and the bathroom question never arose again. The secretaries treated her as a woman in proportion as she acted like one. They had known Donald as all right for a man but below average in grace and consideration. Deirdre was not above average for a woman, but the averages are different. The women faculty brought her into their luncheon groups without fuss. Deirdre slowly learned the American woman's rule of friendly acquaintance: When you run into somebody never rush by self-absorbed, as Donald did; always stop and chat; always be pleased to see the other woman. (Dutch women don't follow the same rule.)

She was worried how the American mailman would treat her, how the dentist and his office staff would treat her, how her car mechanic would treat her, how the exterminator would treat her, how the waiters she knew in Givanni's would treat her, how the staff of Prairie Lights bookstore would treat her. Not at all. She got the usual cheery, Iowa-competent treatment. Paul would ask from behind the order counter at the bookstore, "How can I help you, Deirdre?" and then compliment her outfit. The mailman complained about the ice on her porch, which made lugging the gigantic boxes from Holland dangerous. Deirdre was at first indignant, but quickly not: *After all, he deserves to survive delivering the mail to my house.* She wrote a mollifying note in reply to his angry one and left some cookies for him, and she kept the porch and walk clear. She was being prudent, but more; the world runs on love too. The mailman took to waving at her.

The one tiny nastiness that spring was with the wife of a colleague. The annual banquet in one of Deirdre's departments was given at a cook-your-own steakhouse in West Branch, a teensy place up the interstate, Herbert Hoover's hometown. So Deirdre wore her square dancing outfit, big petticoats and all. *Ironically fun.* As she came into the steamy front of the restaurant she smiled at the department. *Ah, there's Sally,* she said to herself as she hung up her coat. *Nice woman. I'll say hello.* She walked over to the group Sally was standing in and saw at once she was not welcome. Sally wouldn't look at her, and the others were therefore embarrassed. *Good Lord. And for fifteen years I have been pleasant to this "Christian."* Deirdre walked away and had a good time with the rest of the people, the master of ceremonies making jokes about McCloskey's gender change. Later she sent Sally a short note. The religion of Jesus? Consumed with hatred? *Oh, well.* Sally didn't come to the banquet the next year.

And professionally, what would they say? Some man in an interdisciplinary program at the University of Chicago had invited Donald for the spring of 1996, when Holland intervened, but he did not renew the invitation to Deirdre for the spring of 1997. That was Deirdre's fear. But she had been invited two years before as Donald to speak at Western Michigan University in Kalamazoo, and a professor there had renewed the invitation as soon as Deirdre came out to the profession. A class act. Deirdre therefore promised to come to Kalamazoo as soon as she got back to the United States. They put her up at a classy guesthouse and treated her to classy entertainments, and she tried to give classy talks. The little university in the city with the funny name (local T-shirt: "Yes, there actually is a place called Kalamazoo") exhibited more class than Big Deal University in non-funny-sounding Chicago. Nothing was predictable. "Conservative" economists had not missed a beat. The folk of Iowa had acted like sophisticates. The sophisticates had attempted to lock their former faculty member in a madhouse. The sister had acted like a righteous and dogmatic brother, the brother like a sympathetic and flexible sister. Up was down, south was north.

Deirdre was invited that first spring home to give scientific talks at Indiana University and Ohio State University, and at both she also talked to groups of women faculty about her experience. The women, including Deirdre, found it interesting. Groups of academic men could not face such an embarrassing, personal subject. Politics, baseball, postmodernism, the latest joke—*anything* to avoid it. The academic women could face another life and would turn their intellects to What is a woman?

The graduate students at the University of Wisconsin, and particularly the women, invited Deirdre to speak. She slipped over to Madison by plane through Chicago, a reprise as Deirdre of Donaldish activities: he had spoken to the graduate students a few years before, and Deirdre's father had been an alumnus, her sister an alumna. Deirdre felt she belonged. At Wisconsin she spoke about statistical significance to a large and puzzled audience and chatted at lunch with the women graduate students about academic life. The young women used the occasion to talk about how to be both a human and an economist, not easy in a boyish little science. While Deirdre was speaking a woman professor at Wisconsin, who was spending the year abroad and didn't know what the luncheon was about, sent a furious e-mail of protest, on principle. This "Deirdre" should not be allowed to speak to the women graduate students on being a woman economist, she said. What does Deirdre know about that?

Thank you, dear. Not all women were welcoming. A Theory would drive them mad, poisoning the natural grace. A woman economist on the listserve called FemEcon declared in the spring of 1997 that Deirdre was neither man nor woman. Thank you, thank you, thank you very much. The welcoming world of radical feminist women, second wave.

Deirdre learned that a tiny group of separatist feminists of the second wave, such as Mary Daly, Germaine Greer, Andrea Dworkin, Catherine Millot, Heather Draper, and Janice Raymond, make a point of persecuting gender crossers. The slogan of the lesbians among them is "No scent [that is, perfume] and no transsexuals." The separatist feminists regard male-to-female crossers as not, in essence, women. That means they are to be excluded, though feminists of the first wave, among whom Deirdre counted herself, or of the third, would say on the contrary that the Essential Woman is itself the problem. If women are essentially this or essentially that, by a biology locked in at birth, it is hard to see how feminism or anything else can ameliorate their condition. It would be nature all the way down, or so the radical separatists seemed to be supposing. At the Michigan Womyn's Music Festival in 1991, as Pat Califia recounts it, "In what must have been a frightening display of force, security guards ejected [a postoperative crosser] from the festival grounds at midnight, without allowing her to contact her friends or collect her belongings." Califia, a genetic female lesbian who defends gender crossers in her book *Sex Changes: The Politics of Transgenderism,* spoke of her own realization that something was wrong with books like Raymond's *The Transsexual Empire:*

> When it first came out, I read it cover to cover. There were all the things that had been inside my head. But on paper, in black and white, they looked so ugly. No matter how I tried to rationalize it, I couldn't make myself believe that the presence of a transsexual woman ruined a women's event or spoiled a lesbian organization. . . .I didn't want to ally myself with people who were obsessed with hate. I knew what it was like to be hated. . . .It felt wrong to me, as a working-class queer who understood oppression on a survival level, on a street level, to yank the rug out from under somebody else's feet.

■

People say, "I can't understand it!" Sometimes they mean, "That's weird and I disapprove of it." How sad for you, this hateful prejudice. Perhaps you should get some therapy. Sometimes they mean that they can't see themselves wanting to do it. Yeah, right. But other traits of character or preference are equally hard to imagine as one's own, a taste for chocolate ice cream or a toleration for Bauhaus architecture. "How can you *stand* Louis Kahn's addition to the Yale University Art Gallery?" And sometimes they mean that they find gender crossing odd but are willing to listen without a hateful theory. Yes.

39

C O S T S

Ninety thousand dollars. That was the money cost, far above the $20,000 or so for electrolysis and the operation that constitutes the minimum for crossing male to female all the way. An economist would predict that if the monopoly restrictions arising from the Benjamin Standards and the Johns Hopkins–influenced psychiatrists disappear, and if laser hair removal becomes cheaper as it becomes more common, the cost could fall a good deal: perhaps to $10,000 in total some day. That's a debt paid off in five years at about $53 a week, if your credit is poor, ten hours a week at the minimum wage. People finance cars at that level.

The $90,000 for Deirdre was grotesquely higher than the minimum because she had cosmetic surgery and voice surgery from the best, with a lot of surgery to fix their surgery, and because her sister had so courageously opposed it, adding some $25,000 to the bill, and because Deirdre wanted it all to be over quickly. Had she paid every extortionate bill generated by her sister's intervention or by the insurance fraud of hospitals there would have been an additional $22,000. As it was, she battled the hospitals for years. It was like purchasing a top-end Mercedes rather than a Ford, and not bargaining, and then being sued in the middle about one's right to make the purchase, and then being cheated by the car dealer.

But economics correctly teaches that "cost" is not these money costs. It is what you sacrifice by taking the path. Two roads diverged in a yellow wood, and you chose one at the sacrifice of the other. Well, then, Deirdre sacrificed the $90,000 worth of things that could have been bought. A little earlier retirement. A much better car.

But the biggest cost to Deirdre, not to be measured, was the sacrifice of wife and son and daughter.

And cost to whom? Economics also teaches that question: Cui bono, to whose benefit? It was certainly not a benefit to Deirdre's marriage family, in their reckoning. As they accounted it, they paid the cost.

However accounted, they *were* the sacrifice.

■

Donald's wife was angry and ashamed that Donald had become Deirdre. When Deirdre came back to Iowa after the Dutch year and asked to meet, Donald's wife promised, then could not, then would not. Every few months Deirdre would appeal by e-mail across campus: Please, please, just a mild, normalizing chat. Thirty years of marriage. A good marriage. What did I do wrong in all that good time? Please. So we don't meet in the ladies' room. Please.

No. You have hurt me. You did wrong. It's weird. I don't do weird. You should be ashamed. I am ashamed. I can't handle it. No, no, no.

The way she thought of it, she had lost what Deirdre had gained. It was zero-sum, and as Donald/Deirdre became happier the other became more miserable, until she had to break contact. She divorced, she would not meet, she moved to another town, she never shopped in Iowa City. No other contact. It was embarrassing. Mortifying. Wounding. Donald's wife thought of the loss as a death—except that there across campus sat the murderess, alive and happy and unpunished. It was worse than a death. Had Donald died of a heart attack at age fifty-three, as his father had, the wife would have acted the widow for a while, sad to see her life's companion leave, dignified in her grief. But, for God's sake, he became a woman. Deirdre tried to imagine her feelings. Donald's wife would not speak or write, and Deirdre was inexperienced at a woman's imagination. *She feels that her marriage was meaningless. "Was I married all those years," she asks, "to a woman? What does that make me?"* A woman raised in a small town in the 1950s was not relaxed about homosexuality. She felt the crossing made thirty years of her life meaningless. Yes, worse than a death.

For months Deirdre was circumspect when attending committees of the university or passing the Nursing Building on her way to work or shopping for groceries at the Hy Vee. Would she encounter Donald's wife? Couldn't they just acknowledge each other and then go about their lives unrestricted? Deirdre would check the aisles in the grocery store quickly before shopping. At length she realized that her former wife had shifted everything out of Iowa City and only worked there. Deirdre was startled once to see their old car at a distance, with Donald's wife driving to her new home.

■

Their son, a businessman in Chicago, late twenties, was also angry and ashamed. After several months of e-mails in the turbulent fall of 1995, arguing that becoming a woman was irrational, he wrote by e-mail that he would not open letters, would not read anything, not anything at all. Deirdre tried postcards for a while, probably unread; e-mails, probably unread; finally the titles of e-mails, saying "I love you" in a place he could not fail to read.

Silence. Deirdre thought, *Men feel no duty of love, except to those assigned to them by some exchange of favors, and toss love away lightly.* Her friend in Australia, Kate, had one out of three who continued loving. *No, no; not my son.*

A year's silence, and then she returned from Holland hopeful. *Surely now I am home I can heal my broken family. Surely they will love me as they did.* On a night a few weeks after Deirdre's return to Iowa that winter an e-mail appeared in the list from her son.

Wonderful! He's writing! Praise the Lord, she thought as she scrolled through the list and highlighted the title and pressed Return.

No, said the message. I was married last week. Full ceremony. You were not of course invited. This is all I will say.

Married. Not invited. To the wedding. Later she would remember, waking at night with his words, or catching sight of his photo in the upstairs hallway, age three, the little blond boy smiling up at the camera.

That summer in the dining room of the Iowa house during a fit of womanly cleaning Deirdre found his baby cup inscribed with his initials. She knelt a long time in front of the open cabinet, rocking. She would write to her son's new wife. She got up clutching the cup. Surely another woman will understand.

No answer.

Six months later her son returned a final letter from Deirdre unopened, unable to endure Deirdre's plaint, and wrote passionately, this one and last time. You have betrayed me, he said. Love is an exchange.

Men's talk, Deirdre said to herself as she read. **Yet even in such manly terms,** the economist thought, **I stand ready to exchange. No takers.** Deirdre's mother comforted her in the stoic way, "You must expect this in a divorce. The children go with the mother."

■

Deirdre believed her daughter, early twenties, was more hopeful. People said, It will be easier on a daughter. She lived in Lawrence, Kansas, a college student. Deirdre supposed that she did open the monthly letters, with the little presents and the accounts of Deirdre's travels, cheerful invitations to visit at their old home in Iowa City, or to come along on Deirdre's business trips to Europe, a communication every month for a year in each epistolary form. Deirdre remembered a trip to England the two of them had taken when her daughter was twelve, lining up for the Hard Rock Café in London, walking the haunted stones at Avebury, punting on the Isis, father and daughter.

She did not answer. She had learned about the gender crossing two months after her brother did, late in the fall just before Deirdre went to San Francisco and then in the new year to Holland. She had sent one letter, pleading with her father not to do what he intended. She viewed it then as a failure of duty. **How far does duty extend?** Deirdre would wonder. **To avoid their self-defined hurt from embarrassment am I to refuse my life? They could be proud and loving, as my mother is, as many friends are. Instead they are ashamed, making everything worse.** After her one letter the college student wrote nothing, though taking $10,000 a year in support. At one point Deirdre looked into the law of child support and contemplated cutting her off. Once she did, and the bank made it worse by not restarting the transfers when she thought better of it, but then she paid in full with interest, ashamed of the unstoical act. **I'm as confused as my son: love, Deirdre, is not an exchange. No parent with sense expects to be paid back in any coin.** During the two phone calls Deirdre made when back to Iowa she ended by crying, which her daughter did not like. Silence.

Yet Deirdre was hoping, hoping. **Children are that way. I was,** she thought, though the truth did not relieve the throbbing. A woman friend said, "There is nothing more focused on itself than a twenty-something child. It's genetic, not moral. Believe me: I've known a half dozen of them well." Deirdre thought, *I said in effect to my mother at my daughter's age, "See you around, Mom." It's the same.*

Six months back in the United States after the Dutch year, twenty-one months into womanhood and twenty-one months of silence from her daughter, Deirdre wrote again.

> My dearest daughter,
>
> I'm awake at 3:30, unable to sleep. It doesn't happen much. I got back from Mexico and the conference there with a cold and a case of traveler's diarrhea. What really got me up was the ache about you.
>
> You are my only spot of warmth, I hope.
>
> I will be in Kansas later in July for a couple of days, visiting my friend Patty's family in Topeka. I could visit you in Lawrence. A brief meeting, on neutral ground if you want, would be healthy. It would show you that I am presentable and that I love you.
>
> I wonder how you are doing, how I might help. I worry that in turning away from me you may leave yourself regretting later a lost chance to help your parent in need. I regretted not more vigorously trying to help my mother when she was left with two bratty teenagers to raise after my dad died. And in a smaller matter I regretted not visiting my dad in hospital years before when he was sick with appendicitis—it was in a Boston suburb, when I was in college in Cambridge six miles away, and though I didn't have a car I could have gone often. I only went once, with my mother. In both cases (and others: how much cause for regret a human life contains) I hurt myself, by not assuming an adult role for my mother and by not getting closer to my father in his illness. It was intrinsically bad, bad for my soul; and it was imprudent, too. It gave me less of a life.
>
> But all this aside, I love you and want to meet. Can't we?
>
> Love,
>
> Deirdre and Dad

No answer.

■

A few weeks later Deirdre and Patty approached Lawrence in the car on the way from the Kansas City airport to Topeka.

"We've got to stop," said Deirdre.

Patty looked at her. "I don't think it's a good idea. Are you sure?"

"Yes. I'll go in for just a few minutes."

"If she's home. She might be in class."

"It's summer, Patty."

"Yes. But she might not be there."

They found her daughter's address, a worn frame house with a big porch on Kentucky Avenue, divided into three student apartments, and Deirdre ached. *Please, please, dear God.* Deirdre was by this time attending church, and her prayer was more than a figure of speech. She knocked. No answer. She could feel her heart pounding, the weakness. *Oh; wrong door. Hers must be the side apartment.* She went around the porch and knocked. *Wait; no rush; polite.* The cicadas twanged and the air-conditioning roared. Kansas hot. She knocked again. *Not so loud; this isn't a police raid.* Then she tried the door. *Careless; it's open.* She stepped in and called in her new, soft voice from the operation two months before.

"Hello! It's me!"

No answer. The air-conditioning, the disordered student apartment. One room far at the end had the door closed. Deirdre stood in her sundress. *These three,* she thought sardonically, out of tune with her anxiety, *must be the only people in the world who haven't seen me. These I love more than anyone. Is my hair all right? Oh, I wish, I wish she would love me.* Tears. She called again, standing tentatively. *Please. My little girl.*

The door of the far bedroom opened slowly and her daughter shuffled out, wrapped in a blanket as when she was a toddler in the Chicago house coming out of her room at the head of the stair dragging the cozy.

"Oh, no!" she said when she saw Deirdre, "No! I can't handle this!"

"Please, just a few minutes of talk."

"I can't handle this! *Please* go away!"

"Oh, please. It would be so much better if we could talk."

Her daughter seemed weary, not hostile. "No, no. I can't handle it. I can't."

"All right. All right." *It's not going to work,* and Deirdre's hope deflated. *Why should she handle it? It's my life, not hers. Patty was right.* "I'll go. But please, please give me a hug." Her daughter didn't like it. "Please." Deirdre was crying. "My little girl." Her daughter was reluctant, but accepted the hug. Not in the repulsed way. *Not eagerly, exactly,* Deirdre said to herself, *but not repulsed. At least not repulsed.*

"Good-bye, dear. I love you." *She needs to separate as adult children anyway do. Maybe when she has her own children. My God, my God.*

"Good-bye, Dad."

Her daughter changed her phone number and moved to a new address. *Maybe it's just the college student's usual change of apartment with every new year, one step ahead of the rent collector. Maybe it's not repulsed shame.* Donald's wife would not give their daughter's new address. Her daughter didn't want to give it. The phone number was listed under her roommate's name. Embarrassment. *Remember: it's not hatred, and cannot be called that in fairness. Oh, God.* Her son moved too, with his wife by now perhaps pregnant with Deirdre's grandchild. *That would feel more like hatred, to be kept from my grandchild.* Later her son's wife was in fact pregnant, and they tried to keep the knowledge from Deirdre. "I am not authorized by him to tell you," said the ex-wife. *My grandchild. Have you no mercy?* On Saint Patrick's Day of 1998 a grandson was born. Deirdre learned of him nine months later.

But try to feel it as they do, she would tell herself. *Would you do better? Did you?* Donald's wife would not give either child's address. She was stern in forwarding two last pleading notes to the children: All right, "*but*—I will not do this again. If you send me notes to them, I will discard them." *No, no, please, no. I understand your belief that it's best to walk away without loving remembrance from three decades of life. For yourself, you think. But how am I to speak to my children? My grandchild?*

■

Deirdre talked to an elderly neighbor about her mother's disapproving of her marriage to a non-Lutheran.

"She wouldn't speak to me for years after."

"Not speak to you? That's terrible. How many years?"

She reckoned it up. "Thirty."

■

Much later Deirdre talked to Carol about it.

"Your son deserves a more heroic role in your story," said Carol as they finished eating the luncheon salad she had assembled out of leftovers. Deirdre admired Carol's swift efficiency in the kitchen and tried to help by closing cabinets and wiping counters and filling the dishwasher, the unskilled assistant.

"What, for abandoning his father?"

"No, for *not* abandoning his mother and his sister—assuming the role of the man of the family. After all, you had given it up."

Deirdre slumped on the high stool at the counter.

She's right. At my son's age I walked away from my father in the hospital and then from my widowed mother with her teenage children. These are my own stories to my daughter.

"Good Lord, Carol, you're right." *It's only fair that my son and daughter support their mother: she has lost in this. True, she left me, and the children left with her, as much as I wished them to stay.*

But I left her.

Yes, she would think when turning it over again and again, *that's true. But why answer loss with loss, insult with years and decades of reinsults, the hater the loser? Why punish, and make everyone worse off?* the economist thought, *the punisher worst punished? As we forgive those who trespass against us.*

And yet, I have sinned, thought the novice Christian. Her head ached with the complexities. *Mine was the first leaving. We sin against our lovers. The cost of love is sorrow, because it must end in death, literal or figurative. Yet one must love, because "from love one can only escape at the price of life itself," wrote Freya Stark. Are my former wife and my children damaging their lives by their unloving escape? Love is risky, yes, for the endgame is sorrow. But "no lessening of sorrow is worth exile from that stream of all things human and divine."*

And, the professor would think, *it has politics. On a small scale. I didn't do my duty in the civil rights movement of the early 1960s or the antiwar movement of the late 1960s or the gay movement of the 1970s. It would be shameful,* secular stoicism declared, *not to stand up this time.* The rhetoric of the families of the crossgendered or homosexual or Buddhist or whatever is one of victims, but victims not because they are beaten or starved or unloved but because they cannot *bear* the shame. In 1945 a Jew marries a Lutheran and both families say, "Why have you done this to us?" Done this. In 1955 a white man marries a black woman and the families say, "Why have you done this to us?" To us.

In 1995 a lesbian marries her lover in a ceremony in the redwoods, described in Ellen Lewin's book on gay and lesbian marriages, *Recognizing Ourselves: Ceremonies of Lesbian and Gay Commitment.* Muriel's daughter is loving, but her two sons will not bring their families:

my older son called and said he and his wife didn't feel that their children should be exposed to that kind of thing. But he himself would be glad to come. . . . And then followed an hour or so later by my other son with a similar story. . . . I called them both back the next day and told both of them I didn't want either one of them at the ceremony if that's the way they felt.

Lewin continues: "Muriel reminded her sons that . . . as a young white woman marrying a black man in the 1950s she . . . had not given in. . . . She thus found her sons' conventional attitudes particularly ironic."

Deirdre listened, touched, to Lewin telling the story in a public reading at Prairie Lights bookstore. A month later she heard on the radio the story of Billy Tipton, the jazz musician born Dorothy, who from 1928 lived as a man, five times married, adopted children, no one knowing, not even his wives. His wives forgave him when they learned, much later: Billy was a pretty good husband, though with a roving eye. But his son was *angry* hurt. Because Billy had been a bad father? No, because he had been Dorothy. Huh?

And finally, prudence and politics aside: *Let it go, Deirdre. Grow up.* Secular stoicism spoke, or in more sophisticated form her new Christianity. The world contains evil, as the widow learns or the unloved wife learns or the spurned father learns. Deliver us from evil. The evil's there. Donald's wife learned this, and her children did, her sister did, and Deirdre learned it too. *For thine is the kingdom,* Deirdre prayed, *thou God of grownups.*

40

IOWA DRAG

She called the president of Iowa Artistry and got the date of the next meeting. Driving to the motel took her back to her crossdressing year, but now she had no compunction about asking the clerk where the meeting was. He read her as a man in a dress, but she knew better and tripped off down the hall. The meeting, it seemed to her, was a meeting of men, with the usual manly challenges and interruptions. She met two gender crossers, one she had known before and another who had heard of her through the newspaper coverage. Both were intent but at an early stage. The new acquaintance was with his wife. He was important in his little town, a forceful man of about thirty-five, with children. Deirdre talked to husband and wife and thought the situation hopeful. The wife was after all attending the meeting with goodwill; the husband was open to compromise, some tiny bit. They seemed to be taking a different route than Donald and his wife had taken. Hope. But a month later, she heard, their marriage reverted to a hateful dissolve. Deirdre speculated that the relatives couldn't take it and brought pressure on the wife to become nasty. Not that the wife herself didn't have a complaint. It's the tragedy: both sides are right, though both hurt. Sin in the world.

■

Deirdre was asked to give a talk at the local community college, Kirkwood, and she spoke to a full auditorium in her brownish purple dress and brown mock alligator shoes, standing and delivering up to the back rows. She had not prepared much, but she felt energized by the audience. "When I was fourteen years old," she began, in her standard way of preparing an audience for her stutter, "I would fall asleep with two prayers." She aimed at the big boys in the back row, football player sorts: "You are looking at the captain of her high school football team." Laughter. "A very small high school and not a very good team." Still the football players left early. *There's something broken in the masculinity of American men,* she thought as she watched them leave, *which shows in unease and gay bashing and homophobia.* Donald could never understand the animus.

■

She looked for a church. If the First Baptist Church of Berkeley was so good, surely hip little Iowa City would have one like it. The Episcopal church downtown proved welcoming. The balance of tradition and progress in it was pleasing to a historian of England. You can't read English history or English literature from Henry VIII to T. S. Eliot without learning more than you realize about what it means to be an Anglican ("Episcopalian" was the euphemism chosen by Americans during the Revolution to avoid sounding English while fighting them). At Trinity Church the music was good, the priest welcoming, the congregation calm and happy. She was often moved to tears by the atmosphere of love and piety. *Episcopalians in America tend to be hoity-toity,* she thought. *The frozen chosen. The hoity-toity don't need to be rigid or hateful or sneering to feel saved, unlike some separatist feminists and some American fundamentalists.* The next Sunday she tried another church she thought would be welcoming, but it was not. A colleague and his wife were serving the coffee that day, but they did not greet her. The strange silence of many. *It's like having cancer. Not that I reached out when Bob's wife had it.*

■

An instructor at Iowa's Department of Speech Pathology sent Deirdre an e-mail and arranged for her to come into a class to talk about the problems of her speech defect. A baritone is not a speech defect in a woman? It is if you have it, Deirdre replied. In the class the instructor mentioned the local production of the French farce about a gay couple, *La Cage aux Folles,* opening in a couple of days, and Deirdre volunteered herself to go in their party. On the night she wore her blue sequined gown from drag days. As she came into the County Fair cattle barn where the theater was set up, she paused: she had expected other people to be dressed campily, but her sequins stood out among the blue-rinsed ladies from the retirement homes. No one seemed to mind, though, and not even everybody read her. Afterward someone in the cast said to her, "We should have used your dress in the show!" She had a snapshot taken in the lobby with her hairdresser, who played a "cagelle," one of the chorus. *Oh, to have his body,* she thought. *And he doesn't even want to be a girl.*

Afterward there was a dance and fashion show at the university Student Union, a gay rights celebration. It was mainly college kids just now realizing their homosexuality, not much different from college kids just now realizing their heterosexuality. A lot of being cool and looking around. It started at 10:00 P.M. at a decibel level that hurt. Still Deirdre danced, as she had learned at Temptations two years before. It was her duty as a professor to be comfortable, to show the kids that they need not be afraid. *I hope.*

She stayed for part of the fashion show, featuring local merchandise. It was odd to hear the mistress of ceremonies, a strikingly beautiful drag queen named Mercedes, announcing outfits from, well, mah cou-tour-i-ay, Jay Cee Penn-ay. Looking at Mercedes, whose voice was good, too, she thought, *Would I have been happier to cross thirty years earlier? It's a counterfactual impossible to explore,* the amateur philosopher replied sagely, *since I would have been another person.* Donald had a good life as a man, with a good marriage and two good children. But had he been as pretty as Mercedes the temptation would have been strong. *Hmm. Four inches shorter and I would have. When exactly?* It was hard to imagine its being possible in anything but the company of prostitutes in the 1960s, when she was Mercedes' age.

■

A few days later she participated in a class on human sexuality with three crossdressers and another gender crosser from Iowa Artistry. It was to be in the Nursing Building, and Deirdre walked into the building apprehensively, expecting at any moment to run into Donald's wife or a colleague. But the class started at 6:00 P.M., with Deirdre running to make it from a Ph.D. presentation in Economics across campus, and the nursing professors had gone home. *Good Lord,* she thought, *when are we going to meet? In the ladies' room, I suppose.*

The presentation to the class said, We're humans. Yes, this could be your father. Honor thy father and thy mother. Deirdre and the other presenters had a bet among themselves about how quickly a student would ask the bathroom question. It was the third question asked, about average. The football team was in the back row and having a hard time. These boys are cast as heroes of American machodom, and machodom has a problem with gender. Perhaps because it is as ignorant as a post, machodom does not realize that armies and navies and sports teams from Achilles and Patroclus through Nelson's navy to the Gulf War have been built on homoeroticism. Or maybe it does realize it.

Deirdre was familiar with the guys of the last row in large classes. They convey to the other students that it's dumb to pay attention to this stuff, and we cool guys don't. Donald had once thrown out one of the stars on the football team from a four-hundred-person economics class and told him not to come back. "Thrown out" by Uncle Donald's tough words, not literally, for the boy weighed 250 pounds of muscle. Now she thought: *I wonder what Aunt Deirdre would do with such a boy? Probably a little sarcasm, for which I'll be called "that queer bitch." A man gets away with the tough-guy approach to a large audience.*

During the class her eye kept falling on a particularly pretty young man in the second row: *Wow, would he look good in drag!* After the presentation and questions the young man came up and thanked her and introduced himself. He was Mercedes from the fashion show and ball.

■

She was surprised to read homophobic letters from alumni in the *Harvard Magazine,* reacting to a coming-out piece about gays at Harvard, and noted that the virulent ones were from the frightened macho generation, classes of 1946 or '52 or '60: "Does the *H* on my sweater now stand for homosexual?" *You great twit, wearing an H on your sweater.*

■

She spoke in Ames for Coming Out Day at Iowa State. Be not afraid. The 1950s are over. Mostly. *Please, dear Lord.* She delivered the speech in the Student Union at Iowa State to a crowd of several hundred and got the spirit:

> Understand that you will lose people whatever you do in life.
> Any choice that changes your presentation will annoy or

frighten someone. You go to college and find that the people who stayed home to work full time at Casey's are no longer comfortable with you. You marry outside your religion, or move to another part of the country, or do not go into farming as your dad wants you to, and you're going to get some people mad at you.

I say to you: Live your life in a loving but courageous way, combining the feminine and the masculine virtues.

This Sunday I will be baptized in the Episcopalian church. You're all invited: 10:15 service at Trinity Church on Gilbert Street in Iowa City. It's another coming out, which goes on and on, in joy and trepidation. It will be wonderful to be baptized as Deirdre.

When at last we have all come out, when the closets are used for keeping clothes instead of people, when all the hatred based on stupid fear is dissipated, we will all have got our prayer answered, the prayer of identity:

Let us be who we are, dear Lord.
Please, God, let me be the person you made.

41

PROFESSORESSA

She had gone on a weekend in the spring to see friends in New York, staying at their elegant apartment, a floor of a building on Sutton Place with a view of the East River. The two women exhausted themselves scouring a consignment shop on Madison Avenue, then the three of them went to the Statue of Liberty, talking, talking, with breaks for Deirdre to weep at Emma Lazarus's words on the base of the statue: "Give me your tired, your poor, / Your huddled masses yearning to breathe free." Deirdre knew the poem from her father's recitations and from visiting the statue thirty years earlier, when Donald and his wife had climbed the stairs inside the torch. This time she visited Ellis Island too. *The exhibition is unimpressive,* she thought, but then she entered the hall of photographs and stood looking up at the fragments of crossings. A letter in Italian. A passport. A wedding. Fenoaltea. Guptill. Walsh. Ujifusa. In each new class she liked reading out the names of the students, the mixtures of Spanish and Russian and Dutch names, in Iowa mainly German and Scandinavian, and wanted to convey to the students what a fine thing it was, this nation of crossers. Here she stood before the walls of photographs in tearful thought: *People say to me, "How courageous of you." Yeah, sure. These immigrants were really so, crossing from Chinese village or Polish shtetl to Oregon and Chicago.* "Send these, the homeless, tempest-tost to me: / I lift my lamp beside the golden door." Deirdre bought a life and letters of Lazarus and noted what Henry James called her "philosophical mind" and her womanly courage.

■

After school was out Deirdre was invited to give lectures at the University of Catania in Sicily, and she set off with trepidation. Sicilians are short; Italians are fanny pinchers. *First time pinched.* The trip was quick and jolly under the shadow of Mount Etna, and she was delighted when they called her at her encouragement "professoressa," the feminine of the occupation and euphonious *alla Italiana.* She was sick one day from the change of water. The pictures of her sitting with two Italian academic men in a café in Taoromina show a large, tired American lady with a strained smile, with Etna in the background. Second time as Deirdre with traveler's upset.

The John Adams Institute in Amsterdam, which sponsors lectures by American intellectuals, had asked her to speak one evening that week, so she went to Amsterdam by way of Milan and found herself passing. In little Holland with the publicity of her Dutch year she was known. The speech in an elegant old hall was about her transition and its connections with her thinking about bourgeois virtue and the vices of economists. A Dutch member of Parliament commented, and the discussion was lively. Dutch people are like New Yorkers—they listen eagerly to Chautauqua-type speeches and to do so will travel halfway across their country—that is, for an hour. The chair was ending the proceedings when a slim middle-aged woman came up to the question microphone and stood waiting.

"Mevrouw," the chair inquired politely, "do you have a last question for our panelists?"

"Not a question, exactly." The voice was distinctly male. *Good Lord, another gender crosser.* "I am a lawyer here in Holland, once a man. I want to congratulate Professor McCloskey for speaking out."

Deirdre hurried down from the stage and embraced her.

And then to Copenhagen for a meeting of a board for a new department of philosophy and management. She was flattered to be classed with the big-name Stanford theorist of management on the board, who was gallant, and she met an elegant Italian man and numerous tall Scandinavians. The women things were special, such as going with another woman to a cobbler to get Deirdre's heel repaired, and making a meal after the meetings with two other women, peeling potatoes, cooking, washing up, talking, talking about love and life. She lolled in the lovely talk, absent from the sports-jarred, businesslike, back-slapping, love-frightened dealings of nongay men in America. *They have no idea what they're missing,* she thought as Barbara and Guje and Deirdre talked and laughed.

She went back to Holland for two days, jumping off tram number 1 at Prinsengracht to go for interviews at the University of Amsterdam Press, especially a TV crew shooting a story for a midday Dutch program. When she got to the Press she reached in her purse and found her wallet missing. *Oy vey.* First time as Deirdre ripped off. A Swedish friend had had her bag stolen seven times in Europe. *Better than being raped and murdered in America,* she thought as she cursed the subtle thieves of Amsterdam. She remembered that as she boarded the tram she had transferred 500 guilders, about $300, from its bulkiness in her wallet to the inside pocket of her briefcase, the one her mother had given her last Christmas, so the money was safe. Still, the horrid inconvenience: *and my passport!*

The TV crew took her to the local police station to report the theft. Routine, the policeman said in his English: on the trams, especially from the Central Station, you need to watch; keep the flap of your handbag closed and turned inward, which Deirdre then always did in railway stations and undergrounds in Amsterdam or Chicago or New York. *Not so pretty that side out,* the handsome leather bag from Joel's day in The Hague the year before. They went over to the American consulate for a replacement passport, which was difficult for a flight the following day. The people at the consulate, polite if punctilious, knew of her. They had dealt with gender crossers before, and they dealt with lost passports ten or twenty times a day. The State Department is unpopular with American travelers in distress, especially inexperienced travelers who imagine that their taxes provide them a sort of insurance—just go to the American consulate. *Civis Americana sum.* Deirdre noted the libertarian truth: governments are there to make movement difficult, not easy. After the consulate Deirdre and the TV crew drove to The Hague and its much-painted beach, Schevingen, where an annual show of sand castles was displayed, Deirdre posing among the shapes. It was her academic theme that year, knocking down the economists' sand castles. Deirdre didn't see the TV program, but her Dutch friends said it was sweetly done.

■

Late in the summer she taught for a week in Auch, in the southwest of France, graduate students in management from European universities. The school was at a château, and her room was in the Big House, a room almost comically elegant for a lady from Iowa. Then she went to England and visited Susan in Oxford, and the two of them rented a car and drove at speed north to Dundee. Fiona put them up in her house, and she and Suzanne and the other ladies of Dundee welcomed them for drinks and romantic hikes in the country and a final dinner with Deirdre, Susan, Fiona, and Suzanne at a restaurant in the old town at which Deirdre made a fool of herself over the accordion player. She sent a request for him to play "Johnny Lad": "Through the nooks and barley stooks, / Jinkin' you my Johnny lad."

Susan and Deirdre drove across Scotland one day to visit Susan's former mother- and father-in-law, who were jolly and courteous the way upper-class British people can be, traits that served Susan and her former wife well in their troubles. Deirdre remembered, sipping tea and nibbling cake by the garden, pieces of twenty British summers as Donald scattered from 1959 to 1993. First time as Deirdre.

Then she taught for two weeks at a summer institute in Amsterdam, more international graduate students and junior faculty. Deirdre roomed with Judith, her British *vriendinnetje,* in a rented apartment. And then home for school in Iowa to start. No problem. Of course not. She learned of more and more academics who had crossed, an art historian at Swarthmore, a political scientist at Washington, a chemist at Tennessee, a biochemist at Virginia, a sociologist at Berkeley. The newspaper of colleges, the *Chronicle of Higher Education,* ran an article featuring Deirdre and other cases. No scandal. Less and less of a problem for *le professoresse.* What does it matter? Why are you telling me this?

42

SECOND VOICE

*H*er voice was not working. She would be browsing in a women's store and have to ask something, and heads would turn sharply: I didn't know there was a man in here. Sometimes they read her, sometimes not, but the issue was raised. She was surprised at her own embarrassment, since she expected a toughness from stuttering. A stutterer who is too thin skinned will be miserable, and Donald and Deirdre were not miserable.

She wanted to call Dr. Sataloff's office in Philadelphia and try to get the voice corrected. But getting up the courage to call his office was hard, and she whined to Patty: "Their phone system is insane, like trying to call South Station in Boston at the height of railway travel after the war. My parents would call: busy, busy, busy, busy, hold, nothing; busy, busy, busy, busy, hold. I am so afraid, Patty, afraid he will go back on his promise to do it for free, or not be able to do anything, or the voice will end up worse." Boo-hoo.

Deirdre had written a letter to Sataloff, in her academic way, but he hadn't answered. She wrote again, but again no answer. With Patty's help she called and called and finally got an appointment at the end of May, after five months back in the United States, and if approved she would be operated on the following day. When the date came she flew to Newark and spent the evening being Aunt Deirdre to Patty's daughters. Patty's husband was still flummoxed by this professor of his now on Patty's side, spending hours in the living room on the big white couches making talk. They drove to Philadelphia early the next morning, and Deirdre was back in the Dickensian offices of Dr. Sataloff, as in winter eighteen months before, with the harried staff, and the wall of degrees and certifications and commendations to stare at: 9:00 A.M. to noon. South Station.

Sataloff thought he could do a somewhat conservative operation that might work; or he could assure a result, though with more risk and leaving a larger Adam's apple. Deirdre knew she must choose the more conservative procedure, though she wanted the more radical one, because she wanted it all to be finished. *How much more money do I have to spend, how much more doctor fright endure?* The surgery the next day would be the eighth procedure under general anesthesia that Deirdre had experienced through eighteen months, the last.

She and Patty went shopping in Philadelphia, one consignment shop after another. One gigantic place had an entire bridal section, and Deirdre dressed in a white gown with a train. She was happy, and Patty cried in melancholy delight.

Deirdre would be asked, "Do you expect to marry?" The questioner was fishing for her sexual orientation. People, especially male people, want to know about the sex. You reply, "It's about identity," and their eyes glaze over. Yeah, but what about the sex?

On the matter of marriage she would reply cheekily, "I'm open to offers!" thinking: *Yes, yes; I would move anywhere with someone I loved and who loved me. Holland. Saskatoon.* She would say this to girlfriends, a shocking thing for Donald to have said, and they would look at her placidly. Whether or not they approved of giving up career for love, they accepted that many women were willing to do it, as no man has been willing since King Edward VIII in 1936.

Deirdre would add, tough girl: "But realistically my chances are slim to none. The man would have to be tall and late middle-aged and so strongly loving that a big career in his woman would not bother him—or that his woman had been a man." Deirdre thought of what Susan of Oxford said about men not wanting someone who knew men so well. Yet Susan got a boyfriend after her nose job. Deirdre wanted someone to love her. *Am I not lovable?* And especially at night when the thought came she would cry.

For now just being sufficed. Mirrors. She was addicted to mirrors and to every slanted store window that gave her a side shot. She checked her hair, as other women do, and checked her femininity, as other women do not. She would look at herself in mirrors or shop windows as she walked by, not for long periods but glancingly, in different lights, to see the feminine and go on rejoicing. Walking on the Admiralteitskade in Rotterdam the ground-floor windows gave her an angled view, which she would watch out of the corner of her eye. *Do I look all right?* The changing room of one of the Philadelphia consignment shops gave her for the first time a clear look at the back of her legs not tensed by craning around to see. She thought, surprised, *They look good, better than some other women's. Wow.* Patty was amused, at first viewing it as vanity. Not exactly: reassurance.

The evening before the operation she and Patty set out to go to a restaurant on the riverfront and decided to take the subway—a bad idea, because the subway in Philadelphia is confusing and in the evening is deserted. When they got lost a couple of working-class girls helped them find the way. On the empty train the girls looked at them with apparent goodwill, but when Patty and Deirdre got out and the doors started closing, one of the girls shouted, "Good-bye, *sir!*" Patty hadn't heard it and was startled when Deirdre told her. In a teenage way the Philadelphia girls had spoiled their good deed, and Patty understood what Deirdre meant by "being read." Her voice. The damned voice. They ate, then walked the deserted riverfront, Deirdre somber.

The following day Patty took her to the hospital, a new one, not the robber barony of the Graduate Hospital. (Later it turned out that the new one too was a robber barony. Philadelphia hospitals just are, at any rate the ones Dr. Sataloff patronizes. For a year afterward this new one tried to extract $1,300 an hour for six hours of out-patient care, most of it spent sitting around being neglected by the staff. But at the time Deirdre didn't know this and was happy and frightened.) After the operation they drove home to New Jersey, Deirdre on voice rest for two weeks. Patty called Deirdre's mother on the car phone and told her it was all right. In truth they didn't know whether it was going to work until the two weeks of scribbled notes and whispering were up, when Deirdre met Patty in Philadelphia again, and they went back to Dr. Sataloff's.

Had it worked? Patty told Deirdre later that while the shortened vocal cords were being filmed Patty had sat in the waiting room in terror, crying. Sataloff had come out. He was stern. No, it was another patient. The procedure on that patient had not worked. Patty cried. He had come out again, smiling. Deirdre's procedure had worked.

Not completely, but by now Deirdre was accustomed to surgery's not working very well, and Dr. Sataloff offered honorably to try yet again someday. The new operation gave her a hoarse but acceptably feminine voice. Perhaps it could be improved. In stores no heads turned, very far, though people would occasionally say, "My, you have quite a cold there, dear" or "Have you just been sleeping?" and little children would stare at her and then ask naively, "What's wrong with your voice?" A graduate student in economics offered her a cough drop. But the supposition was that this was a woman with a hoarse voice, not a former man. Half the time on the phone they would call her "ma'am," half the time "sir," and she would politely correct them, since it was awkward to go on and on in the wrong gender.

The original surgery on the voice had been a bad idea, but an idea implemented already in December 1995 and by May of 1997 only to be made better by further surgery. Deirdre advised other gender crossers: Don't do the surgery; work with speech therapy. Surgeons don't know reliably how to make a voice feminine. With her original, presurgery voice her many sessions with her speech therapist in Rotterdam would probably have worked better. It's better to have the range of your natural voice, she explained, which you can train feminine. Get a tape recorder. Turn off part of the male instrument, a viola acting as violin. Place your voice forward. Speak in your head instead of your chest. Articulate more clearly. No harsh onsets. It took years to get these. The man who loved her would have to put up, too, with something other than a mellifluous woman's voice. ***Still, sexy when you hear it right.***

43

MAKING IT UP

*P*eople, especially men, would ask how in the world she had learned makeup, as though it were a profound feminine mystery, and she would reply, "It's not rocket science, dear." Makeup was no longer sexy at all, or even very feminine. It was a duty, work, not a joy. Women can find amusement in the game of dressing, where they have choice. But makeup must to be done the one best way you can figure out and then never varied. It's like putting on a uniform. You might change it a little for evening wear, or adjust the eyeshadow to the color of your dress. But compared with the Barbie-doll game of dressing up or down or around, it's like brushing your teeth.

What the makeup routine did do was evoke memories, the way smells do, or song lyrics.

Shave in the shower: If she shaves her face, as she had to until late in the electrolysis, less each cycle, she remembers the male ritual. It gets vaguer and vaguer, replaced by memories of hair removal at Electrology 2000. Later she shaves weekly the peach fuzz that's left, as an exfoliating technique. Models do it. If she shaves her legs, which she has to do once every two weeks or so—with her women's hormones the hair grows much less aggressively—she thinks of the struggle with body hair back when male hormones still ruled her skin, the hours plucking.

Baby wipes to remove eyeliner and mascara: She got the tip from a book about crossdressing; baby wipes do the job as well as more expensive products. A year into the routine she realized that she could cut them into halves or even quarters. It's the little area around the eyes that matters, since soap does the rest.

Wash with soap: She remembers Donald's wife's insistence that she didn't need any beauty treatment but soap and water. Women get tired of cosmetics, indignant at the business of it. Donald's wife was right: her skin didn't need anything else. Deirdre's did. Probably she should buy some expensive cleanser. ***Wait until the electrolysis is done,*** she would say as she examined her skin in the Dutch winter. When it was done, two years on, she stopped soap and used only cleansers, though cheapo stuff from the drugstore.

Alpha hydroxy lotion: Just a little. It's supposed to renew the skin. She's not sure. She started it back in the out cross-dressing era, using man's aftershave lotion with alpha hydroxy (which is made from bananas). She remembers her Iowa City electrologist, whose skin was lovely Cubana anyway, praising the miracles of alpha hydroxy, and so she started. Or was it vitamin E she praised? ***No matter. Keep it out of the eyes.*** Later she got onto Estée Lauder, at $70 a month, which worked. ***Must find a cheap substitute.*** For a couple of years on the hormones her skin improved. "Then," she would joke with other women, "I join the downward march with the rest of you."

Sunscreen: When she remembers. SPF 15. In her fifties she doesn't need more sun damage. She got plenty as a lad working for the highway department hatless in ninety-degree heat, raking blacktop.

Perfume: Unless she's going on a plane and is worried about offending perfume-sensitive people, she always wears it, usually Chanel No. 22. She thinks of it as one more cue saying "woman." The scent is grownup, though she would have chosen No. 5 if that were not her mother's. A girl's got to have her own. "It's Diana's, my sister's," her mother said one day. Chanel No. 22 is impossible to get in Europe, and in the United States it is sold only in old-fashioned stores. An old-fashioned girl.

Foundation: Just on the diamond shape from the middle of the forehead around the nose to the chin, then the neck, especially the sides, to get the red out. She remembers her mother's complaining in Holland about too-thick application. ***No use explaining to her that it had to cover the beard.*** Her mother could not hear the prudent explanation and interpreted heavy makeup as vanity or a failure of taste. Women don't get it, since covering a beard is not their problem.

Lightly, lightly, now, since the hair is almost gone. She looks at the cheap bottle of Revlon Age Defying Extra Cover Creme Makeup (Cool Beige) and thinks of a girlfriend's leading her to the Shiseido counter in Rotterdam and getting her to buy a better kind, at three times the price. *When the electrolysis is all done,* she thinks, *get a make-over by a really good makeup artist, and settle on a routine.* Finally in 1998 she went with Patty down to Georgette Klinger on Madison Avenue, and they both got instruction (Patty was not a makeup type). *For now it's Revlon at the drugstore.*

Powder: Coty Airspun Translucent, another drugstore standby. The powder fixes the foundation. She remembers when she learned to put it on with a brush, from the homosexual makeup artist at the little convention in the Poconos. Dab the brush in the powder. Tap it backward on the handle to get the powder into the brush. Then push, push, push it on, feeling the bristles jam the powder into the pores. The makeup artist was weary: he had explained this hundreds of times. The hesitant, inexperienced crossdressers didn't push hard enough.

Blush: B Box Number 2 from the Bijenkorf ["Beehive"] department store in Rotterdam. It's a wine color, which Deirdre thinks of as mature—*minimize the pinkish tones.* On each successive visit to the cheapo section of the Bijenkorf cosmetic department on trips back to Rotterdam she is less obviously read, if at all. Only the voice, and then not even that.

Eyeshadow: First check your clothing. But there are really only two choices, both from the Bijenkorf, blue or pinkish purple (the Dutch call it aubergine, the French word for eggplant). She remembers experimenting with eyeshadow early in her marriage when Donald's wife was still tolerant of a little open crossdressing, and she thinks of her colleague Dick at the Economics Department at Chicago in 1968 making jokes about one of the secretaries, who wore it in green.

Eyeliner: L'Oréal liquid, the most evocative of her cosmetics. She lines her eyes in 1950s style, which keeps fleetingly coming back into fashion. Occasionally she does it all around, the full raccoon effect, if she's seen some other woman it looks good on, but usually just upper lids. Start a third of the way out from the inner corners, a tip learned from a women's magazine. Thin line, thicker beyond the irises, then a thin line beyond the outer corner. Then back to finish the line into the inner corner. Every time it reminds her strongly, bizarrely, of the Institute for Advanced Study, the Einstein Institute. In 1983 she was a member for a year. Half the time Donald was alone and crossdressed frequently. He had no beard that year and would put on elaborate makeup. He never went out, never looked for a crossdressing club, remained in the closet. Imagine: Einstein and eyeliner. Goodness.

Mascara: Maybelline Great Lash, more drugstore stuff. She had to experiment to find one that didn't irritate her eyes. She always thinks of Donald's wife's ironic "envy" of his long, male lashes. Probably they will go in time. Meanwhile, downstroke, downstroke, then upstroke, upstroke. She thinks of watching a young woman applying mascara on the Sneltram one morning when Deirdre was going out to visit the hospital at the Free University. She was amazed how long she worked at it. Later Deirdre read in the *New Yorker* of a great beauty who would spend forty-five minutes. ***How could you spend forty-five minutes on mascara alone? Down, down. Keep it from glopping or spotting. Dry, if time. Up, up, up.***

Eyebrow pencil: She thinks of the shaping by electrolysis, and of her own plucking before. She thinks of when she was little, watching her mother pluck and pencil in the style of 1950. ***Put the peak just outside the irises. An A shape.***

Lipstick: Like other women she has still not found a lipstick that stays on. The cosmetics ads blare "long lasting." ***Ha.*** Walking into the downtown mall in Iowa City with her sister, finally civil if not really close, the sisters agree that the ads are lies. She thinks of Ousterhout's work on her lips. ***Not his fault that the skin on the lower left lip does not hold lipstick well.*** He did a good job repairing a scar from a childhood injury that went right through the lower lip, though the scar still shows a bit, ghostlike. ***Start there, lower left. Dry the lip with tissue. Pencil first. Fill in. Then upper lips in a bow. Not too big or small. All right. Symmetrical? Darn it: the bow is too high. Wipe the edge carefully, repencil. All right. That'll do.*** Click.

As her grandmother used to say, her war paint is on. She doesn't look like the witch of Endor.

44

H O M E

She could list the misunderstandings she had encountered in her crossing, some of which she had herself believed. They were malicious or innocent, stupid or intelligent; but each was wrong:

- gender crossing has to do with homosexuality
- it is always apparent at an early age
- psychiatrists know about it
- it can be cured by psychiatrists or psychologists
- or by punishments and expulsions
- gays wish to be women
- gender crossers are always effeminate as boys and men
- they are small and feminine looking
- you can tell
- they are lower class, never professors or businesspeople or concert pianists
- the male gender crosser always feels herself a woman trapped in a man's body
- he never really felt like a man
- he was miserable as a man
- he married as a cover-up

- he would not be a normal, loving father of his children
- she ends up as a street prostitute
- she wants a vagina for sexual intercourse alone
- she is miserable as a woman
- she comes to regret her gender change
- suicide often follows the operation
- she is likely to be a homicidal maniac or a sex criminal
- she is in some other sense mentally disturbed
- she is likely to act weird in some other way as well
- for example, she'll be unreliable now at work
- she participates in a masculine conspiracy against women
- she indulges in stereotypes of women
- she does it casually
- she does it for some advantage
- she does it to shock people with the transformation
- she does it to deconstruct the dualism of gender
- she is a third sex, you see
- she is satisfied merely to dress as a woman
- she does not need of course to get married as a woman
- she is not concerned to experience the other parts of a woman's life
- she does it for sexual pleasure
- she does it to get on the Jerry Springer show
- it is a deep worry where she should go to the bathroom
- she wishes to spy on women in the ladies' room
- female-to-male gender crossers are unheard of
- the genital operation is the crux of it all
- the operation for males to females is very expensive
- the operation is rare and experimental
- the operation is unusually dangerous and painful
- the operation makes a man womanly or a woman manly
- cosmetic surgery to achieve a womanly face is just vanity
- the doses of hormones are dangerous
- the doses differ from those of a postmenopausal woman on hormone therapy
- a man's voice rises when he is castrated as an adult
- gender change undermines Christian morality or separatist feminism
- we should, if we can, stop these few people of both birth genders seeking surgical and hormonal and social gender reassignment.

They come down to viewing the male-to-female gender crosser as a weird man rather than as another woman, or for that matter as another human being. They are like other misunderstandings, the knowledge we confidently believe we have of the other. If you've been scorned or misunderstood as a black or a Jew or a short person or a fat person—or as a woman—you've felt it.

■

She went to a conference in New York, at the Columbia Law School. Deirdre was trying out New York. Maybe she would move there. *Though Iowa City has been fine,* she reflected. *Can I pass in Manhattan? New York is gender sophisticated. Remember the restaurant on the Hudson, with Patty and her family, when I overheard a woman in the ladies' room saying, "Did you see the transsexual out there?" But, honestly, I'm not sure if she meant me: when I lingered over hand washing and she came out of the stall she showed no embarrassment and continued talking cheerily with her friend. There are that many of them in New York!* Deirdre left a business card for a college friend who was a professor at the Law School. He came by at the end of the conference.

"Deirdre?"

"Oh! How nice to see you!" The last time had been their twenty-fifth college reunion, in 1989.

"I hadn't heard."

"Good Lord. I thought everyone had."

"I got this card saying 'Deirdre' and called up an economist and he gave me the scoop. I wouldn't have recognized you. You look great!"

He invited her over to his apartment on Central Park for drinks and was genial and unfazed. If you work in New York a long time you stop being fazed. *A job in New York? Lots of tall, gentle, self-confident men?*

■

She went with Patty to a basket party in Patty's town, at which a local woman sold expensive baskets from Ohio. It was cheerful, with a spread of food served in the various designs of baskets, and no one except Patty knew about Deirdre. The experience was peculiar. Deirdre was accustomed by now to interacting superficially in streets and stores with strangers who did not know, and intimately with people who did know. But this was different, being Deirdre beyond paying for the groceries or chatting with salesclerks. It was nerve racking.

Will I make a mistake? Say something only a man would say? Stuttering is so male. Don't say anything unless you're sure you won't. "A deep-voiced woman," they seemed to think. "Seems nice. A little quiet."

A couple of months later she went to Milwaukee to see a woman classmate with whom Donald had wanted to have an affair in the spring of his freshman year. For her he had almost flunked French. She was now a social worker with a grown son, and Deirdre wrote to her as one of the few Radcliffe women she knew. She thought, ***I need women friends from Harvard.*** The classmate had recently converted from Episcopalian to Buddhist and invited Deirdre to a party for the Tibetan New Year. Deirdre expected the Buddhists to be 1960s in dress, but these were indistinguishable from Episcopalians, and their party was like the basket party. Again no one knew, with the complication that this party had men as well as women. Deirdre experienced the casual flirtation, the emotional dance between men and women, which Donald had once performed from the other side. ***Scary.***

It felt like going back into the closet, she realized later. She again had something to hide, namely, that she was not a natural-born woman. People knew in Iowa City or Rotterdam. She didn't like the familiar feeling of the closet, having now spent two years out. ***Still, it's fun to flirt.***

■

She was back in Cambridge for a few days of work and decided to go over to her old private school, called now Buckingham Browne and Nichols, a merger of a girls' school and her boys' school. The fundraising office had adjusted instantly to Deirdre's news when she had sent it two years before. The list of contributors to the annual fund for her class now read "Mr. K., Mr. J., Mr. L., *Ms.* McCloskey, Mr. N., Mr. O." When she visited the office the women were cordial and were pleased to have just received her first book as Deirdre, *The Vices of Economists,* with a flattering photo on the back cover. One of the women offered to give her a tour of the school. In the library Deirdre asked if her books were there—she thought she had remembered sending a pile some years before as Donald. The librarian looked in her computer under "McCloskey."

"We have two by 'Donald,' but none by you," she said perkily, adding with an irony common among women, "Unless you're 'Donald'!"

"Uh . . . but I *was* Donald." The librarian's face went white and then red. Deirdre tried to help: "I'll send a fuller selection when I get back to Iowa. Thank you so much for showing me your splendid library!"

At lunch they sat at the teachers' table and teachers came and went, snatching a bite between classes. Deirdre had to explain three times how it could be that she was of the class of 1960 in this very building, when it was still a boys' school. The dean of students had a chat with her and suggested she come back sometime and speak to the school. Passing. Acceptance. Even affection.

■

November 23, 1997, Deirdre listened to the priest's announcements of parish business on a Sunday and her mind wandered. It was two years to the day full time as Deirdre. "As Deirdre." A month earlier she had been baptized in the name of the Father, the Son, and the Holy Spirit, gathered around the font in Trinity, with an infant to be baptized as well, and their family and Deirdre's friends.

More and more events became routine. Not boring, just routine "as Deirdre." She lived as a woman, without notice or comment. She had lost her marriage family and some sunshine friends and had no special lover. It proved slower to develop *vriendinnetjes* in Iowa City than in Rotterdam, though for a while Patty and she leaned on one another by long distance. She had made numerous less intense friends, kept many others, continued her fulfilling work. People who had known her as a man said she seemed happier.

She was. She could live the rest of her life as a woman.

Good Lord.

Alleluia! Alleluia!

God be praised!

She had crossed.

45

DIFFERENCES

"Do you think," asked Evelyn, "really, seriously think that life
is very different for men?"

Kate stood still, and thought . . . : "I don't know. The
truth is, I do not know."

"No," said Evelyn. "After all these years of thinking about
it, neither do I." They looked at one another soberly, and
sighed.

Margaret Drabble, *The Middle Ground*

She catches falling objects quicker. It's as though they're falling
slower, or as though she's more aware of her surroundings and sees
the anomaly quicker. The pie plate starts to slip off the counter, beginning its fall. She calmly reaches out and catches it.

She is more easily startled by loud noises or sudden movements.
When she comes upon someone she did not expect, she jumps. Donald used to get irritated at his wife for just this—"For God's sake, it's
only me. When are you going to get used to another person being in
the house!"

She cries. There seems to be no verb in English for what she mainly
experiences, like other women: being much more often than a man

on the verge of tears even when not actually weeping. Women's tears are like men's anger, provoked by a bewildering range of circumstances. Her tears had no element of playacting. She had not resisted them as a man—the impulse had not been there to resist. Now it was.

She sweats less. Or rather she "glows," as in "Horses sweat, gentlemen perspire, and ladies glow."

She sleeps more and is tired and stutters a lot if she gets less than eight hours. But she sleeps better.

She stutters less. Or so people tell her. She speaks to a class on human sexuality, and a student comes up to her afterward and says, "I had you as Donald for Economics One. My brother stutters, and it comforted him when I said I had a professor who also did. But you do it less now." "Thank you for saying so." Deirdre thought as she spoke: ***Don't worry, dear, your brother's stuttering has nothing to do with gender crossing.***

She loses weight less easily. The furnace of a man's metabolism is out. True, a man's metabolism didn't stop Donald from getting fat. If you work at it you can overfuel even a man's furnace.

She chooses clothing with an eye, imagining outfits from her closet or the store rack, and can judge instantly when trying them on whether they work. ***White tops make my shoulders look enormous, unless cut just so. This one is not cut just so.*** It surprises and pleases her, since Donald had no interest in clothing and had dull taste in it. Everyone says Deirdre dresses fairly well, and she gets her share of compliments. ***But remember to say it to them, too.*** Oh, what a lovely outfit! ***When it is.***

Her color memory and color vocabulary are a little better. They are still poor by some feminine standards, but when the man at the tire store asks what color her car is, parked out of sight, she can answer without effort what would have been impossible for Donald: "Dark blue, with cream trim."

She works at remembering what people wear. She observes, and comments internally, looking for ideas, but is still not good at remembering.

But she remembers neighborhoods better, without effort, and in driving she starts to navigate by landmark and feel rather than by direction and map.

She likes cooking. Her women friends say, "Wait until you have to do it daily for six people over two decades." Still, they all agree that when you cook for pleasure it is a pleasure, something Donald had not allowed. Too close to the feminine.

She listens intently to stories people tell of their lives, and craves detail. And what did he say to *that*?

She is willing to listen to painful stories of sickness and personal catastrophe. Donald would never let his wife tell stories about the horrors in the hospital, and she resented his squeamishness. ***Guys.***

She is more alert to relational details in stories: Ah, I see, she's his cousin by marriage. She finds herself remembering the family trees, the ex-boyfriends, the big events. Donald had to be reminded of everyone's name, forgetting elementary facts. ***Remember, she had cancer.*** Deirdre would sometimes make the same sort of mistake but would be mortified. She gave a friend a book she herself loved, Elisabeth Berg's *Talk before Sleep,* a real women's book, and only afterward remembered that this friend *had* had cancer and might not love a book about a group of friends around a woman dying of it.

She has gotten no more skillful at telling stories. Some women are not good at it. She wishes she were better and could remember the details she craves and arrange them the way other women do, with no point except the sharing of vision.

She is worse at telling jokes. The usual joke, fashioned by some man, requires a little-boy assertiveness that she finds less attractive now and less comfortable to assume. *Io, io.* The pointedness of jokes, it has been observed, is like a mathematical proof in the Greek style, ending with a sharp little QED. Women's stories are more like computer simulations, a Mesopotamian mathematics of trying things out. Here's what happened to me. I didn't direct it.

She is less single-minded. The word is accurate: of a single mind, as though this single football game or single mechanical puzzle could absorb an entire mind. The guys' way of thinking could be classified in the DSM as a "disorder," monomania, focusing on job or car or golf or hunting or model railroading in a manic way. Many men would therefore need some expensive treatment from mental health professionals. Some you'd want to commit for observation—about 70 percent of the male population, say, just to be on the safe side. Deirdre is more multiminded. In Virginia Woolf's *The Waves* someone says, "Let a man get up and say, 'Behold, this is the truth,' and instantly I perceive a sandy cat filching a piece of fish in the background. Look, you have forgotten the cat, I say." It changes one's attitude toward economics, which is a boys' game and is single-minded. The single-minded game among economists is to find the prudence in everything, even though it's obvious to women that love without prudence is there too. Look, you have forgotten the love.

She is therefore less one-tasked. Donald would work for days on a paper, with no interruptions to care for other people or to create a nest around himself. "No man would trouble about such things," notes the writer-heroine of May Sarton's coming-out novel, *Mrs. Stevens Hears the Mermaids Singing.* "The imaginary man in her mind got up at six, never made his bed, did not care a hoot if there were a flower or not, and was at his desk as bright as a button, at dawn, with a whole day clear before him while some woman out of sight was making a delicious hot stew for his supper." Deirdre could not forget the love, and the duties of order.

She is less impatient. Snowed in at Saint Louis on her way back from Electrology 2000 she waits patiently in the long line for rebooking, not even getting very agitated that TWA as usual does not announce what is happening. People get to the front of the line after forty minutes and find they did not need to be in it at all. The man in front of Deirdre is frothing angry. He shouts and abuses the clerk, a woman. She is relieved to get to Deirdre, and they work together woman to woman, like unloading a dishwasher.

She drives slower and less aggressively. The young women driving in Iowa City are just as bad as the young men, but in her generation only men drove like fools. She punishes a driver passing illegally on the right, speeding up to trap him—of course, him . . . but no, it's another woman! She notes what she is doing. ***Foolish.*** She draws back and lets her pass.

She can't remain angry for long. A bureaucrat at the College of Business has trouble with her gender change and challenges her on silly rules. At first she is indignant, but she can't keep it up the way Donald could, for months and years. ***He's not so bad. He has his own issues. Let him do his job.***

She feels duty bound to wash the dishes. It is no longer a favor, but what her tribe does. She puts the clean crystal and silver away with satisfaction.

She loves, just loves, the little favors of womankind, getting a card for someone, making meatloaf for Charles up the street, helping someone through a day of his life. Not that she is unusually good about it. ***Time I invited Charles again.***

People treat her more kindly. A woman is less threatening and gets smiled at more.

On the other hand, she is treated more casually. Clerks and bureaucrats do not expect trouble from a woman. They are not on guard. They treat a man as dangerous.

She assumes a less confident mask for dealings with salespeople and auto mechanics. It's not This is my right and I'm taking it, dammit, but May I please have some? Oh, *thank* you. The mask is not real uncertainty. You don't immediately forget what you know about car repair. Though it fades.

She has stopped paying attention to guy things—such as cars and sports and war stories. Her knowledge of them starts to depreciate. *By the time I'm seventy I won't know how many baseball leagues there are.*

She is uninterested in sports and finds the sports pages pointless. The only exception is the English game of cricket, but her interest takes a milder and less hobbyish form than exhibited by Donald, who had played on two teams in Chicago. She rediscovered the pleasures of cricket again in the summer of 1996 in Holland watching on the BBC: the beautiful game of white on green, the run-up of the fast bowler, the click of bat on ball, a classic cover drive, the fielder hustling to stop the four with his boot; *and the captain, hmm, he's cute.*

She no longer thinks of social life as strict exchange. Of course, *If she doesn't send that thank-you I'm going to drop her. I can't be bothered with such rudeness.* But contrary to what men think, a woman's life is not mainly composed of such tit-for-tat reasoning. Renea said it to Deirdre driving back from a presentation to Renea's women's club in rural Iowa: "Women are more forgiving."

She dotes on every child she meets. The doting is not forced. A child evokes the warmth without her intending it. Dogs, too.

She reads women novelists, for years *only* women novelists. Partly it is catching up. As Nancy Mairs puts it, "It's not that I resist or refuse works by men, but because my education focused on them, I've had a lot of catching up to do." Partly it is self-instruction: ah, the woman's way of telling. She feels about men's novels the way one of Margaret Drabble's heroines feels about women's novels: "the feeling of great boredom when she opened" one. *Oh, yeah. Courage. Guy stuff. Yawn.*

She takes the woman's side. When married couples quarrel in her presence she sides with the wife, even if it's mainly the husband who is her friend. *After all, she is in my tribe.* But the side taking is not entirely a choice. She sees differently. *For God's sake, can't he see how stupid he's being?*

She is religious. The range in religiousness is wide, and Deirdre feels a novice in this as in much of womanhood (not that there can't be a muscular Christianity). What's the connection, people ask, between finding your gender and finding religion? "I'm not sure," she says, but thinks, *Of course I'm sure: they come from the same rebirth.*

She is neater, her cleaning lady notes, and Deirdre herself notices her determination to make the bed as soon as she gets out of it. *It's so much nicer to come back into the bedroom with the bed made.* Donald could tolerate messes, or assume without thought that his wife or some other woman would take care of it. At first in Holland she was Donald-sloppy, but gradually she got better. *But not obsessive,* she thinks as she scrutinizes the kitchen counter from another angle and wipes it for the third time. Standards vary, and she is not as neat as her mother.

She has more friends, in the women's sense: many instead of none, and a few *vriendinnetjes.* She is willing to confide in them and they in her. She learned slowly how to encourage the confidence she craved: And how do you feel about that? And what did your husband think?

She looks on men as sexually interesting and emotionally stupid.

She thinks less about sex. A female-to-male gender crosser in a documentary called *You Don't Know Dick* said, "As a woman I wanted a relationship first, cuddling, with the sex as a supplement. Now the testosterone says on the contrary, 'I need this now, now, now. When that's taken care of, well, maybe we can think about a relationship.'" Yes.

She cares about love. Men will exercise love if it is assigned to them as a task. "You're the head of the family. Get it? So make decisions for their well-being." "Uh, OK." She thinks: *My son is trying. Give him a break.* Women take delight in love, or anyway assign themselves to do it. Men don't.

She gets as much pleasure from loving as from being loved, delighting in caring for her new Yorkshire terrier, named Janie in honor of Jane Austen. Janie comes with her on trips to France and Holland and Durham, North Carolina, sneaked into the fancy hotel, and is very popular with the conferees. *My baby.*

She cares about relationships and devotes sustained thought to them in a way that Donald could not. The thoughts of most men about their relationships are first drafts, not considered and revised. Crude. Unpracticed. Women think all day about their relationships, and so their remarks are closer to final drafts, amended and reamended by *vriendinnetjes.*

A church friend, a retired Episcopalian priest who attended her monthly spirituality group, told Deirdre as they sheltered under her umbrella after a meeting, "When I met you when you had first come back from Holland you were someone who wanted more relationships. Now you are skilled in them." He meant "womanly," and Deirdre gave him a kiss for his kindness.

46

CHRIST'S MASS, 1997

A woman's calendar is already full: the birthdays, the showers, the other occasions for gifts to friends and for decorations around one's desk, such as Valentine's Day, Saint Patrick's Day, Secretaries' Day, Easter, Mother's Day, Father's Day, Halloween, Thanksgiving, above all Christmas. Some women are sick of making holidays for others, sick of commerce and greed and family, and anyway they've paid their dues, but Deirdre the novice was entranced by Christmas. Patty came out to visit from New Jersey, and together they set up the Christmas tree. The three of them, Patty and Deirdre and Deirdre's roomer Sister Marilyn spent two days baking for a party on the twentieth. On the big night Deirdre wore her draggy blue spangled gown, last worn for *La Cage aux Folles* in the spring, and Patty played Christmas carols for singing. Deirdre thought of it as a party to thank the people who had made her first year back in Iowa happy, though in the rush she missed inviting some. Still, 120 came. She wanted the party to be perfect and worried whether it came up to Martha Stewart standards. (Joke: One of the top ten signs you are being stalked by Martha Stewart is the telltale lemon slice in the dog's water bowl.)

One, two years and across.

■

Christmas Prose from Deirdre, 1997

A poet friend said about my last Christmas letter, "You give up poetry, I'll give up economics."

This year I came back to Iowa. For years and years, my dear friends, I've been explaining to you that Iowa is not what you coasties imagine. While I was away in Holland during 1996 the students here had printed up a money-raising T-shirt with ten reasons, David Letterman style, to be a business major at Iowa, and number two, the second from the top, was "Diversity: We have Professor McCloskey!" When the club officers presented it to me on a trip back to Iowa City I gave them each a kiss. You coasties will be surprised to hear that despite all the publicity in Iowa I have gotten not a single harassing phone call, not a single piece of hate mail.

But when I flew back for good last January 1997 I was terrified. Would my marriage family see me and talk? This above all. But dozens of practical worries. Would the students be cordial? Yes, of course. My graduate students were lovely, always; and the undergraduates just don't care. A Margaret Atwood character observes, "the fences once so firmly in place around the gender corrals are just a bunch of rusty old wire." Thank the Lord.

Would I love my old house, could I live in it alone, could I then get tenants to take the spare rooms, would I be safe there? It worked out fine. In August Sister Marilyn Brinker took a room, and next month Maggie joins as a second roomer. The house is gradually becoming more Deirdre, filled with photographs of you, dear friends (*please* send more!), and yesterday, Thanksgiving, it was filled with smells of pecan and pumpkin pies, Dutch *stomppot* and baking bread. How domestic! Marilyn is *gradually* teaching me to put on my apron before cooking.

Would my colleagues feel comfortable? Yes, on the whole. The men are sometimes boyishly clumsy (I remember the feeling, though it fades), but many are confident and gallant. The women are welcoming, Carol a special example.

Would I have friends? Lord, yes! There are two families where I am Tante Deirdre: Arjo and Marijke's in Holland, and

Patty and George's in New Jersey. In October I was baptized in the Episcopalian church, led by Alice and Lori and Bob. Trinity has accepted me as merely one of the ladies of the church. It was so pleasant to serve food to the workers at our Habitat house this summer—you won't catch *me* wielding a hammer, my dears! My new religiousness is more than social. As you might have expected, though, my approach to Christianity is rather too bookish.

Professionally—your attention wanders, dear friends, and now I know why—it's been fine. The historians are lovely. I gave a keynote address to Women in Economic and Social History this fall in London, and spoke also to my old History Department at Manchester. People wonder how economists would treat me. It's early days yet, but I see no signs of professional catastrophe. I gave lectures elsewhere at the usual rate, but to unusually warm audiences. It was special fun to give a talk at the Mexico meetings of the International Association for Feminist Economics and then wander central Mexico in a van with Nancy and three women from Norway. And above all in September I gave my presidential address to the Economic History Association meeting in New Brunswick, with flashbulbs popping (the story is forthcoming in the March 1998 issue of the business magazine *Worth*). As the people stood to applaud I gave a deep curtsey.

I notice already, without claiming expertise, that a woman's life in the academy is different. Admittedly my perspective is a trifle peculiar just yet. The first time I was chatting in a group of male economists as the only woman and made a point which was ignored, a point commended warmly a few minutes later when Harvey made it, I thought, "*Wonderful:* they're treating me like a woman!" The thrill I can tell you has faded.

I write, I teach. I don't spend *all* my time shopping. Partly because of my sister's intervention, some people worry that I've just gone wacko. No, it's duller than that, though I wouldn't say I'm "just the same person," as some want to put it comfortingly. I'm not Good Old Don (or Wretched Old Don, though I guess the recipients of this letter wouldn't be of that school). I am, so to speak, Don's smarter sister. Who knows if it's the hormones, the social role, the performance of gender becoming second nature, or my true personality able now to express itself. In most matters I can't tell, and I'm in a good position to judge.

Much of my family has been fine. Cousins, for example. My mother has been a rock of support, my brother easy. Even my sister is partly reconciled, and last summer stopped calling me "Donald." We had a visit here in the fall, and we'll spend some days with Mom over Christmas.

The one darkness has been my marriage family. I beg their forgiveness, I beg their love. I will love them always.

But you can see I am not unhappy. On the contrary, I am at peace as never before. My life is full and interesting—I try not to bore my friends! I live well. I wish *you* such a blessed life as mine, and a Merry Christmas and a Happy New Year.

Secular stoicism has its poetry and song and proverb, about which Donald had been proudly expert. "And while the sun and moon endure / Luck's a chance, but trouble's sure." Likewise Christianity has its ritual and prayer and scripture, but about these Deirdre felt humbly amateur. She had no poetry ready for it and watched the novel words. That Christmas of 1997 for Deirdre the two merged, the secular and the religious, though unlike Donald with his baritone she couldn't really sing the carols or hymns—her voice was small and hoarse (though adequately feminine, thank you very much).

"Read a poem twice," an English professor once told Donald when they taught together. "If it's good you'll hear new things each time," in good ritual and prayer and scripture, too, as Deirdre discovered that first year of weekly churchgoing. "Almighty God, unto whom all hearts are open, all desires known, and from whom no secrets are hid." No closets.

Patty and Deirdre had a favorite piece of scripture, chapter 13 of Paul's First Letter to the Corinthians, and traded plaques and pins with bits of it inscribed, above all its peroration, "Faith, hope, and love— these three. But the greatest is love." The opening lines of the chapter were not, Deirdre realized when she consulted learned commentaries, meant as an attack on intellectual presumption, aimed at an academic former man— "Though I speak with the tongues of men and of angels, . . . And though I have the gift of prophecy, and understand all mysteries, and all knowledge . . . and have not love, it profiteth me nothing." And Saint Paul probably did not have Donald's long denial and sudden epiphany in mind when he wrote, "For now we see through a glass, darkly; but then face to face." Yet Patty and Deirdre heard new things each time.

They also had a favorite secular poem, which they carried around in their purses and had made into decorative magnets for their refrigerators. They heard new things in it each time, of Patty's fear of separation, of Deirdre's loss of family, of Donald's wife's loss of a husband, of Deirdre's children's loss of a father, of Donald's sister's loss of a brother; of the "strange" and of a winter of misunderstanding and of love's power to endure, and of autumn, for it was May Sarton's "The Autumn Sonnets Number 2,"[1] read first by Deirdre in Fiona's kitchen in Dundee:

> If I can let you go as trees let go
> Their leaves, so casually, one by one;
> If I can come to know what they do know,
> That fall is the release, the consummation,
> Then fear of time and the uncertain fruit
> Would not distemper the great lucid skies
> This strangest autumn, mellow and acute.
> If I can take the dark with open eyes
> And call it seasonal, not harsh or strange
> (For love itself may need a time of sleep),
> And, treelike, stand unmoved before the change,
> Lose what I lose to keep what I can keep,
> The strange root still alive under the snow,
> Love will endure—if I can let you go.

1. "The Autumn Sonnets Number 2," from "The Autumn Sonnets," © 1972 by May Sarton, in *Halfway to Silence,* first published by The Women's Press Ltd., 1993, 34 Great Sutton Street, London EC1V 0LQ, and in *Collected Poems, 1930-1993* by May Sarton. Reprinted by permission of the Women's Press Ltd. and W. W. Norton & Company, Inc.